Beyond The Village Gate

This book is lovingly dedicated to all of Parmadale's children, yesterday, today and tomorrow, and to children everywhere.

Published by
The Parmadale Christmas Committee
6753 State Road
Parma, Ohio 44134
1985

Proceeds from the sale of this book will benefit the children of Parmadale, a residential village for abused, neglected, dependent young people.

First Printing January 1986 5,000 copies

ISBN: 0-9615123-0-X

Printed in the United States of America
WIMMER BROTHERS BOOKS
P.O. Box 18408
Memphis, TN 38181-0408
"Cookbooks of Distinction"™

Once upon a time there was a small village nestled in the woods. At the end of a winding road were 12 brick cottages, home to the orphans of Parmadale. Smoke curled from the chimneys and the sound of children echoed in the wind.

Christmas is a special time of year and so it was long ago. The holiday began right after Thanksgiving. A list of Christmas presents was posted and the children could ask for one gift. The list was then sent to Santa.

Like children everywhere, the little ones eagerly awaited Christmas day and the birth of the Christ Child. The day began early as they tumbled from their beds in the early morning darkness and gathered for Mass, followed by breakfast in the dining hall. Then the children would return to their cottage to await Santa who arrived with the jingle of sleigh bells. As darkness came again, the children made their rounds of the village singing Christmas carols, their voices ringing clear in the crisp cold air.

The Christmas Committee has brought the joy and love of Christmas to the children of Parmadale for many years. From the time the village first began in 1925, a group of caring, dedicated people shared their Christmas spirit with the children of the village.

The children grew, and over the years the village grew also to meet the changing times. The orphanage of yesterday is today a residential children's village caring for abused, neglected and dependent young people in crisis.

This cookbook, then, grew from the desire to help give these young people a future rich with the promise of tomorrow, to share with them, not just at Christmas time but everyday, the family love and caring so many of them have never before known.

It is with great pride that we share this book with you.
Eileen Barlock

Our sincere thanks to all who shared in this project with us, and who so generously gave of their time and talent. Many hours of dedicated hard work went into compiling this book. These recipes are a reflection of culinary delights from well loved people. We hope they bring happiness to your family, as they have to ours, and warmth to your kitchen.

BEYOND THE VILLAGE GATE

Eileen Barlock
Chairman

Lynne Della Donna
Chairman

Ruth Abbott
Ursula Bartosik
Rosemary Balchak
Judy Braun
Rosemary Corcoran
Nicky Cowan
Jean Croyle
Kay Kelly
Vi Kinsella
Dorothy Loebs

Peggy Koch
Pattie Lovejoy
Sue Mahon
Kay McGorray
Peg O'Shea
Sue Polacek
Lenore Sims
Mary Sims
Betz Spacek

Artwork
Joseph F. Moore

Joe has been a commercial artist for 54 years. Growing up in Boston, he studied at the Boston Normal Art School. After moving to Cleveland in 1931 he worked 18 years for Denison Manufacturing Company. He embarked on a career of free lance package design for 25 years before becoming Art Director at Arrow Engraving. Joe is 77 years old and a volunteer at Parmadale.

TABLE OF CONTENTS

IN THE BEGINNING

A Selection of Appetizers

TASTY HOTS

1 tablespoon dehydrated onions
½ cup shredded Cheddar cheese
½ cup grated Parmesan cheese
3 tablespoons mayonnaise
2 teaspoons chili powder, optional
6 French rolls
24 stuffed olive slices, optional
Paprika

Combine onion, cheeses, mayonnaise, chili powder and salt in small bowl until blended. Cut rolls crosswise into ¼-inch slices. Place on baking sheet and toast one side. Remove from oven and spread cheese mixture on untoasted side of bread. Return to oven and broil until bubbly (about 3 minutes). Sprinkle with paprika and top with an olive slice just before serving. For variation, use party rye bread and garnish tops with bacon crumbs. Yield: 24 servings.
Jean Croyle
Sue Mahon

TASTY CUCUMBER RYE ROUNDS

1 large cucumber
1 (3-ounce) package cream cheese
2 tablespoons Italian salad dressing
1 tablespoon snipped chives
1 teaspoon snipped parsley
Dash of Worcestershire or steak sauce
Salt to taste
Rye rounds
Butter

Score cucumber with a fork; cut off both ends and scoop out seeds from center. Stand cucumber on end and drain well on paper towel. Combine cream cheese, salad dressing, chives, parsley, sauce and salt in small bowl until smooth. Stuff cucumber with this mixture. Wrap tightly in plastic wrap and refrigerate for several hours or until firm. Just before serving, butter rye rounds; slice cucumber crosswise and place one round of cucumber on each rye round.*Delicious and different canapes!*
Lynne Della Donna

ARTICHOKE ROUNDS

1 (15-ounce) jar artichokes packed in water, drained
1 loaf party-size rye bread
1 cup mayonnaise
3 tablespoons grated Parmesan cheese
1 small onion, grated
Paprika

Cut artichokes into quarters. Place ¼ on 1 slice of party rye bread. Combine remaining ingredients in small mixing bowl; spoon mixture over each artichoke quarter. Sprinkle with paprika. Broil for 3 minutes in preheated oven. You may make these ahead and refrigerate, baking just before serving time. Yield: 6 to 8 appetizer servings.
Janet Corcoran

HANKY PANKYS

1 pound ground beef chuck
1 pound hot bulk sausage
1 teaspoon Worcestershire sauce
½ teaspoon garlic salt
1 teaspoon oregano
1 teaspoon salt
1 pound processed cheese food
1 loaf thin-sliced white bread

Sauté beef and sausage in large skillet until browned; drain off fat. Stir in Worcestershire sauce, garlic salt, oregano, and salt, Mix well. Cut cheese into small chunks and stir into mixture. Cook, stirring occasionally, until cheese melts. Spread mixture on bread slices, cut into quarters, place on a baking sheet and freeze until firm (about 2 hours). Remove from freezer and store in freezer proof plastic bags. Just before serving, broil on baking sheet for 2 or 3 minutes. Serve hot. You may use party rye bread or large rye for sandwiches. Yield: 80 to 85 appetizers.
Sister Eleanor
Patti Lovejoy

MUSHROOM CANAPÉS

1 pound mushrooms
¼ cup butter or margarine
3 tablespoons all-purpose flour
¾ teaspoon salt
¼ teaspoon monosodium glutamate
1 cup half and half
1 tablespoon lemon juice
2 tablespoons fresh or dried chives
1 loaf thin-sliced, day old bread, crusts trimmed

Wash mushrooms, pat dry and chop fine. Sauté in butter or margarine in skillet for about 10 minutes. Combine flour with salt and monosodium glutamate; stir into mushrooms. Add half and half, stirring constantly, and cook until thickened and smooth. Stir in lemon juice and chives. Remove from heat and spread on bread. Cut each slice into triangles. Place on baking sheets and freeze. Remove to plastic freezer bags to store. Just before serving, bake at 350 degrees for 10 to 12 minutes. Yield: about 75 or 80 servings.
Dorothy Freeman

CRAB MELT

6 English muffins, halved crosswise
1/2 cup butter or margarine, softened
1 (5-ounce) jar Cheddar cheese spread
1 (6-ounce) can crabmeat or frozen crabmeat, drained or flaked
1 1/2 tablespoons mayonnaise
Dash of garlic salt

Blend margarine or butter, cheese and garlic salt in small bowl. Drain and flake crabmeat; blend with mayonnaise. Add to cheese mixture and stir thoroughly. Spread on muffin halves. Place on ungreased baking sheet and bake at 400 degrees for 10 minutes; cut into quarters and serve hot. These may be made ahead of time and frozen. Cut into quarters before baking - they are easier to cut if frozen first. Bake at 375 degrees for 15 minutes. Yield: 48 or 96, depending upon how they are cut.
Sue McCann

HOT CHILI-ROQUEFORT CANAPES

1 (8-ounce) package cream cheese, softened
1/4 cup Roquefort cheese, crumbled
2 tablespoons catsup
1 tablespoon chili powder
1/4 teaspoon paprika
Dash of garlic powder
20 slices thin white bread, crusts removed

In a small bowl, blend softened cream cheese with Roquefort cheese. Add catsup, chili powder, paprika and dash of garlic powder. Mix well. Toast bread. Spread slices with cheese mixture and cut each slice into 3 finger-length strips. Place on baking sheets and broil until brown and bubbly. Garnish with paprika, if desired. May be prepared ahead, but spread on bread just before baking and serving. Yield: 60 appetizer servings.
Peg O'Shea

CHEESE HORS D'OEUVRES

1 loaf diet white bread
8 ounces sharp cheese, shredded
1/2 pound bacon, fried and crumbled
1 (2 1/4-ounce) package chopped almonds
1 cup salad dressing
1 teaspoon Worcestershire sauce
Salt and pepper to taste

Trim crusts from bread slices. Combine remaining ingredients and spread generously on bread; cut into small squares. Arrange on cookie sheets and freeze. When ready to use, bake at 350 degrees for 10 minutes Yield: about 60 servings.
Barb Radthe

LITTLE HOT MEAT APPETIZERS

½ pound ground pork
½ pound ground beef
1 egg, beaten
½ cup breadcrumbs
1 clove garlic, minced
Salt to taste
Pepper to taste

Blend pork and beef in a medium-sized bowl. Add egg, breadcrumbs, garlic, salt and pepper. Mix until well blended. Shape into small meatballs and add to sauce a few meatballs at a time. Simmer over a low heat for 2 hours. Serve in a heated dish with cocktail picks as servers. Yield: 40 to 50 meatballs.

Sauce:

1 teaspoon sugar
2 (8-ounce) cans tomato sauce
1 (6-ounce) can tomato paste
6 ounces water
¼ teaspoon salt
¼ teaspoon pepper
½ teaspoon red pepper
¼ teaspoon dry mustard
¼ teaspoon garlic salt
¼ teaspoon marjorum
¼ teaspoon oregano
¼ teaspoon thyme
¼ teaspoon basil
4 or 5 dashes of hot pepper sauce

Mix first 4 ingredients in a large Dutch oven. Add salt, pepper, red pepper, dry mustard and garlic salt. Stir in remaining ingredients. Mix well.
Justin Baum

TANGY FRANKFURTERS

1 pound wieners
1 (10-ounce) jar quince or crabapple jelly
1 (6-ounce) jar Dijon mustard
2 tablespoons brown sugar
1 teaspoon lemon juice
1 teaspoon Worcestershire sauce
Dash of garlic powder
1 tablespoon dry onion

Cut wieners into 1-inch pieces and set aside. Simmer jelly, mustard, sugar, lemon juice, Worcestershire sauce, garlic powder and onion over low heat, stirring constantly, for 15 minutes. Add wieners and heat thoroughly. Keep warm in fondue pot or chafing dish. Serve with cocktail picks. Yield: 40.
Sister M. Joachim

SWEET-N-SOUR PARTY MEATBALLS

2 pounds lean ground beef
1/4 teaspoon pepper
1/4 cup soy sauce
1 cup ice water

Sauce:

4 green peppers, seeded and slivered
1 (15-ounce) can pineapple chunks
1 tablespoon vegetable oil
1/4 cup vinegar
1/3 cup brown sugar, firmly packed
2 tablespoons cornstarch
1 tablespoon soy sauce
1/2 teaspoon ground ginger

Combine beef with pepper, soy sauce and ice water; form into tiny meatballs. Bake in shallow pan in 375 degree oven for 10 to 15 minutes. Sauté green peppers in oil just until slightly tender. Drain pineapple chunks, adding sufficient water to syrup to make 1½ cups liquid. Add pineapple to green pepper. Combine pineapple liquid, vinegar, brown sugar, cornstarch, soy sauce and ginger; add to mixture in skillet. Simmer until sauce thickens, stirring constantly. Cook 3 minutes, then stir in meat and cook until meatballs are heated through. (Meatballs may be made up in advance.) Yield: 7 dozen.
Elayne Lewis

STUFFED MUSHROOMS

1 pound large mushrooms
1 (8-ounce) package bulk sausage
1 (32-ounce) jar prepared spaghetti sauce
Pepper and garlic powder, as desired

Clean mushrooms and remove stems. Stuff mushroom caps with sausage. Season with pepper and garlic powder, if desired. Place on cookie sheets and bake in preheated 350 degree oven for 20 minutes. Heat sauce and transfer it to a heated dish. Use tongs to place stuffed mushrooms in sauce. Serve with cocktail picks.
Mary Lou Misciasci

RELISH MUSHROOMS

1/4 cup white vinegar
2 tablespoons sugar
1/4 teaspoon tarragon, crushed
2 (3-or 4-ounce) cans whole mushrooms, drained

Combine vinegar, sugar and tarragon in small bowl, stirring until sugar dissolves. Stir mushrooms into vinegar mixture. Chill several hours to season. Spoon into small serving bowl; garnish with onion rings. Yield: 1 cup.
JoAnn Schoch

PIZZA FONDUE

1½ pounds ground beef
1 medium onion, finely chopped
1 medium green pepper, finely chopped
2 (10½-ounce) cans pizza sauce
2 tablespoons cornstarch
1½ teaspoons oregano
½ teaspoon garlic powder
1 cup shredded mozzarella cheese
1 (10-ounce) package shredded Cheddar cheese
1½ teaspoons fennel seed
1 (6-ounce) can mushrooms, drained

Brown ground beef, onion and green pepper in large skillet; drain off fat and set aside. Blend pizza sauce with cornstarch in saucepan until smooth. Stir in beef mixture, cheeses, oregano and garlic powder. Place over low heat and stir until cheese melts and mixture is blended. Stir in fennel seeds and mushrooms; heat through. Spoon into fondue pot and keep warm. Serve with Italian or French bread which has been torn or cut into bite-size cubes. Use fondue forks for dipping.
Kay Kelly

SWEET AND SOUR MEATBALLS

2 (10-ounce) jars chili sauce
1 (10-ounce) jar grape jelly
2 pounds lean ground beef
1 teaspoon salt
1 teaspoon garlic salt
2 eggs, slightly beaten
½ medium-sized potato, grated (raw)
4 saltine crackers, crushed

Heat chili sauce and grape jelly to boiling point in large heavy saucepan; reduce heat to simmer. Meanwhile, combine beef with seasonings, eggs, potato and crackers in mixing bowl. Shape into ¾-inch balls and drop into boiling sauce. Simmer, covered, for 30 minutes. Pour all into chafing dish and serve with cocktail picks. Yield: 16 servings.
Karen Campbell

FRUIT STACK KABOBS

½ cup plain yogurt
1 tablespoon honey
Grated rind of 1 medium lime, or ½ teaspoon lime juice
Fruit of your choice (strawberries, pineapple, grapes, etc.)
Cheese cubes of your choice (Cheddar, Monterey Jack, etc.)

Combine yogurt, honey and lime rind or juice; refrigerate to allow flavors to blend. Alternate chunks of fruit and cheese on cocktail picks or skewers and arrange on tray. Serve with honey-yogurt dip. *Cool and delicious!*
Ursula Bartosik

CRAB PUFFS

1 cup water
½ cup butter
1 cup all-purpose flour
¼ teaspoon salt
4 eggs
¼ cup Parmesan cheese, grated

Bring water and butter to rolling boil in saucepan. Add flour and salt. Stir vigorously over low heat until mixture leaves sides of pan and forms a ball. Remove from heat. Add eggs, all at one time, and beat until smooth. Beat in cheese. Drop by tablespoonsful on a lightly greased 15x10x1-inch baking sheet. Bake in a preheated 400 degree oven for 18 to 20 minutes, or until golden brown. Pierce puffs with a knife to enable steam to escape. Return to oven for 5 additional minutes. Cool on wire racks. Cut tops off and set aside.

Filling:

6 eggs, hard-boiled and chopped
1 (7½-ounce) can crabmeat, drained and chopped
¼ cup onion, chopped
1 cup celery, finely chopped
½ cup mayonnaise
½ teaspoon dry mustard
½ teaspoon salt

In a bowl, thoroughly combine all ingredients. Using about 2 teaspoonsful per puff, fill each puff with crab mixture. Replace tops and chill. Yield: 2½ dozen.
Eileen Barlock

PICKLED SHRIMP

2 tablespoons instant onion, dehydrated
2 tablespoons water
¾ cup vegetable oil
2 pounds shrimp, peeled and cleaned
½ cup cider vinegar
½ teaspoon black pepper
¼ teaspoon red pepper
1½ teaspoons salt

Dehydrate onion in water. Heat ¼ cup vegetable oil in saucepan. Add onions and shrimp. Sauté 5 to 7 minutes, stirring occasionally. Combine vinegar, black pepper, red pepper, oil, and salt, in bowl. Add shrimp, marinate in refrigerator for 1 day, stirring often. Serve.
Lori O'Shea

SALAMI CORNUCOPIAS

15 thin slices 3-inch round salami
1 (8-ounce) package cream cheese, softened
¼ teaspoon pepper sauce
¼ teaspoon salt
1 tablespoon brandy
3 tablespoons minced parsley
¼ cup finely chopped walnuts

Cut each salami slice in ½ and roll around finger to form cornucopias; press edges together to seal. Place these cones (cornucopias) upright in a wire rack to fill. (May need to fasten with toothpicks.) Using a small bowl, beat cream cheese until light and fluffy; beat in pepper sauce, salt and brandy. Beat well. Stir in parsley and walnuts. Fill each salami cornucopia with cheese mixture, using a teaspoon. Remove from wire rack and set on serving dish in refrigerator for at least 1 hour to chill before serving. Yield: 30 cornucopias, about 12 servings.
Hollis Hura, Registered Dietitian, Parmadale

MEXICAN DEVILS

8 hard cooked eggs
¼ cup whipped salad dressing
2 tablespoons chopped green chilies
½ teaspoon chili powder

Slice eggs in ½ and remove the yolks. Mash yolks in a bowl, blend in salad dressing, chilies and chili powder. Refill egg whites and serve. Yield: 8 servings.
Eileen Barlock

SHRIMP MARINADE

1 cup sour cream
1 pound shrimp, cooked and cleaned
1 cup mayonnaise
1 red onion, thinly sliced
Lemon juice and garlic powder to taste

Mix all ingredients together. Marinate over night. Serve with party rye bread. Yield: 6 servings.
Chicky Weiner
Nancy Kumin
Elaine Wolfe

AVO-TACO APPETIZER

2 avocados, pitted and peeled
1 (8-ounce) package cream cheese, softened
¾ cup dairy sour cream
2 teaspoons lemon juice
Salt to taste
½ head iceburg lettuce, shredded
1 medium onion, chopped
2 tomatoes, chopped, seeded and drained
1 (6-ounce) can pitted black olives, sliced
1 (8-ounce) package Cheddar cheese, shredded
1 (4-ounce) jar mild taco sauce

Blend avocados, cream cheese, sour cream and lemon juice until smooth in small mixing bowl. Spread on 2 pie plates. Sprinkle with salt. Add layers of lettuce, onion, tomatoes, olives, cheese and taco sauce. Serve immediately. Yield: 12 appetizer servings.
Laura Valencic
Lenore Sims

TACO DIP

1 (8-ounce) package cream cheese, softened
1 (16-ounce) carton dairy sour cream
1 (2½-ounce) jar jalapeño peppers
½ envelope dry onion soup mix
4 tablespoons taco sauce
1 tablespoon lemon juice
¼ teaspoon garlic powder
½ head iceburg lettuce, shredded
3 green onions, chopped (include stems)
3 or 4 tomatoes, chopped
1 (8-ounce) package shredded Longhorn cheese

Blend cream cheese and sour cream until smooth in large mixing bowl. Stir in peppers, onion soup mix, taco sauce, lemon juice and garlic powder. Blend thoroughly. Spread on large, flat serving dish which has been coated with non-stick cooking spray. Sprinkle remaining ingredients over this mixture, in order listed. Serve at once with tacos. Keep refrigerated. Yield: 6 to 8 servings.
Judy Braun

BROCCOLI DIP

1 (10-ounce) box frozen cut broccoli
½ cup chopped onion
½ cup chopped celery
2 (4½-ounce) cans mushrooms, drained
4 tablespoons butter or margarine
1 (10¾-ounce) can cream of mushroom soup
1 (6-ounce) roll Cheddar cheese spread
1 teaspoon garlic powder

Cook broccoli until tender; drain and set aside. Sauté onions, celery and mushrooms in butter about 15 minutes; set aside. Combine soup with cheese and garlic powder; heat until cheese melts. Combine sautéed vegetables with soup mixture; add broccoli and simmer about 10 minutes, stirring occasionally, until broccoli falls apart. Serve with crisp raw vegetables or party rye bread.
Ursula Bartosik

MEXICAN CHEESE DIP

1 pound ground beef
1 pound mild Italian sausage
2 pounds processed cheese food, cut into chunks
2 jalapeño peppers, chopped fine and seeds removed
2 whole fresh tomatoes, chopped or 1 (16-ounce) can tomatoes, drained
2 small or 1 large onion, chopped
3 to 5 drops hot pepper sauce

Sauté meat in large skillet until browned; drain off fat. Melt cheese in top of double boiler, over hot water, stirring until smooth. Combine meat, cheese, onions, tomatoes, peppers, and hot pepper sauce in a crock pot or fondue pot. Keep warm. (As mixture cools, it will thicken.) Delicious with taco chips, corn chips or crackers. Yield: 16 appetizer servings.
Karen Bell

PRAIRIE FIRE DIP

1 pound processed cheese food
1 (4-ounce) can chopped green chilies
2 tablespoons chopped onion
1 (15-ounce) can chili without beans

Cut cheese into chunks and place in bottom of a greased 2-quart casserole dish. Stir in onion, green chilies and canned chili. Heat in a 350 degree oven until cheese melts (approximately 20 minutes). Remove from oven and stir until smooth. Serve with corn chips. Yield: 10 to 12 appetizer servings.
Judy Braun

DILL DIP

1 cup real mayonnaise
1 teaspoon dried onions
1 teaspoon dried parsley
½ teaspoon monosodium glutamate
1 cup dairy sour cream
1 teaspoon dried dill weed
½ teaspoon seasoned salt
½ teaspoon Worcestershire sauce
2 or 3 dashes hot pepper sauce
Green food coloring

Blend mayonnaise, onions, parsley, monosodium glutamate, sour cream, dill weed, seasoned salt, Worcestershire sauce and hot pepper sauce in small bowl of electric mixer until smooth. Add a few drops of food coloring. Chill before serving. Yield: 2½ cups (10 to 12 servings).
Peg O'Shea

HOT CRAB SPREAD OR DIP

1 (8-ounce) package cream cheese, softened
1 tablespoon milk
1 (6½-ounce) package frozen crabmeat, thawed and drained
2 tablespoons chopped onion
½ teaspoon prepared horseradish
½ teaspoon salt
½ teaspoon pepper
½ cup slivered almonds, optional

Blend cream cheese with milk in small bowl of electric mixer; add onion, horseradish, salt, pepper and crabmeat. Stir well. Spread into greased baking dish; top with almonds. Bake at 375 degrees for 15 minutes. Serve hot. Yield: 2½ cups or about 10 to 12 servings.
Justin Baum
Becky Dingeldein

DILLED SHRIMP DIP

½ cup milk
2 (8-ounce) packages cream cheese, softened
2 (4½-ounce) cans shrimp, rinsed, drained and chopped
2 teaspoons lemon juice
2 teaspoons Worcestershire sauce
1 teaspoon dill weed
½ cup chopped green onion, including green tops

Blend milk and cream cheese until smooth. Stir in shrimp, lemon juice, Worcestershire sauce, dill weed and onion. Cover and chill at least 2 hours. Yield: about 3 cups.
Teddi Wise

DILLED DIP

1 tablespoon lemon juice
1 teaspoon dry mustard
1 cup mayonnaise
1 cup dairy sour cream
1 teaspoon dill weed, or 1 tablespoon fresh chopped dill
¼ teaspoon salt

Combine lemon juice and mustard, stirring until smooth. Add remaining ingredients and mix well. Serve with vegetables or seafood—shrimp, crabmeat, etc. Yield: 2 cups.
Lynne Della Donna

ARTICHOKE DIP

2 (14-ounce) cans artichokes
1 cup real mayonnaise
1 cup grated Parmesan cheese
1 (6-ounce) package herb stuffing
¼ teaspoon garlic powder

Slice artichokes into quarters and mash in a medium sized bowl. Add mayonnaise and Parmesan cheese; mix well. Place in an 8x8-inch baking dish which has been coated with non-stick cooking spray. Pour herb stuffing over top and sprinkle with garlic powder. Bake 20 minutes at 350 degrees. Yield: 10 to 12 servings.
Teri Andos

DIJON VEGETABLE DIP

1 cup dairy sour cream
½ cup mayonnaise
2 teaspoons Dijon mustard
2 teaspoons prepared horseradish
1 teaspoon dill weed
1 teaspoon lemon juice
1 garlic clove, pressed

In a small bowl thoroughly combine sour cream, mayonnaise, mustard, horseradish, dill weed, lemon juice and pressed garlic juice. Serve with raw vegetables or chips. Yield: 6 to 8 servings.
Lynne Della Donna

MEAT-FILLED PIEROSZKI

2 pounds lean soup beef, cooked
1 large onion, chopped
1 beef bouillon cube
½ cup boiling water
Salt and pepper

Grind beef in food grinder or processor; place in a large bowl. Sauté onion in a small amount of margarine until golden brown; add to meat. Dissolve bouillon cube in water and stir into meat mixture. Add salt and pepper to taste; mix well and set aside.

Dough:

2 cups milk
½ cup butter or margarine
3 tablespoons sugar
1 teaspoon salt
1 envelope active dry yeast
2 eggs
3 to 4 cups all-purpose flour

Heat milk and butter in a saucepan over low heat. When butter is melted, add sugar and salt. Remove from heat and cool slightly; add yeast and allow to dissolve. Place flour and eggs in a large bowl, add yeast mixture and mix well. Let rise until doubled in bulk, no more than 1 hour (pieroszkis will rise during baking). Roll out dough on floured surface to ½-inch thickness and cut circles with a juice glass. Place 1 teaspoon meat mixture on each circle, fold over and pinch edges to seal. Brush tops with egg beaten with a little water. Place on greased cookie sheets and bake at 350 degress 20 minutes, or until golden brown. Serve hot. Delicious as an appetizer, brunch dish, or accompaniment to soups and salads. Yield: about 5 dozen.
Janina Ptak

CHEESE-ASPARAGUS ROLLS

½ cup butter
1 (4-ounce) package bleu cheese
1 (16-ounce) can asparagus spears, well drained
14 to 16 slices white bread
Melted butter for topping
Romano or Parmesan cheese for garnish

Blend butter and bleu cheese thoroughly. After removing the crusts, roll bread out. Spread each slice with cheese mixture. Place asparagus spear at one end of each slice of bread; roll up lengthwise and cut roll into thirds. Place on cookie sheet and brush with melted butter. Sprinkle with Romano or Parmesan cheese and bake at 375 degrees for 12 to 15 minutes, or until slightly browned. Yield: 42 to 50 rolls.
Kay Kelly

FREEZER CHEESE PUFFS

10 slices bacon
1 small onion, minced
½ (8-ounce) package slivered almonds
½ pound sharp Cheddar cheese, shredded
1 tablespoon sherry
1 cup mayonnaise
2 teaspoons Worcestershire sauce
1 loaf white thin-sliced bread

Cook bacon until crisp; drain and crumble. Combine bacon, onion, almonds, cheese, sherry, mayonnaise and Worcestershire sauce in medium bowl. Trim crusts from bread. Spread each slice with cheese mixture and cut into quarters (squares or triangles). Place sandwiches on baking sheet and freeze. Remove from baking sheet and store in airtight plastic bag until needed. Just before serving, bake at 400 degrees for about 10 minutes or until puffed and golden brown. Yield: about 90 cheese puffs.
Ann O'Shea
Peg O'Shea

CHEDDAR PUFFS

1 loaf unsliced white bread (at least 1 day old) French bread
¼ pound sharp Cheddar cheese, cut into chunks
¼ pound butter, cut into pieces
2 egg whites

Trim crusts from bread all around and cut loaf into 1-inch cubes. Combine cheese and butter in top of double boiler. Place over hot, not boiling, water and stir until cheese is melted and mixture is smooth. Remove from heat and cool completely. Beat egg whites until stiff peaks form; slowly fold into cooled cheese mixture. Drop bread cubes into cheese and coat well on all sides. Remove to baking sheet which has been coated with non-stick vegetable spray. Cover loosely with waxed paper and refrigerate overnight before baking. (At this point cubes may be frozen and stored in plastic bags for use later.) Just before serving, remove puffs from refrigerator (or freezer) and bake at 400 degrees for 10 to 12 minutes or until puffed and golden. Yield: enough appetizers for 10 to 12 people.
Gloria Rosenbush

OLIVE-CHEESE PUFFS

2 cups shredded sharp Cheddar cheese
1 cup all-purpose flour
1/2 teaspoon paprika
1/2 cup butter or margarine
3 to 4 dozen small pimiento-stuffed olives

Combine cheese, flour, paprika and margarine; mix well and chill. Use a generous teaspoonful for each puff and shape into ball. Make an indentation in center and place olive inside. Smooth dough around to fully cover olive. Bake at 400 degrees for 15 minutes, or until golden (do not allow to brown). Serve hot. Puffs may be frozen, then thawed and baked as needed. Yield:3 to 4 dozen.
Lynne Della Donna

PARMESAN PASTRY TWISTS

1 (10-ounce, 6 count) frozen pastry shells, thawed
1 egg white, slightly beaten
1/4 cup grated Parmesan cheese
2 teaspoons snipped chives

Roll each pastry shell on a lightly floured board to flatten slightly. Arrange pieces on board so that they overlap slightly to form a rectangle. Press edges together with fingertips to seal. Roll with rolling pin to 12x8x1/8-inch rectangle. Brush lightly with egg white; sprinkle with cheese and chives. Cut rectangle in 1/2 lengthwise. Cut each 1/2 crosswise into 12 sticks. Pick each stick up, twist a few times and place on an ungreased baking sheet. Bake at 425 degrees for 8 to 10 minutes. Yield: 24 twists.
Karen Campbell

EGG ROLL FILLING

2 tablespoons vegetable oil
12-ounces cooked shrimp, minced
2 cups Chinese celery cabbage, finely shredded
8 to 10 water chestnuts, shredded
2 stalks celery, minced
1 cup bean sprouts
1 teaspoon salt
1 tablespoon soy sauce
1 teaspoon sugar
6 to 8 egg roll wrappers
1 egg, beaten, for sealing
2 cups oil for deep-frying

Stir-fry shrimp, cabbage, water chestnuts and celery in 2 tablespoons of heated oil in wok for 2 or 3 minutes, until vegetables become brighter. Add bean sprouts and stir in salt, soy sauce and sugar. Put mixture in egg roll wrapper and seal edges with beaten egg. Deep-fry a few egg rolls at a time in 375 degree oil, until they are brown and crisp. Serve immediately. Yield: 6 or 8 egg rolls. Egg Roll Wrappers on page 25.
Patti Lovejoy

SHRIMP-STUFFED MUSHROOMS

12 large or 24 small mushrooms
2 tablespoons margarine
1½ tablespoons minced onion
½ cup cooked, finely chopped shrimp
2 tablespoons sherry
4 tablespoons grated Parmesan cheese
3 tablespoons breadcrumbs
2 tablespoons chopped parsley
Additional small whole shrimp for garnish

Remove and finely chop mushroom stems. Melt margarine in a small skillet; add onions and mushrooms stems; sauté until tender. Add 3 tablespoons cheese, breadcrumbs and parsley. Remove from heat and stir until all ingredients are moistened. Stuff mushroom caps with cooked mixture. Sprinkle with remaining cheese and top each with a tiny shrimp. Broil 1 minute; serve hot.
Jean Croyle

SAUSAGE STUFFED MUSHROOMS

½ pound mushrooms
⅓ pound mild bulk sausage
1 slice fresh white bread
1 teaspoon parsley flakes
¼ teaspoon garlic powder
1 tablespoon Parmesan cheese

Brown sausage in skillet until cooked through; drain off most of the fat, leaving about 1 teaspoon in bottom of skillet. Shred bread finely with fingers into cooked sausage and fat in skillet. Add parsley, garlic powder and cheese; mix well. Wash mushrooms and remove stems. (Stems may be reserved for use in another dish if desired.) Place mushrooms, underside up, in a shallow greased baking pan or glass dish. Spoon some of prepared filling into each mushroom cap and bake at 350 degrees for about 15 minutes, or until mushrooms are soft and stuffing is lightly browned. Serve immediately. Yield: about 6 appetizer servings.
Hollis Hura, Registered Dietitian, Parmadale

DEVILED BISCUITS

1 (10-count) package refrigerated biscuits
1 (4-ounce) can deviled ham
½ cup butter or margarine
Grated Parmesan cheese

Snip biscuits into quarters and arrange in 2 (8-inch) round pans. Heat deviled ham and butter, stirring until blended. Pour ham mixture over biscuits, coating each piece. Sprinkle generously with cheese. If desired, sprinkle lightly with lemon-pepper marinade. Bake at 400 degrees about 15 minutes, or until golden brown. Serve hot. Yield: 40 servings.
Barb Radthe

SISTER'S COCKTAIL BISCUITS

1 pound bulk sausage
8 ounces Cheddar cheese, shredded
1 medium onion, minced
2 teaspoons liquid red pepper seasoning
3 cups buttermilk baking mix

Preheat oven to 450 degrees. Crumble sausage into a medium bowl. Add cheese, onion, red pepper seasoning and baking mix. Work with hands until thoroughly blended. Shape by level tablespoonfuls into 1-inch balls. Place 1-inch apart on ungreased baking sheets; flatten slightly. Bake 15 minutes, or until golden brown; serve hot. To freeze, cool biscuits thoroughly and freeze in single layer on cookie sheet. Transfer to freezer container or wrap in foil. To reheat, bake at 450 degrees for 15 minutes. Yield: about 4½ dozen.
Sister Joachim

SAUERKRAUT BALLS

4 tablespoons butter
1 medium-sized onion, chopped
1⅓ cups chopped ham
½ clove garlic, minced
4 tablespoons all-purpose flour
½ cup chicken broth
3 cups sauerkraut, drained and chopped
1 tablespoon chopped parsley
2½ cups all-purpose flour
1 egg
2 cups milk
½ loaf soft bread, crusts trimmed and crumbled

Sauté onion in butter in large skillet until golden and tender. Stir in ham and garlic and brown slightly. Blend in 4 tablespoons flour, stirring until smooth. Gradually stir in broth, sauerkraut and parsley; mix thoroughly. Cook for a few more minutes, until mixture resembles a croquette mixture. Remove from heat and spoon into a large flat pan to cool. When cooled, shape into balls about 1-inch in diameter. Beat egg and milk together in small bowl. Dip balls into flour, then into egg and milk mixture, then into breadcrumbs. Deep fry until golden brown. Serve hot. Yield: about 100 balls.
Bill Mahon

HOT CHICKEN WINGS

2½ pounds chicken wings
4 tablespoons red-hot sauce (or more, to taste)
¼ cup melted butter or margarine

Split wings at joints, discard tips and pat dry. Arrange in baking dish and bake, uncovered, 30 minutes at 325 degrees. Remove from pan and place in bowl. Combine hot sauce and butter; pour over wings. Cover and marinate 3 hours at room temperature, or overnight in refrigerator, turning several times. To serve, broil wings 3 to 4 inches from heat, 5 minutes per side, until brown and crispy, basting with marinade. Baste again before serving. *These are famous in Buffalo, New York.*
Lynne Della Donna

SPINACH BALLS

2 (10-ounce) packages frozen chopped spinach
3½ cups herb-seasoned stuffing mix
1 large onion, chopped
½ cup grated Parmesan cheese
½ teaspoon garlic salt
½ teaspoon thyme
¾ cup melted butter or margarine
6 eggs

Cook spinach and drain well, pressing out all water. Combine with remaining ingredients and form mixture into walnut-size balls. Bake at 325 degrees for 15 to 20 minutes.
Jean Rambert

SKILLET EGG ROLL WRAPPERS

2 cups sifted all-purpose flour
2 tablespoons cornstarch
2 teaspoons salt
2 teaspoons sugar
2 eggs, beaten
2 cups water

In a bowl combine dry ingredients and add egg. Stir in water until batter is smooth. Oil small skillet. Place over low heat. Pour ¼ cup batter into center of pan and tilt pan to spread batter evenly. Cook batter over low heat until edges pull away from sides of pan. Turn over and cook other side. Remove wrappers and cool before using. Yield: about 20 wrappers.
Patti Lovejoy

OLD ENGLISH CHEESE BALL

1 (5-ounce) jar Old English Cheddar cheese spread
1 (5-ounce) jar Roka Blue cheese spread
1 (8-ounce) package cream cheese, softened
2 tablespoons wine vinegar
1/4 teaspoon garlic powder
Chopped nuts

Combine all ingredients, except nuts, in mixing bowl and blend well. Refrigerate until firm. Shape into a ball and roll in chopped nuts. Garnish with a maraschino cherry. Serve with your choice of crackers. Yield: 1 medium cheese ball
Lynne Della Donna

BOURSIN CHEESE

2 (8-ounce) packages cream cheese, softened
1 cup butter or margarine, softened
1 teaspoon oregano
2 cloves garlic, crushed
1/4 teaspoon basil
1/4 teaspoon marjoram
1/4 teaspoon dill
1/4 teaspoon thyme
1/4 teaspoon pepper

In a medium-sized bowl, blend cream cheese, butter, oregano, crushed garlic, basil, marjoram, dill, thyme and pepper. When thoroughly blended, place in serving dish surrounded with assorted crackers. Yield: 3 cups. *Like the real thing!*
Florence Douridas

CHEESE-IN-A-BLANKET

1 (8-count) package refrigerated crescent roll dough
1 Gouda cheese round, rind removed

Remove crescent roll dough from tube and unroll; press flat with hands. Place cheese in center of dough and bring up sides so cheese is completely covered. Press seams together with fingers. Place, seamed side down, on baking sheet and bake at 350 degrees for about 10 minutes. Remove from oven and let set for about 5 minutes before serving. Serve warm.
Nancy Kumin

SALMON PARTY BALL

1 (13-ounce) can red salmon
1 (8-ounce) package cream cheese
1 tablespoon lemon juice
2 teaspoons grated onion
1 teaspoon prepared horseradish
½ teaspoon salt
¼ teaspoon liquid smoke or hickory salt
½ cup chopped nuts

Completely drain salmon, removing bones and skin. Place in medium-sized bowl and add softened cream cheese, lemon juice, onion, horseradish, salt and liquid smoke or hickory salt. Mix thoroughly and shape into ball. Roll in nuts. Refrigerate. Yield: 3 cups.
Donna Miller
Nancy Kumin

PINEAPPLE-CHEESE BALL

2 (8-ounce) packages cream cheese
¼ green pepper, chopped very fine
1 small onion, chopped very fine
1 (8-ounce) can crushed pineapple, drained
1 cup crushed pecans or walnuts
½ cup finely crushed nuts

In a large bowl, thoroughly mix cream cheese, green pepper and onion. Add pineapple and 1 cup crushed nuts. Blend thoroughly. Form into a ball and roll in finely crushed nuts. Refrigerate for at least 1 hour before serving. Yield: 3 cups.
Mary Gorbet

BLACK OLIVE CHEESE BALL

1 (4-ounce) package blue cheese
1 (8-ounce) package cream cheese
½ cup margarine
1 small onion, grated
1 (4-ounce) can black olives, chopped
1 cup chopped nuts

Combine blue cheese, cream cheese and margarine in bowl. Add grated onion and chopped olives. Blend. Form into well-shaped ball and roll in chopped nuts until well covered. Chill before serving.
Lynne Della Donna

BACON-DILL CHEESE BALL

1 (8-ounce) package cream cheese, softened
½ cup real mayonnaise
1 tablespoon chopped green onion
½ teaspoon dill weed
6 slices bacon
1 cup slivered almonds

In a large bowl, thoroughly combine softened cream cheese with mayonnaise. Add onion and dill weed. Cook bacon until crisp; drain on paper towels and crumble. Add to cheese mixture and blend thoroughly. Cover and chill for several hours. Brown almonds in 350 degree oven. Form cheese into ball and roll in nuts. Refrigerate until serving time. Yield: 2 cups.
Mary Scherzer

GLAZED BRIE

1 (1½ to 2 pound) Brie wheel
2 cups sugar
½ cup water
Pecans

Remove rind of cheese carefully and place Brie on large sheet of foil. Combine sugar and water in a saucepan; heat to melt, swirling pan carefully. *Do not stir.* As mixture begins to boil, cover pan and allow the condensation to drip back down and melt sugar. After 3 to 5 minutes, uncover pan and cook over high heat until sugar turns golden brown. (Temperature of sugar should be 300 degrees—hard crack state.) Pour caramel over cheese immediately, covering top evenly. Excess will drip down sides and caramel will harden. Be sure to serve within an hour. Arrange pecans on top, around base and serve with cheese knives. May be served as an appetizer or as a dessert with fresh fruit. *The combined flavors are wonderful!*
Karen West

BRIE PÂTÉ

1 (16-ounce) wheel of Brie cheese
½ cup shredded white Cheddar cheese
¼ cup dairy sour cream
1 tablespoon dry sherry
⅛ teaspoon pepper
¼ cup finely chopped scallion

Trim rind from Brie. Combine Brie, Cheddar cheese, sour cream, sherry and pepper in large bowl of electric mixer and beat until smooth. Stir in scallion. Spoon into serving bowl, cover, and chill for at least 1 hour before serving. Garnish with additional scallion, if desired. Yield: 10 servings.
Sue Polacek

SEEDED CHEESE ROLL

1 (8-ounce) package bleu cheese
1 (8-ounce) package cream cheese, softened
1 cup butter or margarine
¾ cup stuffed green olives, chopped
⅓ cup sesame seed, toasted
1 tablespoon snipped chives
1 tablespoon snipped parsley
1 clove garlic, crushed

Beat bleu cheese, cream cheese and margarine or butter in large bowl of electric mixer until smooth. Stir in olives, chives, parsley and garlic. Cover and refrigerate for about 1 hour, or until mixture is stiff enough to roll. Remove from refrigerator and divide into 4 equal parts. Shape each into a roll the diameter of a silver dollar. Roll in sesame seed. Wrap tightly in plastic wrap and store in refrigerator or freezer. If using frozen cheese ball, remove from freezer about 1 hour before serving time. Slice into ¼-inch pieces and serve on crackers. Yield: 25 or 30 servings.
Karen O'Shea

SALMON MOUSSE

1 envelope unflavored gelatin
¼ cup cold water
½ cup whipping cream or milk, scalded
1 (8-ounce) package cream cheese, softened
1 cup sour cream
1 teaspoon lemon juice
1 teaspoon Worcestershire sauce
2 dashes hot pepper sauce
2 shakes garlic salt
½ cup grated onion
3 tablespoons chopped chives
2 tablespoons chopped parsley
1 or 2 tablespoons prepared horseradish
3 (3-ounce) packages sliced, smoked salmon or up to 1 pound of any smoked salmon, coarsely chopped
Stuffed green olives, sliced
Shredded carrot and lettuce, for garnish

Lightly grease a 5-cup shallow mold (fish-shaped, if possible). Soften gelatin in cold water. Heat cream and stir in. Soften cream cheese in a heavy saucepan; stir in sour cream, lemon juice, Worcestershire sauce, hot pepper sauce and garlic salt. Gently fold into gelatin mixture with onion, chives, parsley, horseradish, and salmon. Turn into mold. Cover with plastic wrap. Chill until set. To serve, dip mold quickly into warm water; place serving platter over mold and invert. Garnish mold with olive slices and shredded carrot, tucking lettuce around mold. Serve with wafers or crackers. Yield: 5 cups.
Elaine Wolfe

GAIL'S SUPER CRABMEAT SPREAD

2 (6-ounce) packages frozen crabmeat, thawed
2 (8-ounce) packages cream cheese, softened
2 teaspoons Worcestershire sauce
8 tablespoons catsup
3 tablespoons dairy sour cream
1 small onion, grated

Drain crabmeat well and remove any cartilage. Combine all ingredients in small bowl. Cover with plastic wrap and refrigerate overnight to develop flavors. Serve with crackers. Shrimp may be substituted for crabmeat. Yield: 8 to 10 appetizer servings.
Gail Lynn

EASY TUNA SPREAD

1 (13-ounce) can tuna, drained and flaked
1 small onion, quartered
1 egg, hard-boiled
1/2 cup sliced almonds
1 teaspoon seasoned salt
1/4 teaspoon seasoned pepper
2 tablespoons brandy
1/3 cup mayonnaise or salad dressing
Dash of red pepper seasoning

Combine all ingredients in an electric blender. Cover and process at high speed for 2 minutes, or until mixture forms a stiff paste. Line a 3-cup mold (or bowl) with plastic wrap; pack mixture into bowl and cover with plastic wrap. Refrigerate at least 6 hours. Unmold mixture by lifting plastic wrap from bowl or mold and inverting onto serving plate. Yield: 12 servings.
Jane Ward

CURRIED TUNA SPREAD

1 8-ounce) package cream cheese, softened
3/4 teaspoon curry powder
3 tablespoons milk
1 tablespoon sherry
3 tablespoons chopped chutney
1 (7-ounce) can chunk tuna, drained and flaked

Combine cream cheese with curry powder, milk and sherry; blend until smooth. Stir in chutney and tuna. Serve hot or cold as a spread or dip. Heat in oven until hot, then serve warm or allow to cool. Yield: 2 cups.
Barb Radthe

LIVER PÂTÉ

1 (10¾-ounce) can beef consommé
1 envelope unflavored gelatin
1 medium onion, minced
1 dash Worcestershire sauce
1 (8-ounce) package cream cheese
¾ pound gooseliver or braunschweiger

Heat consommé and gelatin over medium heat, stirring until gelatin dissolves. Remove from heat and pour a small amount of mixture into a 1½-cup decorative mold, covering bottom. Place in freezer for 10 minutes, or until set. In a blender bowl, combine remaining consommé mixture with remaining ingredients; whip until creamy. Remove mold from freezer; add creamy mixture and refrigerate 3 or 4 hours, or until set. May be made on the day of serving. Serve with light crackers. Yield: 1½ cups.
Paula Knight

ZUCCHINI SPREAD

2 cups grated zucchini
¼ cup dairy sour cream
¼ cup plain yogurt
3 tablespoons chopped chives
Salt and pepper, as desired
Chopped fresh basil for seasoning, optional

Place zucchini in strainer and press out as much moisture as possible. In a bowl, mix zucchini with sour cream, yogurt and chives. Season as desired with salt, pepper and basil. Use this spread as a sandwich filling together with ham, chicken or sliced tomatoes; or use as an appetizer by spreading on crackers or cucumber slices.
Ruth Abbott

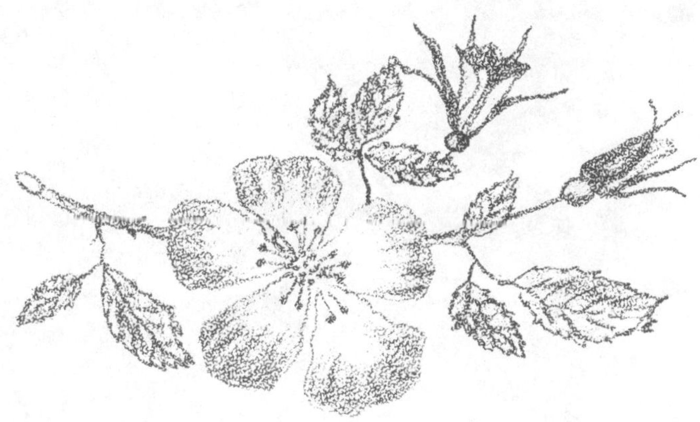

WHET YOUR WHISTLE

Beverages

HOLIDAY PUNCH BOWL

6 (5/8-ounce) envelopes instant daiquiri mix
2 cups light rum
1 (46-ounce) can red fruit punch, chilled
1 (28-ounce) bottle quinine water
1 orange, cut into thin slices

Combine daiquiri mix and rum in a medium-sized bowl. Stir until mix is completely dissolved. Refrigerate until time to serve. To serve, pour rum mixture into a punch bowl. Add the fruit punch and quinine water. Stir until well blended. Carefully, add ice mold and orange slices. Yield: about 25 (4-ounce) servings.

Ice Mold:
Fill an 8-cup mold with water. Freeze for 4 hours or overnight. To unmold, let mold stand at room temperature for about 5 minutes or until ice is movable in the mold. Invert on a baking sheet and carefully slide into a filled punch bowl.
A Friend

TINGLE BELLS PUNCH

2 quarts cranberry juice cocktail, chilled
1 (6-ounce) can frozen lemonade concentrate, thawed
½ cup maraschino cherry juice
2 trays ice cubes
8 (7-ounce) bottles lemon-lime carbonated beverage, chilled

Combine the first 4 ingredients in a punch bowl. Add ice cubes or ice ring and stir gently. Pour lemon-lime carbonated beverage down the side of the bowl to retain bubbles. Garnish, if desired, with lemon slices, orange wedges and maraschino cherries or alternate these on cocktail picks and add 1 to each cup. Yield: 35 (4-ounce) cups.
Rosemary Corcoran

RASPBERRY PUNCH

10 cups cranberry juice cocktail, chilled
5 cups raspberry flavored carbonated beverage, chilled
1 (10-ounce) package frozen raspberries, thawed
1 quart raspberry sherbet

Pour chilled carbonated beverage into a punch bowl. Add cranberry juice and thawed raspberries. Stir gently to blend. Garnish with scoops of raspberry sherbet. Yield: 30 servings.
Eileen Barlock

PARTY PUNCH

4 quarts water
2 cups sugar
2 quarts cranberry juice
1 quart apple juice
1 (12-ounce) can frozen lemonade, thawed
1 (12-ounce) can frozen orange juice, thawed

Heat water and sugar to boiling. Allow to cool to room temperature. Place cooled mixture in a punch bowl. Add remaining ingredients and mix well. If desired, "spike" to taste. Yield: 2 gallons.
Karen Collins

JA NAE'S COLD COFFEE PUNCH

4 cups coffee, prepared and cooled
1 quart chocolate ice cream
1 cup milk
½ cup sugar
½ pint whipping cream, whipped

Fold ingredients together in order listed. Pour into cups and serve with cinnamon sprinkled on top, if desired. Yield: 8 to 10 servings.
Ja Nae Miller

SUMMER SLUSH

1 (12-ounce) can frozen orange juice, undiluted
1 (12-ounce) can frozen lemonade, undiluted
1 (46-ounce) can unsweetened pineapple juice
1½ cups vodka
1 (2-liter) bottle lemon-lime carbonated beverage

Thoroughly mix first 4 ingredients. Store, covered, in the freezer until ready to be served. To serve, spoon into glasses and fill with lemon-lime beverage. Yield: 16 to 20 servings.
Michele Leahy

HOT SPICED NECTAR

3 cups apricot nectar
2 cups orange juice
2 tablespoons lime juice
1 cup water
½ cup brown sugar, packed
1 (2-inch) stick cinnamon
1 teaspoon whole cloves

Combine nectar, orange juice, lime juice and water in a 10 cup percolator. Combine the remaining ingredients in the percolator basket. Allow to complete 1 cycle in an automatic percolator or perk for 10 minutes on the stovetop. Remove basket and serve. Yield: 6½ cups.
Peg O'Shea

SHERBET PUNCH

1 (46-ounce) can punch flavored drink
1 (46-ounce) can grapefruit juice
2 quarts ginger ale or lemon-lime carbonated soft drink
1 quart raspberry sherbet
1 quart lemon-lime sherbet

Mix punch, grapefruit juice and ginger ale; chill. When ready to serve, top with scoops of sherbet. Orange juice can be substituted for the grapefruit juice. Yield: 20 servings.
Edith Demshar

JOANIE'S IRISH CREAM

3 eggs
3/4 cup sweetened condensed milk
1/2 pint whipping cream
1/2 pint half and half
1 tablespoon chocolate syrup
1 teaspoon instant coffee, dissolved in 1 tablespoon hot water
3/4 to 1 cup Scotch

Combine ingredients in blender container. Blend on high until well mixed. Can be served immediately or stored in a glass container which is tightly covered in the refrigerator for up to 1 month. Yield: 1 quart.
Joan Gullett

SPICED APPLE CORDIAL

2 1/2 cups apples, cored, peeled and chopped
1 (6-inch) stick cinnamon, broken
2 cups sugar
2 tablespoons water
3 1/2 cups (750-millimeter bottle) dry white wine
1 1/2 cups brandy

In a saucepan, combine apples, cinnamon and 2 tablespoons of water. Cover and simmer for 5 to 10 minutes. Stir in sugar until dissolved; cool. Combine apple mixture, wine and brandy. Pour into a 2-quart ceramic or glass jar. Cover and store in a cool place for 2 to 4 weeks. Yield: 4 cups.
A Friend

FRUIT NOG

1 (6 ounce) can frozen pineapple juice concentrate, thawed
2 quarts egg nog
1 cup orange liqueur
1/2 cup water
1/2 teaspoon ground allspice
1 pint vanilla ice cream
Ground nutmeg, optional

Pour pineapple juice, egg nog, orange liqueur, water and allspice into a punch bowl. Stir to blend. Garnish with scoops of vanilla ice cream. Sprinkle with nutmeg, if desired. Yield: 20 (4-ounce) servings.
Eileen Barlock

PATIO PUNCH

1 (750 ml) bottle Southern Comfort
2 cups grapefruit juice
1 (2-liter) bottle of lemon-lime carbonated beverage or ginger ale

Combine ingredients in order listed. Mix until well blended. Add ice. Serve chilled. First 3 ingredients can be mixed in advance and refrigerated. Yield: 2 gallons.
Edith Demshar

HOT MULLED CIDER

½ cup firmly packed brown sugar
1 teaspoon whole allspice
1 teaspoon whole cloves
3 inches stick cinnamon
Dash of ground nutmeg
¼ teaspoon salt
2 quarts apple cider
Orange wedges (rind on)

Combine sugar, spices and apple cider in large saucepan. Slowly bring to a boil, stirring to dissolve sugar. Cover, reduce heat, and simmer for about 20 minutes. Remove spices. Serve hot in warmed mugs garnished with a clove-studded orange wedge. Yield: 8 servings.
Connie Bobe

CHOCOLATE NOG

7 cups milk, divided
4 egg yolks
½ cup creamy peanut butter
¾ cup chocolate syrup
2 teaspoons vanilla extract
4 egg whites
1 cup whipping cream
Ground cinnamon

Combine 4 cups milk, egg yolks, peanut butter, chocolate and vanilla. Whip until foamy. Pour into a punch bowl. Add remaining milk and stir to blend. Beat egg whites until stiff. Fold into the milk mixture. Beat whipping cream until stiff and fold in. Sprinkle with cinnamon for garnish, if desired. Yield: 12 (1-cup) servings.
Patti Lovejoy

HOT CHOCOLATE EGGNOG

1 quart dairy eggnog
2 cups milk
½ cup chocolate syrup
Nutmeg, if desired

Blend eggnog, milk and chocolate syrup in a saucepan. Cook over a low heat until thoroughly warmed. Serve in mugs. Garnish with nutmeg, if desired. *Easy and the kids will love it.* Yield: 12 (4-ounce) servings.
Eileen Barlock

VERY SPIRITED EGGNOG

12 eggs, separated
1 (16-ounce) package confectioners' sugar
1 cup bourbon
½ cup rum
¼ cup brandy
2 quarts milk
¼ teaspoon salt
2 cups whipping cream, whipped
Freshly ground nutmeg

Beat egg yolks until light and lemon colored. Gradually, beat in confectioners' sugar. Add bourbon, a little at a time, beating constantly. Allow mixture to stand for several hours or overnight to dispel the egg taste. Add rum, brandy and milk, beating constantly. Refrigerate, covered, for 3 hours. Beat egg whites with salt until stiff but not dry. Fold into the rum mixture. Fold whipped cream into the rum mixture. Dust lightly with freshly ground nutmeg. Yield: 20 servings.
Edith Demshar

YUMMY RUMMY EGGNOG

12 eggs, separated
1½ cups sugar
¼ teaspoon salt
1 quart heavy cream, beaten
1 quart milk
2 tablespoons vanilla or rum extract, or ½ cup rum
Freshly ground nutmeg
Vanilla ice cream, optional

Beat egg whites until stiff. Beat in ½ cup sugar. In another bowl, beat egg yolks, 1 cup sugar and salt until very light and fluffy. Combine egg mixtures, stirring until thoroughly blended. Add cream, milk and vanilla or rum. Beat well. Pour into a punch bowl and serve immediately with scoops of vanilla ice cream floating on top. Eggnog may be stored in the refrigerator in a gallon jug for 1 week. Yield: 30 servings.
Ann Karpac

CHERRY SLUSH

7 cups boiling water
1 cup sugar
2 tea bags (single-serving size)
2 cups cherry flavored vodka
1 (12-ounce) can frozen orange juice concentrate
Water and sugar for rimming glasses

Combine boiling water and sugar with tea bags; let steep for 3 to 5 minutes. Remove and discard tea bags. Cool mixture. Add vodka and orange juice concentrate. Pour into a 13x9x2-inch baking pan. Freeze overnight. To serve, use a large spoon to scrape across the surface of the frozen mixture. Spoon slush into chilled, sugar-rimmed glasses. To rim the glasses with sugar, rub the edge of each glass with water; invert glass in a dish of sugar. Yield: 10 cups.
A Friend

STRAWBERRY DAQUIRIS

1 (16-ounce) package frozen strawberries in syrup
1 (12-ounce) can frozen limeade
1 limeade can filled with rum
1 limeade can filled with water

Mix all ingredients in a 2-quart pitcher. Pour ⅓ of mixture over blender full of ice. Blend on high until "slush" consistency. Repeat with remaining mixture. Can be frozen in covered containers and scooped out with ice cream scooper when served. Yield: 8 to 10 servings.
Carol Mazzella

SPICED WINE MIX

2 cups sugar
2 teaspoons ground cinnamon
2 teaspoons ground cloves
1 teaspoon ground allspice
¼ teaspoon ground nutmeg
1 bottle dry red wine
Cinnamon sticks

Place all dry ingredients except cinnamon sticks in a jar with a tight fitting lid; cover and shake. Store, covered, at room temperature for up to 3 months. For each serving, mix 2 teaspoons dry mix and ½ cup water. Heat in a saucepan to boiling. Add 1 cup dry red wine; heat until hot, but not boiling. Yield: about 50 servings.
Dottie Vanek

BOURBON SLUSH

3 cups boiled water
2 tea bags
1 cup sugar
1 (12-ounce) can frozen orange juice concentrate, thawed
1 (6-ounce) can frozen lemonade concentrate, thawed
½ cup bourbon

Steep tea bags in water; cool. Add remaining ingredients and freeze. To serve, scoop mixture into desired number of beverage glasses and serve with spoons.
Delicious on summer evenings.
Karen West

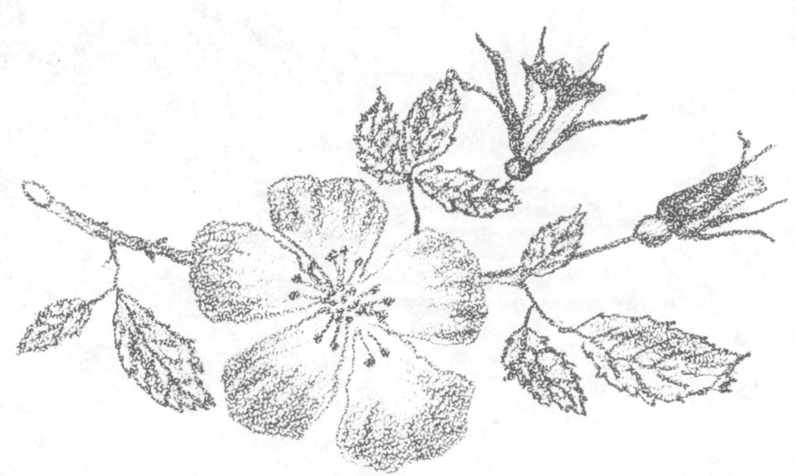

HEARTY FARE

Soups and Sandwiches

ITALIAN WEDDING SOUP

Basic Chicken Soup:

1 stewing hen
1/4 cup salt
4 carrots
3 ribs celery
2 large onions

Clean chicken and soak in cold, salted water for 30 minutes. Rinse thoroughly in cool water. Place chicken in large pot and cover with water. Place over high heat and bring slowly to a boil, skimming top before water comes to a boil. Cover loosely and boil gently 1 hour, adding water as needed. Add vegetables and continue cooking gently for about 3 hours.

Veal Meatballs:

1 pound ground veal
1 egg
1/2 cup fresh grated Parmesan or Romano cheese
1/2 cup breadcrumbs
1 to 2 tablespoons chopped parsley

Combine all ingredients to texture of meatloaf. If mixture is too moist, add breadcrumbs and cheese; if too dry, add water. Form into 1-inch balls; set aside.

Escarole:

1 bunch escarole, endive or mixture of both (escarole has milder flavor)

Clean greens and boil in water until tender. Drain, chop and set aside.

Assembly:

After soup is done, remove chicken and vegetables from pot. Bone chicken and cut into bite-size pieces. Coarsely chop vegetables. Bring soup to a gentle boil and add meatballs. After 20 minutes, or when meatballs begin to rise to surface, add chicken, vegetables and greens. Boil gently approximately 1 hour to allow flavors to combine. If desired, soup may be simmered longer. Add salt to taste while soup is boiling. To serve, top with grated cheese.
Gloria Scali

CREAM OF MUSHROOM SOUP

1½ pounds fresh mushrooms
9 tablespoons butter
2 shallots or scallions, finely chopped
6 tablespoons all-purpose flour
6 cups chicken broth
2 egg yolks
¾ cup heavy cream
Salt to taste

Wash mushrooms; cap and stem. Slice ½ the caps into ½-inch thick slices and coarsely chop remaining caps and stems. Melt 2 tablespoons butter in an 8-to 10-inch skillet (enamel or stainless steel) over moderate heat. When foam subsides, add sliced mushrooms and sauté, stirring with a wooden spoon, for about 2 minutes. Transfer to bowl with slotted spoon; set aside. Melt an additional 2 tablespoons butter in same skillet and sauté chopped caps and stems with shallots for 2 minutes. Set aside. In heavy 4-to 6-quart saucepan, melt remaining butter over moderate heat and stir in flour with wire whisk. Cook, stirring constantly, for 1 or 2 minutes. Do not brown roux. Remove from heat, cool a few seconds, and stir in chicken stock with whisk. Return to heat and stir until this cream soup base comes to a boil. Stir until it thickens and is smooth. Add chopped mushrooms, shallots and butter; simmer, stirring occasionally, for 15 minutes. Blend egg yolks and cream together in small bowl with wire whisk. Gradually add a little of the hot cream soup base to egg yolk mixture, whisking constantly, then add all of this mixture to cream soup, continuing to whisk constantly. Bring to a boil and boil rapidly for 30 seconds, stirring. Remove from heat and add reserved sliced mushrooms. Serve immediately. *This soup is worth all the work involved!* Yield: 4 to 6 servings.
Kathy Johnson

PUMPKIN SOUP

4 tablespoons butter, divided
4 green onions, sliced
1 small onion, sliced
2 tablespoons all-purpose flour
2 (10¾-ounce) cans chicken broth
1 (16-ounce) can pumpkin
1½ cups water
½ teaspoon salt
¾ cup light cream
Croutons
Whipped cream, lightly salted

Melt 3 tablespoons butter in a large saucepan. Sauté the green onion, and onion until tender and golden. Remove from heat and blend in the flour. Return to heat and add chicken broth, pumpkin, water and salt. Bring soup to a boil, stirring constantly. Reduce heat and simmer for 10 minutes. Add cream and remaining butter. Bring to serving temperature. Serve garnished with croutons and whipped cream. Yield: 6 to 8 servings.
Phylis Firalio

CHEESE SOUP

1/2 cup margarine or butter
1/2 cup chopped celery
1/2 cup thinly sliced carrots
1/4 cup chopped onion
1/3 cup all-purpose flour
1 (10 3/4-ounce) condensed chicken broth
3 cups milk
1 (12-ounce) package shredded Cheddar cheese
2 tablespoons bacon bits

Melt butter over medium-high heat in a 2-quart saucepan. Add celery, carrots and onion. Sauté until tender, stirring constantly. Add flour and cook for 1 minute, stirring constantly. Continuing to stir, gradually, add broth. Bring to a gentle boil, reduce heat and simmer for 1 minute. Add milk. Heat to simmering. Remove from heat. Add cheese and stir until cheese melts. Add bacon and heat again, if needed to reach serving temperature. For thicker soup, reduce milk to 2 3/4 cups. Yield: 4 large or 6 small servings.
Jean Croyle

POTATO SOUP

6 potatoes, peeled and sliced
2 carrots, sliced
2 stalks celery, sliced
1 onion, coarsely chopped
1/2 teaspoon salt
Pepper to taste
Parsley to taste
Basil to taste
3 tablespoons butter
2 1/2 tablespoons all-purpose flour
1 1/2 cups milk

Place vegetables in a large saucepan and cover with water. Bring to a boil over medium-high heat, reduce heat and cook, stirring occasionally, for 30 minutes or until tender. Add seasonings. Continue to simmer while melting butter in a small saucepan over medium heat. Stir in flour and cook for 1 minute. Gradually, stir in milk and continue to cook, stirring constantly, until mixture thickens. Add to the soup. Simmer for an additional 5 to 10 minutes and serve. Yield: 6 servings.
Karen Collins

TOUCHED-BY-GOLD CONSOMMÉ

2 (10 1/2-ounce) cans beef broth
2 cups tomato juice
2 tablespoons lemon juice
1/2 teaspoon salt
1/8 teaspoon white pepper
1/4 cup Galliano liqueur

In a small saucepan combine broth, juices, salt and pepper; bring to a boil. Stir in Galliano and simmer 3 minutes. Serve piping hot. *Delicious and elegant beginning for any meal.* Yield: 8 servings.
Ursula Bartosik

CHEESE AND BREW SOUP

¼ cup butter or margarine
⅓ cup grated carrots
⅓ cup grated onion
¼ cup all-purpose flour
½ teaspoon dry mustard
½ teaspoon paprika
4 cups chicken broth
1 cup shredded Cheddar cheese (or more, to taste)
2 cups half-and-half cream
1 (12-ounce) can beer or ale
1 cup diced potatoes, parboiled

Melt butter or margarine in a large, heavy saucepan. Add carrots and onions. Cover and cook 5 minutes over low heat. Blend in flour, mustard and paprika, then stir in 1½ cups broth and the cheese. Stir until cheese melts. Stir in remaining broth and remaining ingredients. Simmer 30 minutes, stirring occasionally. Half-and-half may be diluted with milk, if desired. Yield: 6 servings.
Ruth Abbott

BROCCOLI SOUP

2 pounds fresh broccoli
2 (12½-ounce) cans chicken broth
3 cups milk
2 teaspoons salt
¼ teaspoon pepper
1 cup light cream
½ pound white cheese (Swiss, Monterey Jack)
¼ cup butter or margarine

Cook broccoli, covered, in 1 can chicken broth for about 7 minutes, or until tender. Remove broccoli and chop coarsely. Add remaining chicken broth, milk, salt, and pepper to broth. Bring to a boil; stir in remaining ingredients and broccoli. Heat to serving temperature. Yield: 8 to 12 servings.
Linda Zbin

BREWED CHILI

2 pounds ground chuck
1 (10-ounce) can beer
2 tablespoons vinegar
1 tablespoon ground cumin
1 teaspoon oregano
1 medium onion, chopped
4 cups water
1½ teaspoon chili powder
1 teaspoon garlic powder
2 (6-ounce) cans tomato paste
1 (16-ounce) can kidney beans

Brown meat in Dutch oven and drain off fat. Add remaining ingredients, stirring to blend well. Simmer over low heat for 3 hours.
Loretta Valencic

FRENCH ONION SOUP

2 large onions
2 tablespoons butter or margarine
1 clove garlic, finely minced
Salt and freshly ground black pepper
1 tablespoon all-purpose flour
6 cups beef or chicken stock
¼ bay leaf
¼ teapoon dried thyme
10 to 12 slices French bread, cut ¾ to 1-inch thick
¾ cup shredded Swiss cheese

Peel onions and slice thin. Heat butter or margarine in heavy Dutch oven or kettle; add onions and garlic and cook, stirring for abour 15 minutes or until tender and golden brown. Season with salt and pepper to taste. Sprinkle with flour and continue cooking for about 3 minutes, stirring constantly. Pour in liquid gradually, add bay leaf and thyme. Cover and simmer for 30 to 45 minutes. Preheat oven to 500 degrees and toast French bread, turning to toast both sides evenly. Pour hot soup into 1½-quart ovenproof earthenware casserole or into 4 individual casseroles. Float toast on soup, sprinkle with cheese and place on foil-lined baking sheet to catch drippings. Bake in hot oven until soup is piping hot and cheese is melted and golden brown. Serve immediately. Yield: 4 servings.
Hollis Hura, Registered Dietitian, Parmadale

CHUNKY BEEF-BARLEY SOUP

3 to 4 pounds beef soup meat of your choice
2 long marrow bones
1 (16-ounce) can tomatoes, chopped
½ cup rice
½ cup barley
4 carrots, cut into chunks
4 medium potatoes, cubed
3 parsnips, cubed
2 turnips, cubed
2 stalks celery, coarsely chopped
1 large onion, coarsely chopped
Parsley
Salt, pepper and garlic to taste
Parsley greens

Remove fat from meat; place in large pot and add 8 quarts water. Cook over high heat until water comes to a boil. A foam will form on top; skim off several times until foaming stops. Lower heat, add tomatoes and cook over low heat for 2 hours or until meat is tender. Add vegetables, rice, barley, and seasonings to taste. Cook 1 hour longer. Add parsley greens for final 30 minutes. Yield: 10 to 12 servings
Karen Collins

BRUNSWICK STEW

2 (3-pound) broiler-fryers
2 large onions, sliced
2 cups cut okra (optional)
4 cups chopped fresh tomatoes or 2 (16-ounce) cans tomatoes
2 cups lima beans
3 medium potatoes, diced
2 (16-ounce) cans whole kernel corn
3 teaspoons salt
1 teaspoon pepper
1 tablespoon sugar

Cut chicken into pieces and place in large stockpot with 2 quarts water for thick soup, or 3 quarts water for thinner soup. Simmer 2¼ hours, or until meat can be easily removed from bones. Add vegetables to broth and simmer, uncovered, until beans and potatoes are tender, stirring occasionally to prevent scorching. Add boned and diced chicken and seasonings to soup and heat through before serving. Juices from canned vegetables may be used for part of the water. *Brunswick Stew benefits from long, slow cooking. Its flavor improves if allowed to stand overnight and then reheated.* Yield: 1½ to 2 quarts.
Rosemary Balchak

COLD CUCUMBER SOUP

1½ cups peeled and diced cucumber
2 tablespoons olive oil
1 tablespoon dried dill seed
1 clove garlic, minced or pressed
1 teaspoon salt
¼ teaspoon white pepper
½ cup yogurt
1 cup dairy sour cream
¼ cup chopped, lightly toasted walnuts

Combine cucumber, olive oil, dill seed, garlic, salt and white pepper in a large bowl. Cover and let stand at room temperature for 3 hours. Purée ½ the mixture in a blender and add to the remainder. Stir in yogurt, sour cream and walnuts. Chill at least 8 hours before serving.
Mary Sims

ZUCCHINI SOUP

3 cups chopped celery
1 medium onion, grated
5 tablespoons butter or margarine
2 cups water
1 large zucchini, grated
2 tablespoons chicken bouillon
1 teaspoon sweet basil
1½ cups milk

Sauté celery and onion in butter or margarine until tender. Add water, zucchini, bouillon and basil. Simmer 10 minutes, or until zucchini is tender. Add milk. Thicken with flour, if desired.
Sister Florence

OLD-FASHIONED CROCK POT VEGETABLE SOUP

1 pound lean stew beef, cubed
3 carrots, sliced
3 stalks celery, sliced
1 onion, chopped
2 beef bouillon cubes
1/3 cup barley
1/8 teaspoon pepper
1 quart water
1 (16-ounce) can tomatoes, chopped
1 (16-ounce) can garbanzo beans or chick peas
3 potatoes, pared and cubed
2 tablespoons all-purpose flour
1/2 cup water

Combine the first 8 ingredients in crock pot. Cover and cook on low for 6 hours. Add remaining ingredients and cook, covered, on high for 2 hours. Add 2 tablespoons flour mixed with 1/2 cup water to thicken. Cook for an additional 10 minutes. Chicken soup can be made by cutting the meat from 3 chicken breasts and substituting chicken bouillon for beef bouillon. Yield: 8 servings.
Rosemary Corcoran

MULLIGATAWNY SOUP

1 medium-sized onion, sliced
1/4 cup butter
1 medium-sized carrot, sliced
1 stalk celery, diced
1/2 green pepper, finely diced
1 medium apple, finely sliced
1 cup cooked chicken, cut into bite-sized chunks
1/3 cup all-purpose flour
1/2 teaspoon curry powder
2 cups chicken broth
1 cup canned stewed tomatoes
Salt to taste
Pepper to taste
Parsley to taste

Sauté onion in butter in soup kettle until it becomes tender and translucent. Add carrots, celery, green pepper, apple and chicken. Gradually, stir in flour and curry powder. Continuing to stir constantly, add broth, tomatoes, salt, pepper and parsley. Bring to a boil, reduce heat and simmer, covered, for 20 to 30 minutes. Yield: 5 to 6 servings.
Colleen Fitzgerald

CRAB BISQUE

1 (10¾-ounce) can condensed cream of mushroom soup
1 (10½-ounce) can condensed cream of asparagus soup
1½ soup cans milk
1 cup light cream
1 cup frozen or canned crab meat, flaked and drained
¼ cup dry white wine

Combine soups in a large saucepan. Add milk and cream. Stir until well-blended. Heat over medium heat to a gentle boil, stirring constantly. Add crab meat and heat through. Remove from heat and stir in wine just before serving. Yield: 6 to 8 servings.
Blanche Archer

BOB'S BEST MEATLESS CHILI

1 (16-ounce) package kidney beans, washed and sorted
1 (16-ounce) can whole tomatoes
1 large onion, diced
1 clove garlic, minced
¼ teaspoon cayenne pepper
3 tablespoons chili powder
2 tablespoons hot chili sauce
1 teaspoon cumin

Cover beans with water and soak overnight. Bring to a boil and drain. Add fresh water to cover. Bring to a boil, reduce heat and simmer for 1 hour or until beans are tender. Add tomatoes, onion, garlic, pepper, chili powder, chili sauce and cumin. Mix well. Simmer for 1 hour. Serve with fresh, diced onion, shredded Cheddar cheese and hot homemade bread. *You won't believe how good it is!* Yield: 6 to 8 servings.
Bob Harris

GAZPACHO

1 large clove garlic, cut
6 large ripe tomatoes, peeled and chopped
2 medium cucumbers, chopped
½ cup chopped green pepper
½ cup chopped onion
2 cups tomato juice
⅓ cup vegetable oil
3 tablespoons lemon juice
Salt to taste
Hot pepper sauce to taste
Fresh chopped parsley

Rub a large glass bowl with a cut clove of garlic. Discard the garlic. Add tomatoes, cucumbers, green peppers and onions and mix. Pour tomato juice over vegetables. Add oil, lemon juice and remaining seasonings. Chill several hours, or overnight. Serve in chilled glass bowls. Garnish with fresh parsley. Yield: 8½ cups.
Jo Lawrence

SEAFOOD BISQUE

¼ cup chopped onion
¼ cup finely chopped carrots
2 tablespoons butter
½ to 1 cup shrimp, chopped and divided
½ cup water
Rosemary to taste
Salt to taste
Black pepper to taste
Dash of cayenne pepper
⅓ cup cornstarch
4 cups milk, divided
1 teaspoon lemon juice
¼ cup sherry, optional
½ to 1 cup crabmeat
½ cup scallops, chopped (optional)
Tarragon to taste
Parsley

Sauté onions and carrots in butter in a large stock pot until onions are translucent. Add ¼ cup shrimp, water, rosemary, salt, pepper and cayenne. Simmer for 5 minutes. Blend cornstarch with 1 cup of milk. Add slowly to the pot, stirring constantly. Add remaining milk, lemin juice and sherry. Bring to boiling, stirring constantly. Reduce heat and add remaining shrimp, crab, scallops and tarragon. Cover pot, reduce heat and simmer for 20 minutes to 1 hour, stirring occasionally. Add water as necessary. Bisque should be the consistency of thick gravy. Season to taste. Serve in individual bowls topped with parsley. Yield: 8 to 10 servings.
Paul Zmich

STRAWBERRY SOUP

1½ cups water
¾ cup light-bodied red wine
½ cup sugar
2 tablespoons fresh lemon juice
1 stick cinnamon
2 quarts strawberries, hulled and puréed (reserve a few for garnish)
1 cup heavy cream
¼ cup dairy sour cream

Combine water, wine, sugar, lemon juice and cinnamon stick in a 5-quart saucepan. Boil, uncovered, about 17 minutes, stirring constantly. Add strawberry purée and continue boiling, stirring frequently. Discard cinnamon stick and cool cooked mixture. Whip cream and stir in sour cream. Fold into strawberry mixture. Refrigerate several hours. When ready to serve, garnish with reserved whole strawberries. *A delightfully refreshing summer soup.*
Chef Terrance Clarke

MANHATTAN CLAM CHOWDER

1 cup diced raw potatoes
2½ cups water
1 teaspoon celery salt
1 teaspoon salt
½ cup diced onions
2 tablespoons butter or margarine
2 tablespoons all-purpose flour
1 (6-ounce) can clams, minced
2 tablespoons tomato paste
2 cups water

Combine potatoes, 2½ cups water, celery salt and salt in large heavy saucepan or kettle and bring to a boil, stirring. Reduce heat and simmer for 1 hour. Sauté onions in butter until golden; stir in flour until smooth. Gradually stir in potatoes; add clams, tomato paste and remaining 2 cups water. Return to a boil; reduce heat and simmer for 1 hour more. Yield: 4 to 6 servings.
Helen Wanyerka

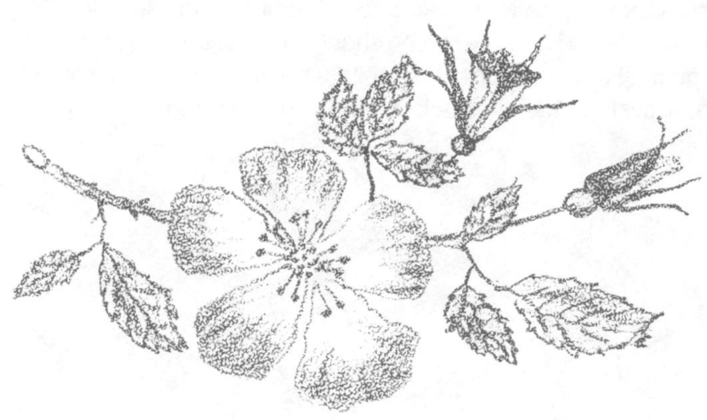

PHILADELPHIA STEAK SANDWICHES

6 Hero rolls
4 tablespoons butter or margarine
4 tablespoons vegetable oil
2 large onions, sliced thin
2 green peppers
½ teaspoon oregano (optional)
Salt and pepper to taste
1½ pounds sirloin steak, pounded and sliced thin
6 ounces provolone cheese

Preheat oven to 350 degrees. Wrap rolls in foil and heat about 10 minutes. Melt butter and oil in a large skillet over medium heat. Add onions and green peppers and sauté until tender. Add oregano, salt and pepper. Remove and keep warm. Sauté beef slices to desired degree of doneness in same skillet, adding more oil if necessary. Top with cheese and cook until melted. Cut rolls in half lengthwise and fill with onions, peppers, and beef-cheese mixture. Serve immediately. Yield: 6 servings.

STROMBOLI

½ cup thousand island dressing
2 tablespoons mustard
1 (16-ounce) loaf frozen bread dough, thawed
4 to 6 slices mozzarella cheese
6 to 8 slices baked ham
4 to 6 slices provolone or Swiss cheese
6 to 8 slices Italian salami

Combine salad dressing and mustard, mix and set aside. On a greased, 15x10x1-inch baking sheet, stretch bread dough to a 12x8-inch sheet. Place mozzarella cheese down the center of the bread dough, leaving 1-inch of dough uncovered on both ends. Spread ½ of the dressing-mustard mix over the cheese. Layer ingredients in the following order: ham, provolone or Swiss cheese, remainder of dressing and salami. Fold the ends of the dough inward. Fold the sides in until they overlap. Seal the edges and turn the seam side down. Cover and let rise for 1 hour. Bake at 375 degrees for 15 minutes or until golden brown on top. Allow to set 5 to 10 minutes before slicing. Serve with sliced tomatoes. Any lunchmeats and cheese can be substituted or added to the recipe. You may also wish to sprinkle with basil or oregano or a combination of both before sealing the stromboli. Yield: 4 to 6 servings.
Jean Croyle

OPEN-FACE MEATLOAF BURGERS

1½ pounds ground beef
⅔ cup evaporated milk
1 egg
½ cup finely crushed cracker crumbs
1½ teaspoons salt
¼ teaspoon pepper
1 teaspoon mustard
¼ cup finely chopped onion
½ cup finely chopped green pepper
6 hamburger buns or toasted English muffins
12 slices cheese

Combine first 9 ingredients in a large mixing bowl. Mix until thoroughly blended. Spread mixture on ½ of a hamburger bun, or toasted English muffin, covering the bun completely. Broil 5 to 7 inches from the broiler for 5 to 8 minutes. Top with a slice of cheese and broil until cheese bubbles. This mix can also be used as a meatloaf. Mix first 9 ingredients until well blended. Shape in a 9x5x3-inch loaf pan. Bake at 350 degrees for 1 hour. Yield: 4 to 6 servings.
June Croyle

HOT HAM, CHEESE AND POPPYSEED SANDWICHES

1/4 cup softened butter or margarine
2 teaspoons prepared mustard
1 teaspoon prepared horseradish
2 tablespoons finely chopped onion
2 teaspoons poppyseed
4 hamburger buns, cut crosswise into halves
4 medium-thick slices Swiss cheese
3/4 pound shaved ham (boiled or baked)

Blend butter, mustard, horseradish, onion and poppyseed well in small bowl. Spread about 1 teaspoon mixture on each 1/2 of buns; layer with Swiss cheese and ham. Wrap individually in aluminum foil. Place on baking sheet and bake at 350 degrees for 15 minutes. Remove from oven, remove foil and serve hot. Sandwiches may be made up ahead of time, wrapped and refrigerated until needed. Yield: 4 sandwiches.
Mary Sims

MOM'S OLD-FASHIONED SLOPPY JOES

1 medium onion, chopped
1/2 green pepper, seeded and chopped
Vegetable oil
1 pound lean ground beef
1 (10-3/4-ounce) can chicken gumbo soup
1 (12-ounce) bottle chili sauce

In a large skillet, brown onions and pepper in oil until golden brown. Add meat and cook until brown and crumbly. Spoon off fat. Return to heat and stir in soup and chili sauce. Cook over medium heat until mixture is heated through, then lower heat and simmer gently 15 minutes. Serve on toasted buns. *Also, great for a party in larger quantities!* Yield: 6 to 8 servings.
Carol Miller

HOOLIO BURGERS

1/2 cup chopped black olives
1 medium-sized onion, chopped
1 (4-ounce) can sliced mushrooms
2 tablespoons margarine, melted
2 pounds lean ground beef
6 onion rolls
1/3 cup dairy sour cream

Sauté olives, onions and mushrooms in margarine until tender. Set aside. Divide ground beef into 6 equal portions and form into thick patties which overhang rolls. Broil or grill for 8 to 10 minutes or until medium-rare. Place burgers on buns. Top with sour cream and sautéed vegetables. *Tuck a napkin into your collar. This is a very messy proposition.* Yield: 6 servings.
Ray Weiss

THE LIGHT TOUCH

Salads

CAULIFLOWER SALAD

1 medium-sized head lettuce, broken up and towel dried
1 large head cauliflower, broken into florets
1 medium-sized onion, chopped
2 cups mayonnaise
1/4 cup sugar
1/3 cup Parmesan cheese
1/4 to 3/4 cup bacon bits

Layer lettuce, cauliflower and onion in a large salad bowl. Spread onion layer with mayonnaise being careful to seal around the sides. Sprinkle sugar, cheese and bacon bits over the mayonnaise. Cover tightly and refrigerate overnight. Toss gently before serving. Yield: 8 to 10 servings.
Mary Sims

ORIENTAL SALAD

1 (10-ounce) package fresh spinach
3 scallions and tops, thinly sliced
1 (16-ounce) can bean sprouts or 1 pound fresh bean sprouts
1 (1-ounce) can sliced water chestnuts, rinsed and drained
2 hard-cooked eggs, sliced
6 slices bacon, cooked crisp and crumbled

Combine ingredients in a salad bowl. Toss to mix. Top with dressing just before serving. Toss. Yield: 6 to 8 servings.

Dressing:

1 cup vegetable oil
1 very small onion, grated
3/4 cup sugar
1/3 cup catsup
1 cup vinegar
1 tablespoon Worcestershire sauce

Combine oil and onion in blender jar. Blend. Add remaining ingredients and blend on high for 1 to 2 minutes until ingredients are well mixed. Half of this dressing seems to be just the perfect amount for a salad that is not too soggy. *This dressing is also good for regular green salads or fruit salad with apples and oranges.*
Rosemary Corcoran

SPECIAL SPINACH SALAD

4-ounces sharp Cheddar cheese, cut into cubes
3 eggs, hard boiled and quartered
2 green onions, sliced
½ cup vegetable oil
⅓ cup wine vinegar
1 teaspoon sugar
½ teaspoon garlic salt
½ teaspoon salt
¼ teaspoon pepper
8 cups torn, fresh spinach or escarole
2 slices bacon, cooked and crumbled

Place cheese in blender container and blend until coarsely chopped; set aside. Blend hard boiled eggs and onion until chopped. Combine with cheese mixture and chill. Place oil, vinegar, sugar, garlic salt, salt and pepper in blender and blend until mixed. Combine spinach with egg and cheese mixture, toss with dressing and top with crumbled bacon. Yield: 6 servings.
Sister Patricia Ann, O.S.U.

ENJOY SPINACH SALAD

1 bunch fresh spinach, washed well and torn into small pieces
3 hard-cooked eggs
½ cup chopped onion
2 unpeeled apples, cored and sliced
½ to 1 cup mayonnaise
Salt and pepper to taste
½ to 1 cup dairy sour cream
2 to 4-ounces bleu cheese (or less, to taste)

Toss and enjoy! Amounts may be varied according to personal tastes. The apples and eggs are essential, and may be increased rather than decreased! Mix immediately before serving.
Marilyn K. Todia

DEE'S PEA SALAD

1 (20-ounce) package frozen peas, uncooked
1 pound bacon, fried crisp and crumbled
1 bunch green onions, sliced with tops
¼ cup diced celery
1 teaspoon sugar
1 teaspoon salt
1 teaspoon pepper
¾ cup mayonnaise
1 (7-ounce) package cashew nuts

Combine the first 8 ingredients in the order listed. Mix until well distributed. Cover and refrigerate for 4 or more hours. Add cashews just before serving. *Absolutely wonderful!!* Yield: 8 to 10 servings.
Dee Teich

GREEK BEAN SALAD

1 pound string beans, cut in half, cooked, drained and cooled
4 tablespoons vegetable oil
2 tablespoons wine vinegar
1 onion, thinly sliced
1 clove garlic, chopped
1 teaspoon fresh parsley, chopped
Salt and pepper
Lettuce leaves
1 hard-cooked egg, chopped
Grated Parmesan cheese

Place beans in a salad bowl. Combine oil, vinegar, onion, garlic, parsley, salt and pepper to taste. Pour over beans and mix lightly. Cover and chill thoroughly in refrigerator—overnight is best. Serve on lettuce leaves on individual salad plates. Sprinkle lightly with chopped egg and cheese before serving. This can be served as an antipasto course. *Excellent!* Yield: 4 servings.
Augusta Cokinos

OVERNIGHT COLESLAW

1 pound cabbage, shredded
1 medium-sized onion, sliced
½ cup sugar
1 cup vinegar
¾ cup vegetable oil
1 tablespoon celery seed
2 tablespoons sugar
½ teaspoon prepared mustard
1 teaspoon salt

Place ½ the cabbage in bottom of large casserole dish; arrange onion slices over cabbage. Layer remaining cabbage over onions. Sprinkle with ½ cup sugar. *Do not stir.* Combine remaining ingredients in saucepan and bring to a boil. Remove from heat and pour over cabbage. Cover tightly and refrigerate overnight (do not stir). Stir just before serving. Yield: 6 to 8 servings.
Sally Vlasik

TUNA MARINADE SALAD

1 (6-ounce) can tuna, drained
1 (16-ounce) can chick peas, drained
1 (14-ounce) can artichoke hearts, drained
1 to 2 (4-ounce) cans button mushrooms, drained
1 small red onion, chopped
1 (8-ounce) bottle Italian dressing

Combine tuna with chick peas, artichokes, mushrooms and onions; add dressing and toss to combine. Cover and refrigerate to marinate overnight. *A great cool summer dish.* Yield: 6 to 8 servings.
Nancy Kumin

HOT POTATO SALAD

5 or 6 potatoes
4 slices bacon
1 medium size onion, chopped
2 tablespoons all-purpose flour
1/3 cup prepared mustard
3/4 cup water
2 tablespoons fresh lemon juice
2 tablespoons vinegar
1 tablespoon sugar
1 teaspoon salt
1/2 teaspoon grated lemon peel
2 tablespoons fresh parsley
Pepper to taste

Cook potatoes in boiling water until tender. Peel and slice into 3/4-inch cubes. Fry bacon until crisp, drain, crumble and set aside. Sauté onion in bacon drippings until lightly brown. Blend in flour and mustard. Add water, lemon juice, vinegar, sugar, salt, lemon peel and pepper. Stir until smooth. Bring to boil, reduce heat and cook until mixture is thick. Add potatoes, mixing gently. Heat until warm. Toss with parsley and crumbled bacon. Serve immediately. Yield: 6 servings.
Dorothy Hunter

POTATO SALAD

10 to 12 large potatoes
French Dressing (recipe follows)
1 large onion, chopped
1 cup chopped celery
2 tablespoons minced green pepper (optional)
1 tablespoon minced parsley
1/2 cup mayonnaise or salad dressing
1/2 cup dairy sour cream
Salt and pepper to taste
3 hard-cooked eggs, sliced
Paprika

French Dressing:

1/4 cup vinegar
1 teaspoon salt
1 teaspoon dry mustard
1/4 teaspoon pepper
3/4 cup vegetable oil

Scrub potatoes, cut in 1/2 and cook in boiling, salted water until tender, about 20 minutes. Meanwhile, combine French Dressing ingredients and shake well to mix. Peel and cube hot potatoes; add celery, onion, green pepper and parsley. Stir dressing and pour over all. Mix until potato cubes are well coated. Cool 1 hour in refrigerator. Combine mayonnaise and sour cream; add to cooled potatoes. Add salt and pepper; mix well. Slice eggs and arrange over potatoes. Sprinkle paprika over all. Chill 1 to 2 hours, or until ready to serve. Yield: 10 to 12 servings.
Jean Croyle

NOODLE CAESAR SALAD

1 (8-ounce) package medium egg noodles
1 clove garlic, peeled
1 egg yolk, beaten
1 head Romaine lettuce, cleaned and torn into bite-sized pieces
1 cup flavored croutons
1/4 cup grated Parmesan cheese
Caesar Salad Dressing

Cook noodles according to package directions. Drain and rinse with cold water. Rub a large salad bowl with garlic. Add noodles and raw egg. Mix well. Add lettuce, croutons, cheese and dressing. Toss until ingredients are combined. Yield: 10 to 12 servings.

Caesar Salad Dressing:

3/4 cup vegetable oil
1/2 cup vinegar
1 teaspoon salt
1 teaspoon anchovy paste
3/4 teaspoon sugar
1/4 teaspoon pepper
1/4 teaspoon dry mustard
1 clove garlic, minced

Combine ingredients in a blender. Blend on high until well-mixed. Chill until ready to serve.
Sue Mahon

RICE SALAD

4 cups cooked rice
1/2 cup chopped onion
1/2 cup diced celery
1/2 cup seeded, finely chopped cucumber
1/4 cup minced green pepper
1/2 cup seeded, chopped tomatoes
Vinaigrette Sauce or bottled dill and vinegar dressing
Chopped fresh tarragon
Chopped parsley

Vinaigrette Sauce:

6 tablespoons olive or vegetable oil
2 tablespoons wine vinegar
1/2 to 1 teaspoon salt
12 grinds fresh pepper

Blend all sauce ingredients in a jar with a tight-fitting lid; shake to thoroughly combine. Combine rice, vegetables and Vinaigrette Sauce; toss well. Arrange on bed of greens or in salad bowl. Sprinkle with tarragon and parsley. For variation, marinade may be poured over hot rice, adding vegetables when cooled. Salad may be prepared a day ahead, using other vegetables of your choice.
Sue Mahon

OLD-FASHIONED NORTH CAROLINA POTATO SALAD

6 to 10 potatoes
1 (6-ounce) jar sweet pickle relish (or 2 diced cucumbers, marinated in vinegar)
4 to 5 tablespoons mayonnaise
2 teaspoons prepared mustard
4 to 6 stalks celery, diced
1 teaspoon brown sugar or molasses
1 teaspoon paprika
4 hard-boiled eggs

Cook potatoes in jackets, in water to cover, until tender. Cool slightly, peel and cube. Dice hard-boiled eggs. Combine pickle relish, mayonnaise, mustard, celery, and sugar in small bowl. Toss gently with potatoes and half the eggs. Spoon into serving bowl. Garnish with remaining eggs and paprika. Refrigerate, covered, until serving time. Yield: 6 to 8 servings.
Arnette Brewer

COLD SPAGHETTI SALAD

1 (8-ounce) package spaghetti
1 cup garlic vinagrette salad dressing
10 fresh mushrooms, cleaned and sliced
1 cup broccoli florets
12 cherry tomatoes, quartered
2 cups cooked, cubed chicken
1/3 cup sunflower seed
1/3 cup fresh basil

Cook spaghetti according to package directions; drain well. Stir with 1/2 cup salad dressing and cover. Chill in refrigerator for at least 2 hours. Combine remaining ingredients with spaghetti just before serving time. Yield: 4 to 6 servings.
Lucille Phillips

HOT CHICKEN CHIP SALAD

2 cups cooked, cubed chicken
3 hard-cooked eggs
1 1/2 cups diced celery
1 (10 3/4-ounce) can cream of chicken soup
1 cup mayonnaise
1/3 cup slivered, toasted almonds
2 tablespoons lemon juice
2 teaspoons grated onion
1/2 teaspoon salt
1/4 cup chopped pimiento (optional)
1/2 cup shredded American or Cheddar cheese
1 cup crushed potato chips

Combine all ingredients except cheese and potato chips. Turn into a 13x9x2-inch baking dish or 3-quart round casserole dish. Top with cheese and sprinkle with crushed potato chips. Bake at 425 degrees 20 minutes. Turkey may be substituted for chicken. Yield: 6 servings.
Lynne Della Donna

PINEAPPLE-CRANBERRY SALAD

2 (3-ounce) packages fruit flavored gelatin
2 (16-ounce) cans whole berry cranberry sauce
2 (20-ounce) cans crushed pineapple, drained and juice reserved
2 cups boiling water
1 cup reserved pineapple juice
1 cup diced celery
1 cup chopped walnuts

Dissolve gelatin in boiling water in large mixing bowl. Add pineapple juice and cool. Stir in cranberry sauce, pineapple, celery and nuts. Pour into 15x10x2-inch glass dish and refrigerate until set. For a tangy taste, substitute ginger ale for the water. This salad looks lovely when made in a pretty crystal bowl for a holiday table.
Dorothy Hunter

BINGO CHERRI-O MOLD

2 (3-ounce) packages black cherry-flavored gelatin
1 (16-ounce) can pitted black cherries, drained (reserve juice)
1 (3-ounce) package cream cheese
Pecans

Dissolve gelatin in 2 cups boiling water. Add sufficient cold water to reserved cherry juice to make 2 cups. Pour 2 cups of gelatin mixture into mold and refrigerate until thickened, but not set. Meanwhile, stuff each cherry with cream cheese and a pecan. Add stuffed cherries to thickened gelatin mixture and cover with remaining gelatin mixture. Chill until firm. (To make a firmer mold, add 1 envelope unflavored gelatin to first mixture.) Yield: 1 (5-cup) mold.
Blanche Archer
Sue Mahon

RASPBERRY-RASPBERRY GELATIN

1 (6-ounce) package raspberry flavored gelatin
1 cup boiling water
1 (10-ounce) package frozen raspberries or 1 pint fresh raspberries
1 (16-ounce) can applesauce

Combine gelatin and water in a large bowl. Stir until gelatin dissolves and add raspberries and applesauce. Blend gently but thoroughly. Pour into a 12x8x2-inch baking dish. Cover and refrigerate until firm. Gelatin is tarter and firmer when fresh raspberries are used *but oh-so-good!* Yield: 8 servings.
Betty Logue

PRETZEL SALAD

2 cups crushed pretzels
3/4 cup margarine, melted
3 tablespoons sugar
1 (8-ounce) package cream cheese, softened
1 cup sugar
1 (9-ounce) carton frozen, whipped, non-dairy topping
1 (6-ounce) package strawberry flavored gelatin
2 cups boiling water
2 (10-ounce) packages frozen strawberries, thawed

Mix first 3 ingredients and pat into a 13x9x2-inch baking dish. Bake at 350 degrees for 8 to 10 minutes or until browned. Cool. Combine cream cheese and 1 cup sugar. Beat until well-blended and smooth and creamy. Fold cream cheese into the non-dairy topping. Spread this over the cooled pretzel crust. Cover and refrigerate. Dissolve the flavored gelatin in boiling water. Add strawberries and cool to room temperature. Gently pour the cooled mixture over the cream cheese and whipped topping. Cover and return to the refrigerator until entire mixture is completely set. Yield: 6 to 8 servings.
Sister Patricia Ann O.S.U.

PORTOFINO MOLD

2 (3-ounce) packages raspberry flavored gelatin
1 1/4 cups boiling water
1 (20-ounce) can crushed pineapple with juice
1 (16-ounce) can cranberry sauce
3/4 cup port wine
1 cup chopped pecans, optional

Combine flavored gelatin and water. Stir until gelatin is completely dissolved. Add pineapple with juice, cranberry sauce and wine. Pour into a 2 quart casserole. Cover and refrigerate until slightly thickened. Stir in pecans, if desired. Chill until completely set. Top with layer of cream cheese topping before serving. Yield: 6 to 8 servings.

Topping:

1 (8-ounce) package cream cheese
1 cup dairy sour cream

Combine ingredients until well-blended. Spread over gelatin mixture and refrigerate until chilled before serving.
Justin Baum

GRASSHOPPER SALAD

1 (6-ounce) package lime flavored gelatin
2 cups boiling water
1½ cups cold water
2 tablespoons créme de menthe liqueur
1 envelope whipped topping mix, prepared according to directions

Dissolve gelatin in boiling water. Add cold water and liqueur. Mix until well blended. Chill until slightly thickened. Pour ½ of mixture into a lightly oiled, 6 cup mold. Cover and refrigerate until almost set. Fold remaining gelatin mixture into the whipped topping. Pour over gelatin in mold. Return to refrigerator and chill until completely set. Serve on lettuce-lined dish. Yield: 6 to 8 servings.
Justin Baum

STRAWBERRY SALAD

1 cup fresh strawberries, cleaned, hulled and halved
½ head Romaine lettuce, cleaned, drained and torn into bite-sized pieces
1 medium Spanish onion, sliced into rings
2 (11-ounce) cans mandarin oranges, drained
Poppy Seed Dressing to taste

Combine first 4 ingredients in a large salad bowl. Toss gently until well mixed. Top with enough dressing to coat but not make soggy. Toss until all ingredients are covered with dressing. *Fabulous!* Yield: 6 servings.
Judy Braun

SEVEN ROCK SHRIMP EXTRAORDINARE

1 pound cooked shrimp, peeled and deveined
½ pound fresh mushrooms, sliced
1 (4½-ounce) can artichoke hearts, drained and cut in half
1 cup carrots, cut into 1-inch sticks
1 medium-sized onion, thinly sliced and separated into rings
¾ cup diced celery
¼ cup chopped pimiento
3 small cloves of garlic, minced
1¼ cups white distilled vinegar
¾ cup water
¼ cup vegetable oil
1 teaspoon lime juice
1 (8-ounce) bottle Italian dressing
Chopped parsley and leaf lettuce for garnish

Combine above ingredients (except garnish) and toss with Italian dressing. Serve over a bed of leaf lettuce and sprinkle with chopped parsley. Yield: 4 servings.
Chef Terry Lawrence Clarke

RENE'S HORSERADISH MOUSSE

1 pint whipping cream
5 (3-ounce) packages lemon flavored gelatin
5 cups boiling water
1 (5 or 8-ounce) jar prepared white horseradish
1 cup real mayonnaise

Whip cream until stiff. Refrigerate. Dissolve gelatin in hot water in large mixing bowl. Chill in refrigerator until it begins to get firm around edges. Remove from refrigerator and beat until fluffy. Fold in whipped cream, horseradish and mayonnaise until smooth and blended. Spoon into a fluted tube pan which has been coated with non-stick cooking spray. Cover with plastic wrap and refrigerate. Just before serving, turn out onto large serving plate and garnish with fresh sprigs of parsley, olives and watercress. *This is a wonderful accompaniment to roast beef or ham.*
Rene O'Day

CRANBERRY-RASPBERRY SHERBET SALAD

1 (6-ounce) package raspberry flavored gelatin
1½ cups boiling water
1 (16-ounce) can whole berry cranberry sauce
1 pint raspberry sherbet, softened
1 (15½-ounce) can crushed pineapple, drained
½ cup broken walnuts
1 cup dairy sour cream, optional

Dissolve gelatin in boiling water, substituting some of the reserved pineapple juice if desired. Add cranberry sauce and stir until blended. Stir in raspberry sherbet until completely melted. Fold in pineapple and nuts. Pour mixture into a 13x9x2-inch glass casserole dish and refrigerate until set. Spread sour cream over top just before serving. Cut into squares to serve. Yield: 12 servings.
Dorothy Franco

RAZMATAZZ GELATIN

1(3-ounce) package raspberry flavored gelatin
1 (3-ounce) package lemon-flavored gelatin
1½ cups boiling water
1 (10-ounce) package frozen raspberries
1 cup frozen cranberry-orange relish
7-ounces lemon-lime soda

Dissolve gelatins in boiling water; add raspberries and stir. Add relish and mix well. Chill until cold, but not set. Slowly pour soda into bowl and stir. Pour into mold and refrigerate until set. Yield: 1 (5-cup) mold.
Regina Ryan

FROZEN FRESH FRUIT SALAD

1 (8-ounce) package cream cheese, softened
1/4 cup lemon juice
1 teaspoon grated lemon rind
1/2 cup sugar
1/4 teaspoon salt
1 1/2 cups dairy sour cream
1 pint fresh blueberries
2 cups fresh peaches, chopped
1 cup seedless grapes, halved
1/4 cup chopped maraschino cherries

Combine first 5 ingredients in mixer bowl. Beat until well blended. Add sour cream and beat thoroughly. Fold in fruit. Generously fill 24 paper lined muffin tins with the mixture. Freeze. Remove paper liners and serve on greens. Allow to stand at room temperature for 40 minutes before serving. Easier to eat and has a better flavor if they are partially thawed. These are especially nice for holiday time. Frozen peaches and blueberries can be used. Yield: 24 servings.
Rosemary Corcoran

PECAN AND CHEESE FRUIT CUPS

1 (16-ounce) can fruit cocktail
2 envelopes unflavored gelatin
2 cups orange juice
1 (3-ounce) package cream cheese, cubed and softened
1/2 cup mayonnaise or salad dressing
1/4 cup lemon juice
2 tablespoons sugar
1-ounce bleu cheese, crumbled (1/4 cup)
1/2 cup broken pecans

Drain fruit cocktail, reserving 1 cup syrup. Soften gelatin in 1/2 the reserved syrup. Heat orange juice to boiling point and add to softened gelatin, stirring until gelatin dissolves. Slowly add hot mixture to cream cheese, beating with electric mixer until smooth. Add remaining reserved fruit syrup, mayonnaise, lemon juice, sugar, and dash of salt. Beat gelatin mixture again until smooth. Chill until partially set. Stir in drained fruit cocktail, bleu cheese, and nuts. Spoon into 10 1/2-cup molds. Chill until firm. Yield: 10 servings.
Lenore Sims

ORANGE BOWL SALAD

½ cup vegetable oil
⅓ cup frozen orange juice concentrate, thawed
⅓ cup honey
2 tablespoons vinegar
1½ teaspoons salt
1½ teaspoons sugar
1 teaspoon dry mustard
1 teaspoon paprika
Dash of pepper
5 cups torn salad greens
1 (11-ounce) can mandarin oranges, drained
1 small onion, thinly sliced and separated into rings

Combine first 9 ingredients in container with tightly fitted lid. Cover; shake well. Reserve a few orange sections and onion rings for garnish. In a large bowl, toss greens, oranges, onion rings and dressing; toss lightly. Garnish. Yield: 5 to 6 servings.
Lenore Sims

SHRIMP MOLD

1 (8-ounce) package cream cheese, softened
1 cup mayonnaise
1 cup condensed tomato soup
1 (¼-ounce) envelope unflavored gelatin, dissolved in ¼ cup cold water
1 cup diced celery
½ cup diced onion
1 pound cooked shrimp, diced

Blend cream cheese with mayonnaise in mixing bowl. Heat tomato soup in small saucepan to boiling; add dissolved gelatin. Remove from heat and blend into cream cheese mixture; fold in remaining ingredients. Pour into a greased 6-cup mold. Refrigerate, covered with plastic wrap. Before serving, unmold and cut into 6 or 8 servings. Place on lettuce lined salad plates. Yield: 6 to 8 servings.
Lissa Keller

AVO-TACO SALAD

1 pound ground beef
1 (1¼-ounce) package taco seasoning mix
½ head iceburg lettuce, shredded
1 small onion, chopped
1 medium tomato, cut into thin wedges
1 cup shredded Cheddar cheese
1 avocado
1 cup taco chips, broken (more if desired)
French dressing to taste

Brown ground beef in large skillet, add taco seasoning and prepare as directed on seasoning packet. Toss lettuce, tomato and onion together in large salad bowl. Place 1 serving of salad mixture on individual serving plates; spoon some meat over top and sprinkle with cheese. Sprinkle with chips and garnish with sliced avocado and salad dressing. Taco sauce and/or sour cream may be spooned over the top, if desired. Yield: 4 to 6 servings.
Judy Braun

CHICKEN-GRAPE SALAD

2½ cups chicken, cooked and cubed
1 cup green seedless grapes, sliced
½ cup sliced walnuts or almonds
1 (5-ounce) jar mayonnaise
1 cup diced celery
½ pint whipping cream, whipped
Lettuce

Combine first 5 ingredients in a medium-sized mixing bowl. Mix until well blended. Gently fold in the whipped cream. Chill. Serve over lettuce leaves. Yield: 3 to 4 servings.
Becky Gingeldein

KOBS' CRUNCHY CHICKEN SALAD

3 cups cooked, chopped chicken
3 cups cooked rice
2 (10¾-ounce) cans cream of chicken soup
2 cups diced celery
1 cup mayonnaise
4 tablespoons minced onion

Combine all ingredients and place in a 13x9x2-inch baking pan.

Topping:

2 cups cornflake cereal
4 tablespoons melted butter

Mix together and sprinkle over chicken mixture. Top, if desired, with 2-ounces slivered almonds. Bake at 375 degrees 30 minutes. Yield: 6 to 8 servings.
Lil Kobs

ORIENTAL CHICKEN SALAD

1/4 cup soy sauce
1 teaspoon sugar
1 teaspoon prepared mustard
1 tablespoon vegetable oil
2 1/2 cups cooked chicken, cut in thin strips
3 cups cooked rice, cooled
1 cup chopped celery
1/2 cup sliced green onions, including tops
1 (14-ounce) can fancy mixed Chinese vegetables, rinsed and drained

Blend soy sauce, sugar, mustard and oil in cup. Pour over chicken and toss lightly. Cover and refrigerate for about 1 hour. Stir in remaining ingredients. Serve over salad greens and garnish with mayonnaise, if desired. Yield: 6 servings.
Mary Sims

IT'S A DOOZIE SALAD

4 chicken breasts, cooked, skinned and boned
1 head lettuce, washed and torn
3 green onions, sliced thin
1 (3-ounce) can chow mein noodles
1 (4-ounce) package slivered almonds
1/4 cup poppy seeds

Dressing:

4 tablespoons sugar
1 tablespoon salt
1/2 teaspoon pepper
4 tablespoons vinegar
1/2 cup vegetable oil

Combine dressing ingredients in a jar with a tight-fitting lid; shake to combine thoroughly. Combine cubed chicken, lettuce and onions. Stir in noodles, almonds and poppy seeds; add dressing and toss to coat.
Dee Teich

THE COVER STORY

Dressings and Sauces

POPPY SEED DRESSING

¾ cup sugar
1 teaspoon dry mustard
⅓ cup vinegar
½ tablespoon onion juice
1 cup vegetable oil
1½ tablespoons poppy seeds

Combine first 4 ingredients. Mix until well blended. Slowly, add oil, stirring constantly. Continue mixing until ingredients are thoroughly distributed. Add seeds. Cover and refrigerate until ready to serve. Shake before serving.
Dottie Vanek

CELERY SEED DRESSING

1 cup catsup
¾ cup sugar
1 tablespoon salt
1 tablespoon grated onion
1 egg
3 cups vegetable oil
¾ cup cider vinegar
1 tablespoon celery seed

Combine first 7 ingredients in blender container. Blend on high for 1 to 2 minutes or until ingredients are evenly distributed. Add celery seed. Store in container with a tight fitting lid. Shake before serving. Yield: 6 cups.
Sister Karen Kellereskie, C.S.F.N.

SUMMERFIELD'S DIJON DRESSING

1 (9-ounce) jar Dijon mustard
3 cups vegetable oil
1 cup wine vinegar
¼ cup Parmesan cheese
Pepper to taste

Place ingredients in a blender container or a jar with a tight fitting lid. Blend on low or shake until all ingredients are well mixed. Refrigerate, covered, until time to serve. Shake before serving. Yield: 4 to 5 cups.
Summerfield Inn, New Hampshire

CELERY-HONEY DRESSING

½ cup sugar
1 teaspoon dry mustard
1 teaspoon paprika
¼ teaspoon salt
⅓ cup honey
1 tablespoon lemon juice
¼ cup vinegar
1 cup vegetable oil
1 teaspoon grated onion
1 teaspoon celery seeds

Combine first 7 ingredients in container of electric blender; blend well. Slowly add oil, continuing to blend until thick. Stir in onion and celery seeds. Cover and store in refrigerator. Yield: Approximately 3 cups.
Peg O'Shea

GARLIC FRENCH DRESSING

1 (10¾-ounce) can tomato soup
¾ cup vinegar
½ to ¾ cup sugar
1 tablespoon salt
1 teaspoon pepper
1 teaspoon paprika
1 tablespoon yellow mustard
1 tablespoon Worcestershire sauce
1 onion, finely grated
2 to 3 garlic cloves, finely grated
1 cup vegetable oil

Combine ingredients in order listed. Mix until well blended. Place in container with tight fitting lid and refrigerate until needed. Shake well before using. Garlic can be left out to make a basic French dressing. Yield: 2½ to 3 cups.
Sue Polacek
Lee Creadon

COUNTRY FRENCH DRESSING

6 shallots, peeled
6 cloves garlic, peeled
1 teaspoon salt
¾ tablespoons pepper
2 tablespoons sugar
1 tablespoon Dijon-style mustard
1 tablespoon water
¾ cup tarragon vinegar
3 cups vegetable oil

Place all ingredients except oil in blender container; blend 1 minute. Slowly add oil with blender running; blend 2 minutes more. Store in refrigerator in covered container. Yield: 1 quart.
Karen West

SCRATCH BLEU CHEESE DRESSING

¾ cup dairy sour cream
½ teaspoon dry mustard
½ teaspoon black pepper
½ teaspoon salt
⅓ teaspoon garlic powder
1 teaspoon Worcestershire sauce
1⅓ cups mayonnaise
4-ounces Danish bleu cheese

In mixing bowl blend sour cream, mustard, pepper, salt, garlic powder and Worcestershire sauce, beating 2 minutes at low speed. Add mayonnaise and blend 30 seconds at low speed, then 2 minutes at medium speed. Crumble cheese by hand into very small pieces, then add to creamed mixture. Blend at low speed no more than 4 minutes. Let stand 24 hours before serving. Yield: 2½ cups.
Rosemary Balchak

STRAWBERRY DRESSING

½ cup sliced strawberries
⅓ cup water
¼ cup vegetable oil
2 tablespoons cider vinegar
¾ teaspoon onion powder
½ teaspoon salt
½ teaspoon sugar
Dash of garlic powder
2 tablespoons walnuts, chopped fine

Combine strawberries, water, oil, vinegar, onion powder, salt, sugar and garlic powder in blender container. Mix at high speed until smooth, about 10 seconds. Pour into a small bowl and stir in walnuts. *Great with fruit salad!* Yield: 1½ cups.
Lynne Della Donna

PEANUTTY FRUIT SALAD DRESSING

¼ cup peanut butter
3 tablespoons honey
¼ cup milk
½ cup dairy sour cream

Combine peanut butter and honey. Slowly, add milk, stirring constantly. Add sour cream and mix until well blended. Refrigerate several hours or overnight before serving. Yield: 1½ cups.
A Friend

LEMÓN MARINADE

½ cup soy sauce
¼ cup dry red wine
3 tablespoons vegetable oil
2 tablespoons Worcestershire sauce
1 clove garlic, mashed
2 green onions, sliced (or 1 small onion, sliced)
Pepper to taste

Place all ingredients in a jar. Mix well and use over meat, especially beef, to marinate.
Ellen Mahon

SEAFOOD SAUCE (ZUPPA DE COYZE)

1/4 cup chopped onion
1/4 cup chopped celery
1 teaspoon minced garlic
1/2 cup olive oil
1 tablespoon chopped basil
Black pepper, coarsely ground
1/2 cup dry white wine
2 cups canned plum tomatoes, undrained, chopped

Combine onions, garlic, celery, basil and pepper. Heat oil in a steel or enamel pan and cook vegetables over moderate heat 8 to 10 minutes, stirring frequently. Add wine and boil until liquid is reduced to about 1/4 cup. Add tomatoes and their liquid; simmer, uncovered, over low heat 20 to 25 minutes, stirring frequently. Drop in scrubbed clams, mussels, shrimp, fish or any desired seafood. Cover and raise heat. Cook, shaking pan frequently, 15 minutes or until shells open and fish is cooked. *Good served with small pasta and bread. Also good as a light spaghetti sauce, adding meat or sausage if desired.* Yield: about 2 cups sauce
Mary Simonetti

BEST EVER BARBECUE SAUCE

1/3 cup vegetable oil
1/3 cup margarine, melted
1/2 cup vinegar
1 cup orange juice
1/4 cup catsup
1/4 cup finely chopped onion
1/4 cup Worcestershire sauce
2 teaspoons hot sauce
2 teaspoons salt
1 teaspoon red pepper
1/4 teaspoon ground oregano
1/8 teaspoon chili powder

Combine all ingredients in a saucepan. Bring to a boil, stirring constantly. Reduce heat and simmer for 10 minutes, stirring occasionally. Use on chicken, pork chops or ribs. Yield: 2 1/2 cups.
Evelyn Maroush

YOGURT DIP FOR FRUIT

1 (8-ounce) carton fruit flavored yogurt
1 (8-ounce) carton frozen, whipped, non-dairy topping
Assorted fruit, cut into bite-sized pieces

Thoroughly blend yogurt and whipped topping. Transfer to a small bowl and place in the center of a platter of fresh fruit. Provide cocktail picks for serving. Yield: 2 cups.
Blanche Archer

QUICK HOLLANDAISE SAUCE

½ cup butter or margarine
3 egg yolks
2 tablespoons lemon juice
¼ teaspoon salt
Dash of white pepper
½ teaspoon prepared mustard

Melt butter in a small saucepan and heat until bubbly but not browned. Combine egg yolks, lemon juice, salt, white pepper and mustard in a blender container. Cover and blend on medium for 5 seconds. Slowly, add butter in a steady stream while blending at low speed. Blend on high for 5 seconds. Serve immediately on cooked vegetables, fish, etc. Yield: ¾ cup.
Lynne Della Donna

EASY BÉRNAISE SAUCE

¼ cup white wine
¼ cup tarragon vinegar
¾ teaspoon dried tarragon
1 tablespoon green onion, white only
½ teaspoon dried chervil
⅛ teaspoon salt
Dash of white pepper
2 egg yolks
½ cup butter, melted
Dash of cayenne pepper
1 tablespoon lemon juice
2 to 3 tablespoons dairy sour cream

Combine first 7 ingredients in a medium-sized saucepan. Bring mixture to a boil, stirring constantly. Continue to boil until mixture measures 2 tablespoons. Cool slightly and add egg yolks. Beat with a whisk while cooking over a low heat. Cook until yolks thicken. Blend in butter, a little at a time, mixing well after each addition. Stir in cayenne pepper and lemon juice. Add sour cream. Serve warm or at room temperature. Prepare ahead of time and place in an insulated container to keep warm without curdling. Yield: 6 to 8 servings.
Chicky Weiner

MARINARA SAUCE

1 clove garlic, minced
1 tablespoon minced parsley
¼ cup olive oil
½ teaspoon dried basil
2 cups chopped tomatoes
1 teaspoon salt
⅛ teaspoon pepper

Sauté garlic and parsley in oil over medium heat until garlic is lightly browned. Add basil, tomatoes, salt and pepper. Reduce heat and simmer for 30 minutes. Yield: 1 to 1½ cups.
Elaine Della Donna

EASY BLENDER SPAGHETTI SAUCE

4 large onions, quartered
4 cloves garlic, peeled and halved
1 green pepper, quartered
1 carrot, quartered
2 stalks celery, cut into chunks
3 (16-ounce) cans whole tomatoes
2 (6-ounce) cans tomato paste
1½ pounds ground chuck
2 tablespoons parsley
1 tablespoon dried basil
1 tablespoon ground oregano
1 tablespoon salt
2 (4-ounce) cans mushrooms, optional
Spaghetti, cooked according to package directions

Combine first 7 ingredients in blender container. Blend on high until ingredients are liquified. Brown ground meat in Dutch oven over medium heat. Drain excess fat. Pour vegetable-tomato mixture over meat. Add seasonings and mushrooms. Reduce heat and simmer for 3 to 4 hours or until the desired consistency is reached. Serve over hot, cooked spaghetti. Yield: 10 to 12 servings.
Ann Karpac

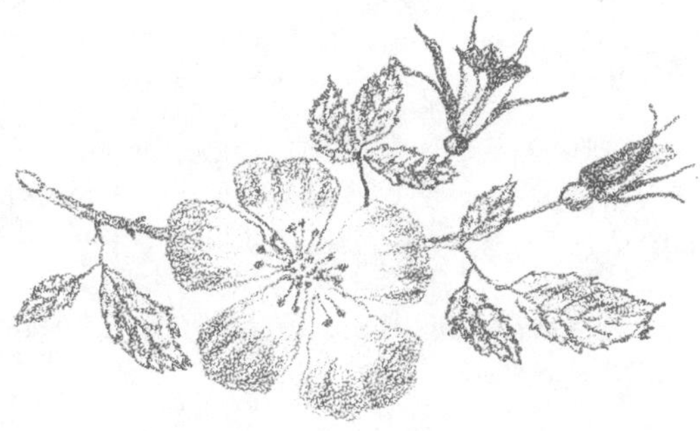

HOT MUSTARD SAUCE

3-ounces hot dry mustard
¼ cup all-purpose flour
1½ cups sugar
Dash of salt
4 eggs, slightly beaten
¾ cup vinegar

Combine mustard, flour, sugar and salt in top of double boiler; add eggs and vinegar, stirring until blended. Cook, stirring constantly, over boiling water until mixture thickens. Cool and pour into glass jar with tight-fitting lid. Refrigerate until ready to use. Bring to room temperature before using and thin, if necessary, with a drop of water. Good with egg rolls or on hot dogs and sandwiches. Yield: about 3 cups.
B. J. Arth
Judy Braun

PESTO SAUCE

5-ounces fresh basil, or 3 tablespoons crushed dried basil
½ cup pine nuts (from health food store)
½ cup grated Parmesan cheese
2 small cloves garlic
5 tablespoons olive oil
Salt and pepper to taste
12-ounces thin spaghetti, vermicelli or angel hair, cooked and drained

Place basil, pine nuts, cheese and garlic in blender container; blend according to manufacturer's instructions for pulverizing dry ingredients. Slowly add oil, blending on high speed until mixture is smooth. Season with salt and pepper; pour over spaghetti and toss until well coated.
Lynne Della Donna

BOUQUET GARNI

½ teaspoon parsley
½ teaspoon rosemary
½ teaspoon marjoram
1 teaspoon thyme
2 bay leaves, crushed
4 or 5-inch square cheese cloth

Place dried herbs in center of cloth. Bring up corners of cloth and tie with string. Use to season soups and stews.
Eileen Barlock

RICH SWEET-AND-SOUR SAUCE

½ cup chutney
½ cup plum jam
¼ cup cold water
1 tablespoon sugar
1 tablespoon vinegar

Combine all ingredients in a saucepan and simmer 1 minute. Cool and refrigerate. Yield: 1½ cups.
Patti Lovejoy

RAISIN SAUCE

1 cup sugar
½ cup water
1 cup raisins
2 tablespoons butter or margarine
2 teaspoons vinegar
1 teaspoon Worcestershire sauce
½ teaspoon salt
¼ teaspoon cloves
Pinch of pepper
1 cup fruit jelly

Combine sugar and water in a saucepan. Bring to a boil over medium high heat, stirring constantly. Add remainder of ingredients. Bring back to boiling. Reduce heat and simmer for 10 to 15 minutes. Serve with ham. Yield: 3½ to 4 cups.
A Friend

HOT FUDGE SAUCE

2 cups sugar
¾ cup cocoa
¼ cup all-purpose flour
Dash of salt
2 cups milk
4 tablespoons butter or margarine
2 teaspoons vanilla extract

Combine sugar, cocoa, flour and salt in heavy saucepan; stir. Add milk and butter, place over medium-high heat and bring to a boil, stirring constantly. Reduce heat and boil for 8 minutes, continuing to stir. Remove from heat and stir in vanilla. Keep stored in refrigerator, heating sauce as needed. Serve over ice cream or brownies.
Karen Gallagher

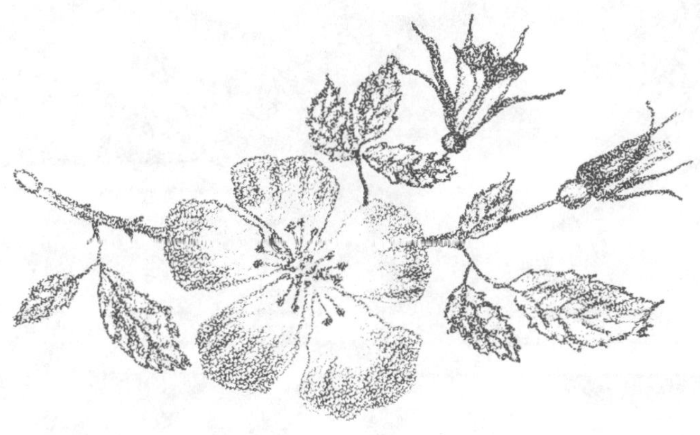

IN THE DOUGH

Yeast Dough, Bread and Rolls

EASY KOLACKY

Dough:

1 package hot roll mix
2 tablespoons warm water (105 to 115 degrees)
½ cup butter or margarine
½ cup milk
¼ cup dairy sour cream
1 egg
Preserves or canned fruit filling

Grease a 15x10x1-inch jelly roll pan or a 13x9x2-inch pan. Dissolve yeast from hot roll mix in warm water. In large bowl, cut butter into flour mixture until the size of peas. Stir in milk, dissolved yeast, sour cream and egg. Blend well. Knead on floured surface for 1 minute. Press dough into pan. Cover and let rise in warm place until light and doubled in size, about 1 hour. Preheat oven to 375 degrees. Cut risen dough in pan, into 24 squares. Using fingers, make large indentation in center of each square. Place 1 heaping teaspoon of preserves or canned fruit in each indentation. Bake immediately, in 15x10x1-inch pan 17 to 30 minutes; or in 13x9x2-inch pan 25 to 35 minutes, until golden brown.

Glaze:

1½ cups powdered sugar
3 to 4 teaspoon milk
½ teaspoon vanilla extract

In a medium bowl, combine powdered sugar, milk and vanilla. Drizzle glaze from a spoon onto rolls. Yield: 24 rolls.
Betz Spacek

SWEET DOUGH

1¼ cups warm water
½ cup sugar
1 teaspoon salt
2 envelopes dry yeast
4 eggs, beaten
1 cup all-purpose flour
½ cup vegetable shortening, softened
4½ to 5 cups all-purpose flour

Combine sugar and salt in a large mixing bowl. Add warm water and mix. Add eggs and 1 cup flour; beat until mixture is almost smooth. Add shortening. Beat until well-blended. Add enough flour to make a soft dough. Beat with a wooden spoon. Cover and let rise in a warm place for 1½ to 2 hours or until double in bulk. Punch down. Cover and let rest for 10 minutes. Shape as desired. Cover and allow to rise for 30 minutes or until double in bulk. Bake at 375 degrees for 25 to 30 minutes. *This dough can also be used for pecan rolls, tea rings and kuchens.* Yield: 18 rolls.
Alice Waight

SOURDOUGH STARTER

½ teaspoon dry yeast
1½ cups warm water
2 cups all-purpose flour
1 teaspoon salt
3 tablespoons sugar

Dissolve yeast in warm water. Sift together flour, salt and sugar and stir into yeast mixture. Pour into a covered container. Keep mixture in warm place for 3 days, stirring once or twice daily. Starter will be thick and bubbly. Starter may be frozen. When ready to use remove from freezer and thaw for 48 hours. The evening before you are ready to bake place starter in warm spot and add 2 cups flour and 1½ cups warm water. It will be ready to use in the morning. Yield: about 3½ cups starter.
Eileen Barlock

SOURDOUGH PANCAKES

1 cup sourdough starter
⅓ cup butter, melted
2 teaspoons salt
¼ cup dry powdered milk
1 teaspoon baking soda
2 eggs
2½ tablespoons sugar

Combine all ingredients and mix well. Pour by ¼ cupfuls onto a hot, greased griddle or skillet. Cook for 2 to 3 minutes or until golden; turn; cook until browned.
Eileen Barlock

SOURDOUGH BISCUITS

2 cups sourdough starter
2 cups all-purpose flour
2 teaspoons baking powder
1 tablespoon sugar
½ teaspoon salt
½ cup butter

Combine dry ingredients in a large mixing bowl. Cut butter into mixture until is crumbly and resembles coarse corn meal. Add starter and stir well. Turn dough out onto a floured board and knead for 8 to 10 minutes or until mixture is smooth and elastic. More flour can be added if dough is too sticky. Roll dough to ½-inch thickness. Cut with a biscuit cutter or rim of a drinking glass. Place on a greased 15x10x1-inch baking sheet. Cover and let rise in a warm place for 30 minutes. Bake at 425 degrees for 20 minutes or until browned. Yield: 20 biscuits.
Eileen Barlock

FRIENDSHIP CAKE

Place sourdough starter in large bowl and cover loosely. Do not refrigerate!

Day 1:

Add *1 cup all-purpose flour*
1 cup sugar
1 cup milk

Mix ingredients thoroughly until smooth.

Day 2, 3 and 4:
Stir each day gently. Do not beat.

Day 5:
Repeat day 1.

Day 6, 7, 8 and 9:
Same as days 2, 3 and 4.

Day 10:
Remove 3 cups of batter - one for each of 3 friends.

Include recipe to remaining portion: add and mix well.

1 cup sugar
2 eggs
2 teaspoons vanilla extract
2/3 cup vegetable oil
2 cups all-purpose flour
2 teaspoons baking soda
1/4 teaspoon salt
2 teaspoons ground cinnamon

After well mixed, add:

1 (20-ounce) can crushed pineapple, drained
1/2 cup chopped nuts
1/2 cup raisins

Pour into 13x9x2-inch greased and floured baking pan. Bake at 350 degrees for about 45 minutes.

Topping:
1/2 teaspoon ground cinnamon
1/2 cup melted butter
1 cup brown sugar
1 teaspoon all-purpose flour

Topping is optional—*the cake is very good!*
John Laco

MASHED POTATO DINNER ROLLS

½ cup milk
2 tablespoons margarine, softened
2 tablespoons sugar
1 teaspoon salt
1 envelope dry yeast
1 egg, beaten
½ cup mashed potatoes
2 cups all-purpose flour
Melted butter or margarine

Scald milk and cool to lukewarm. Add margarine, sugar and salt; stir until well mixed. Add yeast. Blend in egg, potatoes and flour; mixing until well blended. Cover and place in refrigerator or cold place for 2 hours or overnight. Divide dough into 2 parts. Roll each into a circle ¼-inch thick on a lightly floured board. Brush with melted butter. Cut into 8 wedges. Roll each piece from the wide end into a horn. Place on a lightly greased 15x10x1-inch baking sheet with the point side down. Bake at 375 degrees for 15 minutes. Yield: 16 horns.
Sister M. Claudia, C.S.F.S.

POPPYSEED OR NUT ROLLS

4 cups all-purpose flour, sifted
¼ teaspoon baking soda
½ teaspoon salt
1 package active dry yeast
1 cup butter or margarine
5 egg yolks
1 cup dairy sour cream
Powdered sugar

Stir flour, soda, salt and yeast together in a bowl. Cut in butter or margarine until mixture resembles coarse meal. Stir in egg yolks and sour cream; blend well, using hands. Divide dough into 4 parts; wrap each in waxed paper and refrigerate overnight. To bake, sprinkle powdered sugar on counter or board. Cut each package of dough in ½. Roll 1 piece at a time until paper thin. Spread with filling mixture and roll up. Repeat with remaining dough. Place 2 rolls on a well-greased baking sheet and bake at 350 degrees 20 minutes, or until golden brown. Sprinkle powdered sugar while warm. Yield: 8 rolls.

Poppyseed Filling:

1 pound freshly ground poppy seed
1 cup milk
1 teaspoon vanilla extract
1 ripe banana, mashed (optional)

Mix ingredients well and spread over dough. Makes enough filling for 8 rolls.

Nut Filling:

1 pound ground walnuts
5 egg whites, beaten stiff
1 cup sugar

Mix ingredients together and spread over dough. Makes enough filling for 8 rolls.
Kaye Sarby
Bea Moncol

TASTY PEACH MUFFINS

1/3 cup butter or margarine
1/2 cup sugar
1 egg
1 1/2 cups all-purpose flour
1 1/2 teaspoons baking powder
1/2 teaspoon salt
1/4 teaspoon ground nutmeg
1/2 cup milk
1/2 cup chopped fresh peaches

Combine butter and sugar in a mixing bowl. Cream until smooth. Add egg and beat until well-blended. Combine flour, baking powder, salt and nutmeg; add to the butter mixture alternately with milk. Mix well after each addition. Stir in peaches. Fill greased muffin cups 2/3 full and bake at 350 degrees for 30 minutes. Top with Cinnamon Topping. *Dee-lish!!* Yield: 12 muffins.

Cinnamon Topping:

1/2 cup sugar
1 teaspoon ground cinnamon
1/2 cup butter or margarine, melted

Combine sugar and cinnamon. While muffins are warm, dip top into melted butter then in cinnamon-sugar.
Betz Spacek

NUTTY PUMPKIN MUFFINS

2 eggs, slightly beaten
1 cup sugar
1/2 cup peanut or vegetable oil
3 tablespoons water
1 (16-ounce) can pumpkin
1 3/4 cups all-purpose flour
1 teaspoon baking soda
1/2 teaspoon salt
1/2 teaspoon ground allspice
1 cup dates, chopped
1/2 cup roasted peanuts, chopped

Place eggs in a mixing bowl. Gradually, add sugar, oil, water and pumpkin, beating well after each addition. Combine flour, soda, salt, allspice, dates and peanuts. Stir into egg mixture. Fill greased muffin cups about 3/4 full. Bake at 375 degrees for 25 minutes or until toothpick inserted in the middle comes out clean. Remove from the oven and cool on racks for 10 minutes in the pans. Invert pans to remove and cool completely. Yield: 18 muffins.
Ruth Abbott

TEA ROOM MUFFINS

4 cups all-purpose flour
2 tablespoons baking powder
1½ teaspoons salt
1 cup sugar
2 eggs
1½ cups milk
1 cup margarine or butter, melted

Combine first 4 ingredients and mix until well-blended. Combine eggs and milk; beat well. Add to dry ingredients and mix until all ingredients are moistened. Stir in melted butter or margarine. Pour into greased muffin cups filling until ⅔ full. Bake at 375 degrees for 25 minutes or until well-browned. Yield: 24 muffins.
Nicky Cowan

WHEAT GERM CRESCENTS

¾ cup brown sugar, firmly packed
½ cup margarine
½ cup butter
½ teaspoon salt
1 teaspoon vanilla extract
2 teaspoons almond extract
1¾ cup all-purpose flour
½ cup wheat germ

Cream butter and margarine with brown sugar. Add remaining ingredients and form into crescent shapes. Bake on ungreased cookie sheet at 350 degrees for 15 minutes, or until lightly browned. Roll in powdered sugar while still warm.
Shirley Herbst

FRENCH APPLE BREAD

1¼ cups all-purpose flour
1 cup bran cereal
1 teaspoon baking powder
1 teaspoon baking soda
½ cup sugar
¾ cup margarine, melted
3 eggs, slightly beaten
¼ cup applesauce
1 cup peeled, diced apples
½ cup grated Cheddar cheese
½ cup chopped nuts
6 thin apple slices

Combine first 4 ingredients; set aside. Cream sugar and margarine. Add eggs, applesauce, diced apples, cheese and nuts. Mix until well blended. Add flour mixture; mix well. Spoon into a greased 9x5x3-inch loaf pan. Place apple slices on top. Bake at 350 degrees for 50 to 55 minutes or until loaf tests done. Cool completely.
Dianne Barnett

NO FAT BANANA BREAD

3 ripe bananas, cut into chunks
¾ cup sugar
2 eggs
2 cups all-purpose flour
1 teaspoon salt
1 teaspoon baking soda
½ cup chopped nuts

Combine bananas and sugar in a mixing bowl; mix with electric mixer until well-blended using medium speed. Add eggs and continue beating. Combine dry ingredients and add to banana mixture. Beat until thoroughly mixed. Stir in chopped nuts. Pour into a greased 9x5x3-inch loaf pan and bake at 325 degrees for 1 hour. When cool, wrap in foil and let stand 24 hours before slicing. Slice in thin slices for serving. Yield: 1 loaf.
Marge Geraghty

CASHEW BUTTERSCOTCH BREAD

1 (18.5-ounce) package butterscotch or spice cake mix
2 eggs
1 cup water
1 (8¾-ounce) can crushed pineapple, drained
1 cup chopped cashews

Combine first 3 ingredients in mixing bowl. Blend with electric mixer until smooth. Stir in drained pineapple and cashews. Pour into a greased and floured 9x5x3-inch loaf pan. Bake at 350 degrees for 50 minutes. Remove from pan and cool on baking rack. Yield: 1 loaf.
J. Barbieri

STRAWBERRY BREAD

3 cups all-purpose flour
1 teaspoon baking soda
½ teaspoon salt
1 tablespoon ground cinnamon
2 cups sugar
3 eggs, beaten
1 cup vegetable oil
2 (10-ounce) packages frozen strawberries, or 1½ to 2 cups fresh strawberries, sliced

Combine flour, soda, salt, cinnamon and sugar; add eggs, oil and berries and mix until well blended. Turn into 2 well-greased 9x5x3-inch loaf pans. Bake at 350 degrees 1 hour, or until wooden pick inserted in center comes out clean. Serve warm. Freezes well. Yield: 2 loaves.
Mary Sims

APRICOT NIBBLE BREAD

2 (3-ounce) packages cream cheese, softened
1/3 cup sugar
1 tablespoon all-purpose flour
1 egg
1 teaspoon grated orange peel
1 egg, slightly beaten
1/2 cup orange juice
1/2 cup water
1 (17-ounce) apricot-nut quick bread mix

Combine cream cheese, sugar and flour in a small bowl. Add egg and orange peel. Beat until well-blended; set aside. Combine the beaten egg, juice and water in a medium-sized bowl. Add the quick bread mix and stir until just moistened. Turn 2/3 of the apricot batter into a greased and floured 9x5x3-inch loaf pan. Pour cream cheese mixture over the top; spoon in remaining apricot batter. Bake at 350 degrees for 1 hour. Allow to cool for 10 minutes; remove from pan. Cool completely. Wrap in foil and refrigerate until serving. Yield: 1 loaf.
Rosemary Corcoran

LEMONY BREAD

2 1/2 cups all-purpose flour
1/2 teaspoon salt
1/2 teaspoon baking soda
1 tablespoon baking powder
1/2 cup wheat germ
1/2 cup vegetable shortening or margarine
1 cup sugar
2 eggs
1/2 cup lemon juice
1/2 cup water
1/2 cup shredded lemon peel

In large bowl, mix together flour, salt, baking soda and baking powder. Stir in wheat germ. In another bowl, cream shortening and sugar until light and fluffy. Add eggs, one at a time, beating well after each addition. Combine lemon juice and water, add to shortening mixture. Stir in lemon peel. Pour into flour mixture and stir just enough to moisten dry ingredients. Do not beat. Pour into well-greased 9x5x3-inch loaf pan. Bake at 350 degrees for 1 hour or until done. Yield: 1 loaf.
Ruth Abbott

CHUNKY PEANUT BUTTER BREAD

2 cups all-purpose flour
3 teaspoons baking powder
1/2 teaspoon salt
3/4 cup chunky peanut butter
1/4 cup butter or margarine, softened
3/4 cup sugar
1 large egg
1 teaspoon vanilla extract
1 cup milk

Stir together flour, baking powder and salt. In a medium-sized bowl, beat together peanut butter and margarine with wooden spoon until blended. Beat in sugar; add egg and vanilla. Add flour mixture. Using a pastry blender, mix until fine crumbs form. Add milk and stir only until mixture is moistened. Preheat oven to 350 degrees. Spread batter in a greased 9x5x3-inch loaf pan. Bake for 55 to 60 minutes. Place pan on wire rack to cool for 5 minutes. Turn bread out of pan and cool completely.
Jane Boyd

PUMPKIN BREAD

3/4 cup vegetable shortening
2 2/3 cups sugar
4 eggs
2/3 cup water
3 1/2 cups all-purpose flour
1/2 teaspoon baking powder
1 1/2 teaspoons salt
1 teaspoon ground cloves
2 teaspoons baking soda
1 teaspoon ground cinnamon
1 (16-ounce) can pumpkin
1 cup chopped nuts
1 cup chopped dates or raisins

Combine shortening, sugar and cream until smooth and fluffy. Add eggs, one at a time, beating well after each addition. Add water. Sift dry ingredients together and add to batter mixing thoroughly. Blend in pumpkin. Add nuts and dates. Pour into 3 lightly greased and floured 9x5x3-inch loaf pans. Bake at 350 degrees for 1 hour. This freezes well. Yield: 3 loaves.
Rosemary Corcoran

BOON TAVERN SPOON BREAD

3 cups milk
1 1/4 cups white cornmeal
3 eggs, well beaten
1 teaspoon salt
1 3/4 teaspoons baking powder
2 tablespoons melted butter

Place milk in a heavy saucepan and bring to a boil over a medium heat. Stir in cornmeal. Cook for 8 to 10 minutes or until stiff, stirring constantly. Remove from heat and cool. Add remaining ingredients and beat at high speed of electric mixer for 15 minutes or until smooth. Pour into a greased 1 1/2-quart casserole. Bake at 375 degrees for 30 minutes. Yield: 1 loaf.
Dolores Sygula

A SIMPLE ZUCCHINI BREAD

3 eggs, well beaten
2 cups sugar
1 cup vegetable oil
1 teaspoon vanilla extract
2 cups grated zucchini with excess liquid squeezed out
3 cups all-purpose flour
2 cups chopped nuts
1 teaspoon ground cinnamon
1 teaspoon salt
1 teaspoon baking powder
1 teaspoon baking soda
½ cup dairy sour cream

Combine all ingredients in a large mixing bowl; mix for 3 minutes or until well blended. Pour into 2, greased and floured 9x5x3-inch loaf pans. Bake at 350 degrees for 50 to 60 minutes or until done. Let cool in pans. If desired, add 1 cup raisins and 1 cup chopped nuts may be substituted for the 2 cups nuts. Yield: 2 loaves.
Justin Baum
Kathy Korzekwa
Carol Brady

IRISH OATMEAL BREAD

3 cups sifted all-purpose flour
1¼ cups quick cooking oats
1½ tablespoons baking powder
1½ teaspoon salt
1 egg
¼ cup honey
1½ cups milk

Combine dry ingredients in a large bowl. Mix egg, milk and honey in separate mixing bowl until well-blended. Pour egg mixture into oat mixture. Stir with wooden spoon just until the dry ingredients are moistened. Pour into a greased 9x5x3-inch loaf pan and bake at 350 degrees for 1 hour and 15 minutes or until crusty or until a tester inserted in the center of the loaf comes out clean. Cool on a wire rack. While warm, brush top with melted butter. Yield: 1 loaf.
Nicky Cowan

MONKEY BREAD

1¼ cups brown sugar, packed
¾ cup chopped nuts
1 teaspoon ground cinnamon
4 (10 biscuit) cans refrigerated biscuits
¾ cup margarine, melted

Combine ¾ cup brown sugar, nuts and ½ teaspoon cinnamon. Mix until ingredients are evenly distributed. Cut each biscuit in 2 pieces and roll in brown sugar mixture. Place in lightly greased bundt pan. Mix margarine, remaining brown sugar and remaining cinnamon. Pour over biscuits. Bake at 350 degrees for 40 to 45 minutes. Yield: 1 loaf.
Frances Willson

CUSTARD ROLLS

½ box filo
Melted butter
3 cups milk
4 eggs, slightly beaten
1¼ cups sugar
½ cup farina or cream of wheat
1 tablespoon sweet butter
2 teaspoons vanilla extract

To make filling, heat milk with sugar and eggs in heavy saucepan over low heat, stirring constantly. When almost boiling, stir in farina. Remove from heat, add butter and vanilla and cool. Refrigerate until chilled thoroughly before using.

To make rolls, remove 1 sheet of filo dough at a time. Brush with melted sweet butter and cut into 4 equal lengths. Place about 1 tablespoon filling on end of each strip and roll as for jelly roll (from long side). Place on greased baking sheet. When all rolls are made, bake at 350 degrees for 30 minutes or until golden brown. Dust with confectioners' sugar while warm. Do not cover or store in closed container. May be covered lightly with paper towels. If all are not eaten immediately, keep stored in refrigerator.
Sally Zetl

PUFFS ITALIANO

1 (16-ounce) loaf frozen white bread dough, thawed overnight in the refrigerator
⅔ cup Swiss cheese
½ teaspoon salt
⅛ teaspoon cayenne pepper
½ cup grated Parmesan cheese
1 egg yolk
1 teaspooon water
Parmesan cheese

Allow dough to stand at room temperature on a lightly floured pastry board for 1 hour. Roll and pat out dough to ½-inch thickness. Sprinkle with Swiss cheese, salt and cayenne pepper. Fold dough over to enclose cheese. Knead into a ball. Sprinkle surface of board with ½ cup grated Parmesan cheese. Continue to knead until dough has incorporated all the cheese. Roll dough to a 12-inch square. Cut into 1½-inch squares or use a 1½-inch round cutter. Reroll dough trimmings for more cut pieces. Place on greased baking sheets. Cover and let rise 30 minutes in warm place away from drafts. Combine egg yolk and water in a cup; brush cheese puffs, then top each with a sprinkling of Parmesan cheese. Bake at 400 degrees for 12 minutes or until golden. Remove from oven and let cool on racks. Store in metal container with tight-fitting lid. Serve with soups and salads. Yield: Approximately 6 dozen.
Peg O'Shea

PULL-APART BUTTERSCOTCH BUNS

1 (16-ounce) loaf frozen white bread dough, partially thawed
½ cup chopped nuts
1 (4-ounce) package butterscotch pudding mix
½ cup firmly packed brown sugar
½ teaspoon ground cinnamon
6 tablespoons butter or margarine, melted

Generously butter 12 cup fluted tube pan or 9-inch square pan. Sprinkle nuts in pan. Cut loaf of bread into 24 pieces by first cutting lengthwise into 3 evenly divided strips, then making 7 crosswise cuts completely through all 3 strips of dough. Place pieces in pan. Sprinkle evenly with dry pudding mix, brown sugar and cinnamon. Drizzle melted butter or margarine over pieces. Cover and let rise in warm place until double in size, 3 to 4 hours. Bake at 375 degrees for 25 to 30 minutes. Remove from oven; let stand 3 to 5 minutes. Turn onto plate lined with waxed paper. Yield: 8 to 10 servings.
Sue Mahon

HERBED MELBA PITA TOAST

5 large round pita bread
½ cup butter or olive oil
Crumbled dried basil (or other herb of your choice)
Garlic salt (optional)

Tear bread rounds in ½ and cut into triangles of preferred size. Brush insides of bread with butter or olive oil and sprinkle with basil or other herb and garlic salt. Place in single layer on cookie sheets and bake at 275 degrees 20 to 30 minutes, or until lightly browned. Remove, cool and store in airtight containers. Keeps for several days at room temperature or for weeks in refrigerator. Use with any dip instead of potato chips.
Rosemary Balchak

SESAME MELBA TOAST

1 loaf thin party white bread
½ cup butter
½ cup margarine
Sesame seeds

Cut bread slices in ½. Melt butter and margarine together. Brush butter mixture over bread slices; place on ungreased cookie sheets. Sprinkle with sesame seeds. Bake at 350 degrees 10 to 15 minutes.
Peg O'Shea

THE MELTING POT

Casseroles, Egg Dishes and Quiche

PEPPERONI CASSEROLE

1 pound hot Italian sausage
1 green pepper, diced
1 medium onion, diced
1 (4-ounce) can mushrooms, drained
1 clove garlic, crushed
¼ pound thinly sliced pepperoni
1 (16-ounce) can Italian cooking sauce
1 (16-ounce) can stewed tomatoes
1 (8-ounce) package sea shell macaroni
1 (8-ounce) package shredded mozzarella cheese

Lightly grease a 13x9x2-inch baking dish. In a large skillet, cook first 6 ingredients together until sausage is no longer pink. Pour off excess fat. Add cooking sauce and stewed tomatoes; simmer ½ hour. In a large saucepan, cook macaroni according to directions on package. Drain well. Add shells to sauce and mix gently. Pour mixture into greased baking dish. Top with mozzarella cheese. Bake in 350 degree preheated oven for 20 minutes. Let stand 5 minutes before serving. Yield: 6 servings.
Judy Porter

ZUCCHINI PIE

Pie crust
4 cups thinly sliced zucchini
1 cup chopped green onion
2 cloves garlic, minced
3 tablespoons butter or margarine
½ cup snipped parsley
¾ teaspoon basil
½ teaspoon salt
½ teaspoon oregano
¼ teaspoon pepper
2 eggs, beaten
1½ cups shredded mozzarella cheese
2 teaspoon Dijon mustard

Sauté zucchini, onion and garlic in butter or margarine in a skillet for 10 minutes. Stir in parsley, basil, salt, pepper and oregano. Combine eggs and mozzarella cheese. Stir into zucchini. Bake pie crust 5 minutes; pour zucchini mixture into crust and bake 20 to 25 minutes at 375 degrees, until knife comes out clean. Let stand 10 minutes before serving. Yield: 4 to 6 servings.
Betz Spacek

VEGETARIAN MOUSSAKA

3 medium-sized eggplants, sliced ½-inch thick
2 pounds mushrooms, sliced
1 large onion, chopped
2 cloves garlic, minced
1 tablespoon butter or margarine
1 (6-ounce) can tomato paste
¼ cup fresh chopped parsley
Dash of oregano
Dash of basil
½ teaspoon salt
Pepper to taste
Dash of ground cinnamon
¼ cup dry red wine
½ cup breadcrumbs
½ cup grated Parmesan cheese
4 eggs, beaten

Arrange sliced eggplant on greased baking sheet, salt lightly, bake at 350 degrees for 15 minutes. In a large skillet, sauté mushrooms, onion and garlic in butter. Add tomato paste, parsley, oregano, basil, salt, pepper, cinnamon and wine, simmering until liquid is absorbed. Add breadcrumbs, grated cheese and eggs. Stir and remove from heat.

White Sauce:

1 cup butter or margarine
½ cup all-purpose flour
2½ cups warm milk
4 egg yolks

Melt butter over low heat and stir in flour. Slowly add warm milk, stirring constantly. Cook until thick, then beat in egg yolks. In a large buttered casserole, cover the bottom with eggplant slices. Add ½ mushroom sauce, remaining eggplant and remaining mushroom sauce. Top with white sauce and sprinkle with cheese. Bake, covered, at 350 degrees for 35 minutes. Uncover and continue baking for another 15 minutes. Yield: 8 servings.
Thomas More Program

MUTINY ON THE BOUNTY CASSEROLE

1 pound ground beef
1 cup chopped onion
1 cup chopped green pepper
1 (14½ or 16-ounce) can tomatoes
1 teaspoon salt
1 tablespoon chili powder
½ teaspoon garlic powder
3 cups cooked rice
4 cups shredded cabbage
½ cup dairy sour cream
1 cup shredded Monterey Jack cheese

In a large skillet, sauté ground beef, onions and green pepper until meat is lightly browned; drain off fat. Stir in tomatoes, seasonings, rice and cabbage. Cover and cook for 10 to 15 minutes or until cabbage is tender-crisp. Stir in sour cream. Sprinkle with cheese. Cover and allow cheese to melt (2 to 3 minutes). Yield: 6 to 8 servings.
Lynne Della Donna

HEARTY VEGETABLE CASSEROLE

1 (16-ounce) bag frozen cut broccoli
1 (16-ounce) bag frozen brussels sprouts
1 (16-ounce) bag cauliflower
1 (8-ounce) jar processed cheese spread
1 (8-ounce) can mushroom soup

Thoroughly thaw vegetables; layer in a 3-quart casserole. Blend cheese and soup over low heat until smooth; pour over vegetables. Do not stir. Bake at 350 degrees 30 minutes, or until vegetables are fork-tender. *Great with ham! A terrific buffet dish!* Yield: 14 to 16 servings.
JoAnn Schock

SOUR CREAM ENCHILADAS

1 (10¾-ounce) can cream of chicken soup
1 pint (2 cups) dairy sour cream
1 (3-ounce) can chopped green chilies (hot)
1 (4½-ounce) package flour tortillas
Oil
⅓ cup green onions, chopped
4-ounces sharp Cheddar cheese, shredded

Heat soup, sour cream and chilies in small saucepan until heated through over medium heat, stirring occasionally. Fry tortillas in oil; drain. Spoon some of the soup mixture over each tortilla, top with a little cheese and some onions. Roll and place in greased 13x9x2-inch glass baking dish. Pour remaining soup mixture over tortillas and bake at 350 degrees for 20 to 25 minutes, or until hot and bubbly. Yield: 8 to 10 tortillas.
Judy & Butch Nekvinda

SLOVAK EASTER CHEESE

1½ quarts milk
12 eggs
1 cup sugar
¼ teaspoon salt
1 tablespoon pickling spices
Cheesecloth

Scald milk. Combine eggs, sugar, salt and vanilla. Stir into cooled milk mixture. Tie pickling spices in a small cheesecloth bag and hang in cooking pot. Cook over a medium heat, stirring constantly, until curds form. Place cheesecloth in a colander and pour the hot mixture into the cheesecloth. Bring the ends of the cheesecloth together and tie. Hang over a bowl for 12 hours or overnight. Refrigerate. Yield: about 1 pound cheese.
John Laco

GREEK SPINACH PIE

2 (10-ounce) packages frozen chopped spinach (or about 2½ cups fresh)
1 medium onion
½ pound butter
3 large eggs
1 pound ricotta, cottage cheese or Monterey Jack cheese
½ pound crumbled feta cheese
Salt to taste
Pepper to taste
20 sheets filo dough

Cook spinach according to package directions. If fresh, clean, chop and blanch about 3 bunches. Dice onion and sauté in 2 tablespoons butter; add spinach and cook until moisture has evaporated. Beat eggs; add ricotta and feta cheese to eggs. Add spinach to mixture and season with salt and pepper. Carefully spread filo dough out flat and cover with moistened dish towel so it doesn't become brittle. Melt remaining butter. Butter an 13x9x2-inch baking pan and place a sheet of dough on bottom. Brush lightly with melted butter and continue layering sheets of dough, buttering each sheet until you have a stack of 10. Spread spinach mixture evenly on top and stack with another 10 sheets of dough and butter. Bake at 375 degrees for 15 minutes in a preheated oven; reduce heat to 350 degrees and bake for another 30 minutes. If top layer gets too brown cover with brown paper. Remove from oven and let rest for 15 minutes before serving. Yield: 12 servings or 16 appetizers.
Joan Murphy

NOODLE-LESS LASAGNA

1 pound lean ground beef
1 (16-ounce) jar spaghetti sauce
1 (12-ounce) carton cottage cheese
¼ cup grated Romano cheese
1 egg
1½ pounds zucchini, cut lengthwise into ¼-inch slices
2 tablespoons all-purpose flour
1 (4-ounce) package shredded mozzarella cheese
¼ cup grated Romano cheese

Preheat oven to 350 degrees. Grease a 9x9x2-inch baking pan. In a large skillet, brown meat. Drain off fat. Stir in spaghetti sauce and simmer until heated through. In a small bowl, beat egg and blend in cottage cheese and ¼ cup Romano cheese. In baking dish, layer the following: ½ of zucchini, flour, cottage cheese mixture, meat sauce and mozzarella in that order. Repeat layers. Bake uncovered for 45 minutes. Let stand for 15 to 20 minutes before serving. Cut into squares. Yield: 6 servings.
Kathryn Kurdziel

RINGS AND THINGS BEEF CASSEROLE

2 cups macaroni
1½ pounds lean ground beef
1 (10¾-ounce) can tomato soup
1 (10¾-ounce) can cream of mushroom soup
1 medium green pepper, diced
½ cup water
¼ cup chopped pimento
1 (4-ounce) can chopped mushrooms, drained
2 cups shredded Cheddar cheese
1 (6-ounce) can fried onion rings

Cook macaroni according to package directions. Brown ground beef in large skillet; drain, and set aside. Butter a 13x9x2-inch (or 2-quart) baking dish. Combine macaroni with beef and all other ingredients, except cheese and onion rings, in large bowl. Pour into prepared baking dish. Sprinkle with ½ the cheese, then ½ the onion rings. Repeat layers. Bake at 350 degrees for 35 minutes. Yield: 6 to 8 servings.
Betz Spacek
Kay Holman

QUICHE LORRAINE

1 (9-inch) unbaked pie shell
½ pound bacon, cooked and crumbled
1 cup shredded Swiss or Gruyere cheese
4 eggs
1 tablespoon all-purpose flour
1½ cups half and half
¼ teaspoon salt
Freshly ground black pepper
⅛ teaspoon ground nutmeg
1 tablespoon melted butter or margarine

Preheat oven to 350 degrees and bake prepared pie shell for 3 or 4 minutes (do not brown). Remove from oven. Scatter crumbled bacon and shredded cheese over bottom of pie shell. Beat eggs, flour, cream, salt, pepper and nutmeg together until smooth in small bowl with wire whisk. Pour over bacon/cheese mixture; add melted butter. Bake for 35 minutes or until knife inserted near center comes out clean. Cool on wire rack about 5 minutes before serving. Yield: 6 servings.
Kay McGorray

CRUSTLESS MUSHROOM QUICHE

3 cups sliced fresh mushrooms
1 cup chopped green onions
1 clove garlic, crushed
2 tablespoons butter or margarine
3 slices bacon, cooked and crumbled
1½ cups milk
1 cup shredded Cheddar cheese
⅔ cup biscuit mix
4 eggs, slightly beaten
1 teaspoon Dijon mustard
1 teaspoon dried parsley flakes
½ teaspoon thyme
½ teaspoon salt
⅛ teaspoon pepper

Sauté mushrooms, onions and garlic in butter in skillet. Spoon into a greased quiche pan (one without removable bottom). Cover with bacon crumbs. Combine milk, cheese, biscuit mix, eggs, mustard, parsley, thyme, salt and pepper in blender until mixed well. Pour over mushroom mixture. Bake in a preheated 350 degree oven for 50 to 60 minutes or until a knife inserted just off-center comes out clean. Remove from oven and allow to stand for 10 minutes before serving. Cut into 6 slices to serve. *This is good cold, too!* Yield: 4 to 6 servings.
Sally Vlasik

ONION-BACON QUICHE

1 (10-inch) unbaked pie shell
¼ cup chopped onion
1 (16-ounce) package bacon, cooked and crumbled
1 cup shredded Swiss cheese
4 eggs
2 cups light cream or half and half
¾ teaspoon salt
¼ teasoon cayenne pepper
Pinch of ground nutmeg

Layer onion, bacon and cheese into bottom of prepared pie shell. Beat eggs, cream, salt, pepper and nutmeg together in small bowl; pour into pie shell. Bake at 375 degrees for 40 minutes (do not preheat oven) or until toothpick inserted near center comes out clean. Do not mix ahead of time and leave in pie shell before baking; crust will become soggy. Yield: 6 servings.
Karen Collins

FAST AND FURIOUS

Microwave

WASSAIL

1 quart apple cider
1 teaspoon ground allspice
½ teaspoon ground cloves
¼ teaspoon ground nutmeg
2 cinnamon sticks
½ cup orange juice
2 tablespoons lemon juice
½ cup sugar
2 tart, medium-sized apples, peeled and thinly sliced

Combine all ingredients in a 3-quart casserole. Microwave on high for 15 to 18 minutes or until hot. Strain and serve. Yield: 6 to 8 servings.
Sue Polacek

FRESH POLISH SAUSAGE AND CABBAGE

3 tablespoons butter or margarine
1 large onion, chopped
1 head of cabbage, chopped
½ teaspoon salt
Dash of pepper
1 pound fresh Polish sausage

In an 8-inch glass baking dish, melt butter in microwave oven for 1½ minutes on high. Add onions and microwave, uncovered, for 1½ minutes on high. Coarsely shred cabbage and stir into onion mixture. Add salt and pepper. Cut ¼ inch slashes into sausage at about 2-inch intervals. Place on top of cabbage. Cover and microwave on high for 14 to 15 minutes. Turn sausage once or twice during cooking. Yield: 3 to 4 servings.
Kay Holman

MICROWAVE MINI RUEBENS

1 (6-ounce) box rye melba toast rounds
¼ pound thinly sliced, cooked, corned beef
1 (8-ounce) can sauerkraut, rinsed, drained and snipped
1 cup finely shredded Swiss cheese
2 teaspoons prepared mustard
1 tablespoon caraway seed

Arrange 8 toast rounds around edge of plate lined with paper towels. Place 2 or 3 more rounds in center. Cut corned beef into 1½-inch squares and place over each toast round. Top each with 1 teaspoon sauerkraut. Combine cheese and mustard together by tossing lightly. Spoon about 1 teaspoon cheese mixture over sauerkraut; sprinkle with caraway seed. Microwave on medium for 1 to 2 minutes or until cheese is melted, rotating once. Repeat with remaining ingredients. These may be baked in a conventional oven for 4 to 6 minutes at 350 degrees. Yield: about 48 toast rounds (servings for 20).
Karen Campbell

CHINESE BEEF AND VEGETABLES

1 pound flank steak, baked until rare
1 cup sliced onions
½ cup diagonally sliced celery (¼-inch slices)
2 tablespoons water
1 cup sliced mushrooms
1 clove garlic, minced
1½ tablespoons soy sauce combined with 1½ tablespoons water
1½ tablespoons cornstarch
½ teaspoon beef bouillon granules
2 cups Chinese pea pods
18 cherry tomatoes

Cut flank steak lengthwise into 2-inch strips. Carve meat against the grain. Place onion, celery and water in a 3-quart casserole. Cover and microwave on high for 3 minutes or until vegetables are tender-crisp. Stir in remaining ingredients, except pea pods and tomatoes; mix lightly. Cover and microwave on high for about 8 minutes or until meat loses its pink color. Add pea pods; cover and microwave on high for 2 minutes. Add tomatoes; stir lightly and microwave on high, uncovered for 2 minutes. Drain liquid into a 1 cup measure; cover meat mixture and set aside. Microwave liquid on high for 2 minutes or until mixture bubbles. Stir liquid back into the meat mixture and serve. Yield: 4 servings.
Jean Croyle

CHAMPAGNE JELLY

1¾ cups champagne
3 cups sugar
½ bottle liquid fruit pectin

Combine champagne and sugar in a 3-quart casserole. Mix well. Cover and microwave on high for 4 minutes. Stir; return to microwave for 3 to 4 minutes or until mixture begins to boil. Continue cooking for an additional minute. Stir. Gradually, stir pectin into hot mixture; mix well. Ladle into prepared glasses and seal with parafin. Yield: 4 cups jelly.
Sue Polacek

MICROWAVE PECAN PIE

3 tablespoons margarine
3 eggs, slightly beaten
1 cup dark corn syrup
¼ cup brown sugar
1½ teaspoons all-purpose flour
1 teaspoon vanilla extract
1 cup pecan halves
1 baked 9-inch pie shell

Place margarine in glass mixing bowl. Microwave for 30 seconds or just until melted. Stir in remaining ingredients. Mix well. Pour filling into pie shell. Microwave on defrost for 25 minutes, or until knife inserted comes out clean.
Jean Croyle

ELEGANT CHICKEN

2 (10-ounce) packages frozen asparagus spears
1/4 cup butter
1/4 cup blanched, slivered almonds
1/4 cup all-purpose flour
1/2 teaspoon salt
1/8 teaspoon pepper
1 (10 1/2-ounce) can chicken and rice soup
1 cup chicken broth
3 cups cooked chicken, cut into bite-sized pieces
Paprika

Slit tops of boxes of asparagus. Microwave on high for 5 minutes. Open boxes and rearrange spears. Microwave on high 5 minutes more. Set aside. To make sauce, melt butter in a 9-inch pie pan, on high for 1 minute. Add almonds. Microwave on high for 1 1/2 minutes, stirring every 30 seconds. Mix flour, salt, pepper, and add to buttered almonds. Add soup and broth, stirring well. Microwave on high for 3 to 5 minutes, stirring every 2 minutes, until thick. In a 12x8x2-inch casserole, alternate layers of chicken and asparagus. Cover with butter sauce. Sprinkle with paprika. Cover with plastic wrap and microwave on high 5 to 6 minutes. Turn dish one-half turn after 2 1/2 minutes. Garnish with almonds and parsley. Yield: 5 to 6 servings.
Jean Croyle

GRASSHOPPER TARTS

4-ounces milk chocolate candy bars
2 tablespoons butter or margarine
20 large marshmallows
1/3 cup milk
2 tablespoons white crème de cacao
2 tablespoons crème de menthe
1 cup whipping cream, whipped
6 muffin size paper liners or 18 to 24 tart size paper liners

With a potato peeler make a few chocolate curls for garnish. Set aside. Microwave remaining chocolate and butter in a 2-cup glass measuring cup, 1 to 1 1/2 minutes on high until softened. Stir until smooth. Divide chocolate among muffin or tart papers. Spread chocolate evenly over bottom and up the sides of paper liners, using back of spoon. Refrigerate until set. Combine marshmallows and milk in a glass mixing bowl. Microwave on high, uncovered 1 1/2 minutes or until marshmallows are puffed. Stir until smooth. Blend in crème de cacao and crème de menthe. Refrigerate until partially set, about 45 minutes. Fold in whipped cream. Spoon into chocolate cups. Refrigerate 2 to 3 hours. Remove tarts from cups and peel off papers. Top with chocolate curls. Chocolate becomes brittle when refrigerated. For ease in serving, allow the tarts to stand at room temperature 20 to 30 minutes before serving.
Debbie Simunek

HOT MUSHROOM CANAPES

2 cups sliced mushrooms
Salt
1 cup whipping cream
3 to 4 dozen small, toasted bread rounds or melba toast

Place mushrooms in a 12x8x2-inch glass baking dish. Sprinkle lightly with salt and cover with whipping cream. Microwave, uncovered, on high for 12 to 14 minutes, stirring occasionally, until the cream becomes thick and browned. Transfer to a chafing dish to keep warm until served. To serve, spoon onto toast rounds. Yield: 48 mushroom rounds.
Sue Mahon

MICROWAVE LASAGNA

1½ pounds ground beef
1 (28-ounce) can tomatoes, undrained, or 1 (15-ounce) can tomato sauce
1 (6-ounce) can tomato paste
1½ teaspoons salt
2 teaspoons basil
¾ teaspoon oregano leaves
¼ teaspoon garlic powder
¾ cup water
2 cups cottage cheese or 2 cups Ricotta cheese plus 2 tablespoons water
¼ cup grated Parmesan cheese
1 egg
1 tablespoon parsley flakes
8 uncooked lasagna noodles
3 cups shredded mozzarella cheese

Crumble beef into 1½-quart glass casserole; microwave on high for 5 to 6 minutes, or until meat is no longer pink, stirring once. Stir to break meat into small pieces; drain. Stir in tomatoes or tomato sauce, tomato paste, salt, basil, oregano, garlic powder and water. Cover and microwave on high 4 to 5 minutes, or until mixture boils. Combine cottage cheese, or Ricotta, Parmesan cheese, egg and parsley; mix well. Pour 1½ cups tomato sauce mixture into 12x8x2-inch glass baking dish, spreading evenly. Arrange 4 uncooked noodles evenly over sauce. Do not overlap noodles! Top with ½ the cottage cheese mixture, spreading evenly. Sprinkle with ½ the mozzarella cheese. Spoon 1 cup sauce evenly over cheese. Arrange remaining noodles over sauce; top with even layers of cottage cheese mixture, mozzarella cheese, and tomato sauce. Cover tightly with plastic wrap. Microwave on high 15 minutes; rotate dish. Microwave on medium (50% power) 15 to 20 minutes, or until noodles are tender. Remove plastic wrap. Sprinkle with an additional 2 tablespoons Parmesan cheese. Microwave, uncovered, 1½ to 2 minutes, or until cheese melts. Cover with foil, shiny side down. Let stand 10 to 15 minutes before cutting into squares for serving. Standing time very important. Yield: 6 to 8 servings.
Betty De Marco
Debbie Simunek

CHICKEN CORDON BLEU

2 to 4 whole chicken breasts, boned and split
4 slices baked or boiled ham, halved
4 slices, Swiss, muenster or Monterey Jack cheese, halved
4 tablespoons margarine, melted
½ cup Cheddar cheese cracker crumbs
2 tablespoons margarine

Pound chicken breasts until thin. Place a slice of ham and a slice of cheese on each cutlet. Fold edges in and roll tightly, securing with wooden picks. Dip chicken rolls in melted margarine, then roll in crumbs. Arrange in baking dish, dot with remaining margarine, cover and cook 8 to 14 minutes, or until tender, in microwave oven or bake in conventional oven at 350 degrees for 45 minutes. Yield: 8 servings.
C.E.I. Microwave Seminar

MICROWAVE QUICHE

12 slices bacon
1 cup shredded Swiss cheese
½ cup shredded Cheddar cheese
⅔ cup chopped onion
1¾ cups milk
½ cup biscuit baking mix
4 eggs
½ teaspoon salt
Paprika

Layer bacon between paper towels on bacon rack or plate. Microwave on high for 8 to 9 minutes or until crisp. Cool. Combine cheese and onion. Crumble bacon and mix with cheese. Sprinkle evenly in lightly greased 9-inch glass pie plate. Combine milk, baking mix, eggs and salt in mixing bowl. Beat at high speed of electric mixer for 1 minute. Pour over bacon-cheese mixture. Sprinkle with paprika. Microwave, uncovered, on high for 12 to 14 minutes or until almost set, rotating dish 3 to 4 times. Let stand five minutes before cutting. Yield: 4 to 6 servings.
Jean Croyle

SEAFOOD SUPREME

1 pound frozen crabs, or 2 (6½-ounce) cans crabmeat, drained
1 pound frozen lobster, or 2 (6½-ounce) cans lobster, drained
1 pound shrimp, or 2 (6½-ounce) cans shrimp, drained
1 cup mayonnaise
½ cup finely chopped green pepper
¼ cup finely chopped green onion
1 cup minced celery
½ teaspoon salt
1 tablespoon Worcestershire sauce
2 cups crushed potato chips

Chop seafood into ½-inch pieces, reserving 6 whole shrimp. Combine chopped seafood with mayonnaise, green pepper, green onion, celery, salt and Worcestershire sauce; turn into 2½-quart casserole. Microwave on roast (80% power) setting 8 minutes. Sprinkle crushed potato chips over casserole; heat 1 minute. Garnish, if desired, with lemon twists, parsley and reserved shrimp. Recipe may be halved and cooked in individual shells or ramekins. Microwave 4 to 6 shells 2 to 3 minutes on roast (80% power) setting. Yield: 8 to 12 servings.
C.E.I. Microwave Seminar

SCALLOPS IN CHEDDAR WINE SAUCE

3 tablespoons butter or margarine
8-ounces fresh mushrooms, sliced
1 pound small scallops
½ cup dry white wine
2 tablespoons all-purpose flour
½ teaspoon salt
½ cup shredded Cheddar cheese
Chopped parsley

Melt 1 tablespoon butter or margarine in an 11x7x2-inch baking dish in microwave oven for 30 seconds. Add mushrooms and cook 4 to 5 minutes, uncovered, on high, stirring 2 to 3 times, until limp. Remove mushrooms and set aside. Reserving ½ the cooking liquid in same dish, stir in scallops and white wine. Cover and cook 2½ minutes, stirring 2 or 3 times. Drain cooking liquid into glass measuring cup; set scallops aside with mushrooms. In same dish, melt remaining butter 1 minute on high. Stir in flour and salt; cook, uncovered, 1 minute on high. Slowly stir in 1 cup of reserved liquid, adding wine if necessary to make 1 cup. Cook 3 minutes, uncovered, until thickened, stirring 2 or 3 times. Stir in cheese. Heat 1 minute on high or until cheese melts. Add mushrooms and scallops to sauce and spoon into individual ramekins. Garnish and serve, or cover and refrigerate. When ready to serve, heat uncovered 1 to 2 minutes, until heated through. Yield: 4 servings.
Sue Mahon

SALMON QUICHE

1 (9-inch) pastry shell
2 cups salmon chunks, cooked and boned, or 1 (16-ounce) can salmon, drained
½ cup ripe olives, sliced
2 tablespoons snipped parsley
1 cup shredded Cheddar cheese
3 eggs
¾ cup evaporated milk
¼ teaspoon salt
¼ teaspoon onion powder

Bake pastry shell and set aside to cool. Lightly mix salmon, olives and parsley; sprinkle over bottom of pastry shell. Top with shredded cheese. Combine eggs with milk, salt and onion powder. Pour over mixture in pastry shell. Cook in microwave oven on medium setting 18 to 20 minutes, or until knife inserted in center comes out clean. Yield: 6 servings.
Sue Mahon

HOT THREE BEAN SALAD

4 strips bacon, snipped into small pieces
½ cup sugar
1 tablespoon cornstarch
1 teaspoon salt
¼ teaspoon pepper
⅔ cup vinegar
1 (16-ounce) can cut green beans, drained
1 (16-ounce) can red kidney beans, drained
1 medium-sized onion, sliced thin

In a 2-quart casserole, microwave bacon pieces on high for 3 to 4 minutes, stirring after 2 minutes. Remove cooked bacon with a slotted spoon and drain on paper towels. Add sugar and cornstarch to bacon dripping; blend well. Stir in salt, pepper and vinegar. Microwave on high for 3 to 4 minutes or until thick. Add all drained beans and onion slices to sauce in casserole; stir well. Cover and microwave on high for 6 minutes, stirring after 3 minutes. Allow to stand 10 minutes. Sprinkle bacon over top before serving. *This tastes better if prepared ahead and reheated.* Yield: 8 to 10 servings.
Carolyn Sadler

VEGETABLES SUPREME

1 (16-ounce) bag frozen mixed vegetables
1 (5-ounce) can water chestnuts, sliced
1 (10¾-ounce) can cream of celery soup, undiluted
1 (6-ounce) can French fried onion rings

Place frozen vegetables in a 2½-quart casserole. Cover with plastic wrap and microwave on high for 8 minutes, turning dish ¼ turn after 4 minutes. Uncover and spread water chestnuts over vegetables and then soup over water chestnuts. Top with onion rings. Microwave on high uncovered, 4 minutes. Turn dish ¼ turn after 2 minutes. Yield: 6 to 8 servings.
Margaret Fallon

MUSHROOMS WITH HERBS

1½ pounds mushrooms, 1-inch in size
2 tablespoons butter or margarine
1 tablespoon instant minced onion
1 teaspoon dry basil
1 teaspoon oregano leaves
¼ teaspoon thyme
¼ teaspoon garlic salt
¼ teaspoon liquid hot pepper
1 tablespoon lime juice
2 tablespoons dry sherry

Twist out mushroom stems. Wash caps, pat dry. In a 12x8x2-inch baking dish, melt butter in microwave, 1 minute on high. To the butter, add onion, basil, oregano, thyme, garlic salt and liquid pepper. Mix well. Add mushrooms and coat well with mixture. Microwave uncovered, 5 to 6 minutes, stirring often. Serve in a chafing dish or over candle warmer. Yield: 7 dozen.
Ann O'Shea

CAULIFLOWER AU GRATIN

1 (10 to 12-ounce) package frozen cauliflower or broccoli
3 tablespoons water
1 cup herb-seasoned bread cubes
½ cup shredded Cheddar cheese

Place cauliflower or broccoli and water in a 1½-quart casserole. Cover and microwave on high for 8 minutes, stirring after 4 minutes. Drain liquid and reserve. Combine bread cubes, liquid and cheese. Sprinkle on vegetables. Cover and microwave on high for 2 minutes. Uncover and turn dish ¼ turn. Microwave on high 1 minute more. Yield: 3 to 4 servings.
Susan Miceli

GARDNER'S SPECIAL PLATTER

1½ pounds fresh broccoli
½ medium head cauliflower
2 medium zucchini
3 tablespoons butter or margarine
½ teaspoon garlic salt
¼ teaspoon thyme leaves
2 medium tomatoes, cut into wedges
¼ cup Parmesan cheese

Trim broccoli, cut into pieces about 2½-inches long and with stalks about ¼-inch thick. Arrange toward edge of 12-inch glass serving plate with flower ends toward center of dish. Cut cauliflower into similar-sized flowerettes. Place between broccoi stalks. Slice zucchini and mound in center of plate. Cover all with plastic wrap. Combine butter, garlic salt and thyme in glass dish. (Can stand several hours at room temperature.) Microwave 9 to 11 minutes at 100% power, or until vegetables are just about tender. Microwave butter mixture about 1 minute or until melted. Drain excess liquid from vegetables. Remove plastic wrap. Arrange tomato wedges over other vegetables. Drizzle vegetables with butter, sprinkle with Parmesan cheese. Microwave, uncovered 1½ to 2 minutes or until tomatoes are heated.
Debbie Simunek

ZUCCHINI CHEESE CUSTARD

6 cups shredded unpared zucchini (about 2 pounds)
1 teaspoon salt
4 eggs, well beaten
6-ounces Cheddar cheese, shredded
¼ cup all-purpose flour
¼ cup chopped fresh parsley
Dash white pepper

Spread zucchini on baking dish or tray; sprinkle evenly with salt and set aside one hour. Transfer zucchini to colander and rinse, pressing with the back of a spoon to release moisture. Transfer zucchini to an 8-inch square baking dish; cover with vented plastic wrap. Microwave on high 10 minutes, stirring after 5 minutes. Turn zucchini into colander and drain. Dry baking dish and coat with non-stick cooking spray. In medium bowl, combine zucchini, eggs, 4-ounces cheese and remaining ingredients. Pour mixture into baking dish and microwave on medium (50% power) stirring every 2 minutes, for 6 minutes or until mixture thickens. Sprinkle with remaining 2-ounces cheese and continue to microwave on medium about 1 minute or until cheese is melted. Yield: 4 servings.
A Friend

POTATOES PERFECT

1/4 pound bacon, diced
2 medium onions, sliced thin
4 medium potatoes, sliced thin
8-ounces Gruyère or Cheddar cheese, sliced thin
Salt and pepper to taste
Butter

In a 10x6x2-inch or 8-inch round glass baking dish, place layers of 1/2 the bacon, 1/2 the onions, 1/2 the potatoes and 1/2 the cheese. Season with salt and pepper and dot with butter. Repeat layers of bacon, onions, potatoes and cheese. Dot with butter. Cover dish with waxed paper and microwave on high setting for 18 to 22 minutes, giving dish a quarter-turn every 3 minutes. Yield: 4 to 6 servings.
C.E.I. Microwave Seminar

MICROWAVE PORCUPINE MEATBALLS

1 pound ground chuck
1/4 cup uncooked rice
1 small onion, chopped
1 teaspoon salt
1/4 teaspoon pepper
1 egg
1 (10 3/4-ounce) can tomato soup
1 1/4 cups water

Combine ground chuck, rice, onion, salt, pepper and egg. Form into about 24 balls, 1-inch in size. Arrange in shallow 1 1/2-quart glass casserole. Add soup and water. Cover. Microwave on high for 25 to 30 minutes, or until rice is tender. These meatballs simmer right in the sauce. (With quick rice, increase rice to 1/2 cup, reduce water to 3/4 cup and cooking time to 15 to 20 minutes). Yield: 4 to 5 servings.
Michele Leahy

POTATO-MUSHROOM AU GRATIN

5 cups thinly sliced potatoes
12-ounces thinly sliced mushrooms
1 medium-sized onion, finely chopped
1/4 cup parsley, finely chopped
3/4 cup heavy cream
1 cup shredded Cheddar cheese

Combine ingredients in order listed. Pour into a buttered, 2-quart casserole. Cover and microwave on high for 20 minutes. Stir and microwave on high an additional 10 minutes. Sprinkle with additional cheese to garnish. Cover and let stand 5 minutes before serving. Yield: 6 to 8 servings.
Helen Zorn

MICROWAVE CARAMEL APPLE SQUARES

Crust:

½ cup butter
1½ cups all-purpose flour
¼ cup sugar
1 egg yolk

Microwave butter on high for 45 seconds to melt. Blend into flour, sugar and egg yolk. Press into bottom of a 12x8x2-inch dish. Microwave on high for 5 to 6 minutes. Turn dish ½ turn after 2½ minutes. Add filling; top with Cinnamon Topping and microwave on high for 10 to 12 minutes. Yield: 24 bars.

Filling:

30 caramels
2 tablespoons water
6 medium-sized apples, peeled and sliced
1 tablespoon lemon juice

Unwrap caramels and combine with water. Microwave for 2 to 2½ minutes on high, stirring twice during cooking. Arrange apples on crust. Drizzle with lemon juice and caramel mixture.

Topping:

1 cup all-purpose flour
⅓ cup brown sugar, firmly packed
½ cup butter
Cinnamon-sugar

Combine flour and brown sugar. Cut in butter. Sprinkle over apples and caramel mixture. Sprinkle with cinnamon sugar.
Jean Croyle

FLAMED BANANAS

4 ripe bananas
4 tablespoons butter
Powdered sugar
¼ cup brandy, fruited brandy, or Kirsch

Peel bananas and slice lengthwise, then cut crosswide. Melt butter in a baking dish in microwave oven. Coat all sides of bananas with the butter and arrange in a circle like the spokes of a wheel, cut ends toward outside of dish, and flat side down. Cover loosely with waxed paper and microwave on high 2 minutes, or until tender (take care not to overcook). Sprinkle heavily with sugar. Warm brandy 15 seconds in a handled cup in the microwave. Pour around bananas and flame. Top with whipped cream or serve over ice cream. Yield: 4 servings.
C.E.I. Microwave Seminar

TOFFEE CAKE

1 (19-ounce) package Devil's Food cake mix with pudding
3 eggs
1/3 cup vegetable oil
3/4 cup water
1/2 cup dairy sour cream
1/3 cup brown sugar, firmly packed
1 teaspoon instant coffee powder
3 (1 1/8-ounce) chocolate-covered toffee candy bars, crushed (reserve 2 tablespoons for garnish)

Lightly grease 12-cup bundt pan; sprinkle with 1 tablespoon sugar to coat. In a large bowl, blend cake mix with remaining ingredients; beat until smooth, then fold in crushed candy. Pour batter into prepared pan and microwave on roast (80% power) setting for 5 minutes. Rotate pan then microwave 5 minutes more. Rotate pan again and microwave on high for 5 minutes, or until wooden pick inserted in cake comes out clean. Cool 10 minutes in pan, then invert cake onto plate and frost with glaze. Garnish with reserved candy. Yield: 12 to 16 servings.

Glaze:

1 cup powdered sugar
1 (1-ounce) square unsweetened chocolate, melted
1/4 teaspoon instant coffee powder
1/2 teaspoon vanilla extract
2 tablespoons water

Blend all ingredients until smooth and pour at once over hot cake.
C.E.I. Microwave Seminar

SURPRISE DOUBLE CHOCOLATE CAKE

2 cups chocolate cake mix (without pudding)
1/3 cup vegetable oil
3/4 cup water
1 egg
1 (6-ounce) package chocolate morsels

Mix chocolate cake mix, oil, water and egg until well blended. Fold in chocolate morsels. Pour into greased 8-inch round glass cake dish. Microwave on high power 6 to 7 minutes, or until moisture disappears and cake begins to pull away from sides of the dish. Let stand on counter to cool slightly, 5 to 10 minutes. Invert on platter and spread chocolate over top. *A nice surprise is to discover that this cake makes it's own frosting.*
Debbie Simunek

CHEESE-SHRIMP PUFFS

32 crackers
1/4 cup butter or margarine
1 cup shredded Cheddar cheese
1 egg, separated
1 (14 1/2-ounce) can small cooked shrimp

Arrange crackers on 2 napkin-lined plates or trays. With electric mixer, soften butter 10 seconds on high. Cream butter and cheese together. Add egg yolk and mix well. Beat egg white until soft peaks form; fold into cheese mixture. Drain shrimp well and divide among crackers. Top each with a spoonful of cheese mixture, allowing space for mixture to spread during heating. Microwave on high, 1 plate at a time, uncovered, 30 seconds or until hot. These may be assembled up to 2 hours ahead and left at room temperature until ready to cook. Yield: 32.
C.E.I. Microwave Seminar

CARAMEL APPLES

1 (14-ounce) package caramels
1 tablespoon hot water
4 or 5 medium apples
Wooden sticks
1 cup finely chopped nuts

Set power level on high. In 1 1/2-quart casserole dish, microwave caramels and water for 2 to 3 minutes, or until melted, stirring twice until smooth. Insert sticks into apples. Dip each apple into caramel, turning and tipping dish to coat apples. Sprinkle with chopped nuts and place on greased waxed paper. Yield: 6 apples.
Shirley Holler

MICROWAVE PEANUT BRITTLE

1 cup sugar
1/2 cup white corn syrup
1 cup salted cocktail nuts
1 teaspoon butter
1 teaspoon vanilla extract
1 teaspoon baking soda

Mix sugar and corn syrup; microwave on high 4 minutes. Add peanuts, stir, and cook 3 minutes longer. Stir in butter and vanilla; cook 1 minute. Stir in soda. Spread quickly on greased cookie sheet. Cool and break into pieces.
Kay Kelly

CRUNCHY CHOCOLATE SAUCE

¼ cup milk
1 (1-ounce) square unsweetened chocolate
¾ cup light brown sugar, packed
¼ cup crunchy peanut butter
¼ teaspoon vanilla extract

Measure milk in a 2 cup measuring cup. Drop in chocolate. Microwave on high for 1½ minutes. Stir until well-blended. Add sugar and stir to blend. Microwave on high for 30 seconds or until mixture boils. Add peanut butter and vanilla. Stir until well-blended. Serve warm or cold over ice cream or pound cake. Yield: 1 cup sauce.
Sue Polacek

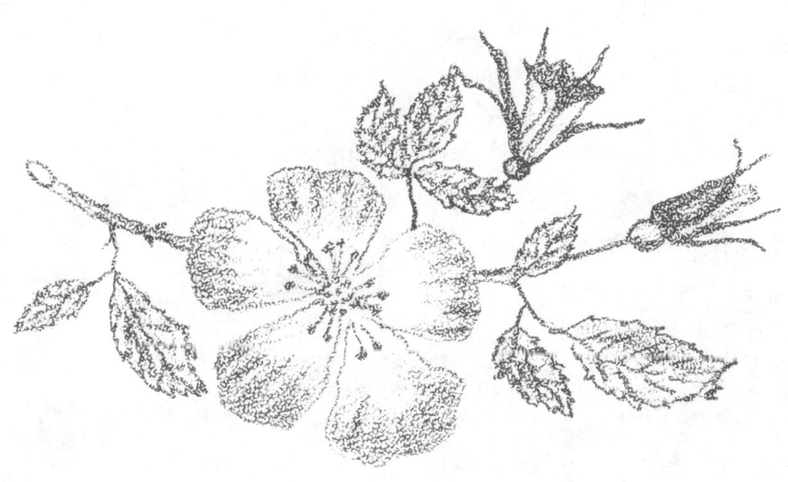

THE MAIN EVENT

Entrees

GLORIA'S BAKED LASAGNA

1 pound lasagna noodles
1 pound ricotta cheese
2 eggs, well beaten
1 teaspoon salt
1/4 teaspoon pepper
2 hard boiled eggs, grated
1 pound mozzarella cheese, coarsely shredded
1/2 cup grated Romano or Parmesan cheese

Meat Sauce:

1 pound ground chuck
1/2 pound mild bulk Italian sausage
3 (6-ounce) cans tomato paste
6 tomato paste cans of water
1 teaspoon salt
1/2 teaspoon pepper
1 teaspoon dried basil
2 teaspoons sugar
1/2 small onion, finely chopped
2 cloves garlic, cut in halves

Brown ground beef and sausage in small amount of oil, mashing with fork. Add onion and garlic. Sauté until lightly brown. Drain any excess fat. Stir in tomato paste, water, salt, pepper, basil and sugar; mix well. Cover pan and cook over low heat for about 1 hour, stirring occasionally. Remove garlic, if desired. Combine ricotta with beaten eggs, salt and pepper in small bowl. Boil lasagna noodles in 6 quarts of salted water to which a tablespoon of oil has been added. Cook for 15 minutes or until barely tender; drain. Slightly cover bottom of 9x13-inch pan with meat sauce, then alternately layer as follows; lasagna, ricotta, Romano cheese, lasagna, grated eggs, mozzarella cheese, meat sauce. Continue and end with lasagna, top with layer of mozzarella cheese. Cover and bake in moderate oven, 350 degrees, for about 15 to 25 minutes or until hot and bubbly.
Gloria DeLambo

FETTUCCINE

1 (10-ounce) package fettuccine noodles
6 tablespoons butter
1 cup dairy sour cream
1 cup heavy whipping cream
1 1/3 cups grated Parmesan cheese
2 tablespoons finely snipped chives
Dash of ground nutmeg
Dash of salt and pepper

Cook noodles as directed on package; drain and set aside. Melt butter in large saucepan; add noodles and stir. Add sour cream and stir over low heat for 1 minute. Stir in cream and continue cooking, slowly, for 5 minutes, stirring occasionally. Add cheese, nutmeg, salt, pepper and 1 tablespoon chives. Continue stirring until cheese is melted. Remove from heat and pour into warm tureen. Sprinkle with remaining chives and serve immediately. Yield: 4 servings.
Lynne Della Donna

NANCY'S LASAGNA

½ pound bulk Italian sausage
½ pound ground beef
1 tablespoon dried basil
1½ teaspoons salt
1 (16-ounce) can tomatoes
1 (12-ounce) can tomato paste
1 (10-ounce) box lasagna noodles
2 eggs
3 cups cottage or fresh Ricotta cheese
½ cup grated Parmesan or Romano cheese
2 tablespoons parsley flakes
1 teaspoon salt
½ teaspoon pepper
1 pound mozzarella cheese, thinly sliced

Brown meats slowly in medium-size skillet. Spoon off excess fat. Add next 4 ingredients. Cover and simmer for 15 minutes, stirring once. Cook noodles according to package directions and set aside. In a medium-size bowl, beat eggs and add remaining ingredients, except mozzarella. Blend thoroughly but gently. Layer ½ the noodles in a greased 13x9x2-inch baking pan; spread ½ of the cottage cheese filling over noodles; next, layer ½ of the mozzarella cheese followed by ½ of the meat sauce. Repeat layers in above order. Bake in a 375 degree oven for 30 minutes. (May be assembled early and refrigerated. Then bake for 50 minutes.) Let stand 10 minutes before serving. Yield: 8 to 10 servings.
Nancy Lee Corcoran

PASTA SALAD

½ pound vermicelli or thin spaghetti
1 cup bottled Italian salad dressing, divided
6 to 8 split chicken breasts, cooked, boned and cubed
1 cup mayonnaise
1 (8-ounce) can artichoke hearts, drained and quartered
Sliced scallions to taste
2 cups fresh mushrooms, sliced

Cook pasta according to package directions and drain. Cool slightly and add ⅓ cup salad dressing. Toss until pasta is well coated. Cover and refrigerate overnight. Add chicken, mayonnaise, artichokes, scallions and mushrooms. Add remaining salad dressing and mix until well blended. Garnish with parsley, paprika, sliced avocado or whatever adds a touch of color. Yield: 6 to 8 servings.
Shelly Galvin

MEATBALL LASAGNA

Meatballs:

½ pound ground chuck
¼ pound ground veal
2 tablespoons chopped onion
1 clove garlic, crushed
2 tablespoons chopped parsley
1 teaspoon dried oregano
¾ teaspoon salt
Dash of pepper
2 tablespoons grated Parmesan cheese
1 egg

Combine all ingredients in a medium bowl, mixing well. Shape into about 30 (¾-inch) meatballs.

Tomato Sauce:

¼ cup olive oil
¼ cup chopped onion
1 clove garlic
1 (28-ounce) can whole tomatoes, undrained
2 (6-ounce) cans tomato paste
2 teaspoons dried oregano
1 teaspoon dried basil
1 tablespoon sugar
2 teaspoons salt
1 teaspoon galic powder
¼ teaspoon pepper

In hot oil in a heavy skillet, brown meatballs and remove with slotted spoon. Add onions and garlic to skillet and sauté 5 minutes. Add remaining ingredients along with ½ cup water and meatballs. Stir gently to combine. Bring to a boil, reduce heat, and simmer, uncovered, 1 to 1½ hours, stirring occasionally.

Lasagna:

8-ounces lasagna noodles
1 pound mozzarella cheese, shredded
1 pound ricotta cheese
1 cup grated Parmesan cheese

Preheat oven to 350 degrees. Cook lasagna noodles according to package directions; rinse and drain. In a greased 13x9x2-inch baking dish, layer ½ the noodles, ½ the mozzarella, ½ the ricotta, ½ the tomato sauce and meatballs, and ½ the Parmesan. Repeat layers. Bake 30 to 35 minutes. Yield: 6 servings.
Kathy Scali

SPAGHETTI WITH LOBSTER SAUCE

1 tablespoon olive oil
1 large clove garlic, quartered
1 (1 pound 13-ounce) can tomato sauce
1 (15-ounce) can tomato sauce
2 to 4 lobster tails
1 pound thin spaghetti

In a heavy saucepan, heat olive oil and sauté garlic pieces. Add tomato sauce and cook over low heat. Snip "fins" from underside of lobster tails and slit down the middle. This makes it easier to remove after cooking. Add tails to sauce and cook, covered, over low heat, for 1 hour. Stir occasionally. Uncover and cook another 30 minutes to thicken. Cook spaghetti according to package directions. Remove lobster tails from sauce and lobster from shells. Serve whole with spaghetti or cut into small pieces and mix with sauce before mixing with spaghetti. Yield: 4 to 6 servings.
Phyllis Mazzella

LINGUINE CARBONARA

6 slices bacon, diced
2 cloves garlic, pressed
¼ cup onion, chopped
3 eggs
¾ cup grated Parmesan cheese
¼ teaspoon red pepper flakes
⅛ teaspoon freshly ground pepper
1 pound linguine noodles, cooked and drained

In a medium skillet, combine bacon, garlic and onion. Cook over low heat for 12 minutes. In a small bowl, beat eggs, add cheese, pepper flakes and pepper. In a large bowl toss cooked pasta with bacon mixture. Quickly add egg mixture and toss again. (Heat from noodles cooks eggs). Serve immediately with additional cheese. Yield: 4 servings.
Lynne Della Donna

LINGUINE WITH WHITE CLAM SAUCE

¼ cup olive oil
2 garlic cloves, chopped
3 (6½-ounce) cans chopped clams
2 tablespoons fresh parsley
1 tablespoon butter
1 (16-ounce) box linguine, cooked and drained
Parmesan cheese

Place olive oil in a saucepan. Heat gently; add garlic and sauté until golden brown. Add chopped clams, undrained. Bring to a boil. Add parsley and continue to boil gently for 5 minutes. Add butter to sauce just before serving, if desired. Serve over linguine. Sprinkle with Parmesan cheese. *Great served with a chilled bottle of white wine and garlic bread.* Yield: 4 servings.
Lynne Della Donna

CRESCENTOLI

1 egg yolk
1 egg white
½ cup cottage or ricotta cheese
⅛ teaspoon salt
¼ teaspoon garlic salt
¼ teaspoon onion salt
2 teaspoons parsley
Dash of pepper
2 tablespoons grated Parmesan cheese
½ cup diced mozzarella cheese
½ cup diced Swiss cheese
2 (8-count) tubes crescent dinner rolls
1 (15-ounce) can pizza sauce

Beat egg yolk in medium-size bowl; stir in cottage or ricotta cheese. Blend in seasonings and Parmesan. Add mozzarella and Swiss cheeses and mix well. Open 1 tube crescent rolls and unroll dough; separate into 4 squares. Press perforations with fingertips to seal; cut each square into 8 rectangles. Spoon 1½ teaspoons cheese mixture on one end of each rectangle. Fold dough over and seal three open edges with a fork. Repeat until both cans of rolls and all cheese is used. Lay rolls on ungreased 15x10x1-inch baking sheet about ½-inch apart. Brush each with beaten egg white. Bake at 375 degrees for 10 to 13 minutes or until golden brown. While Crescentoli is baking, heat pizza sauce in small saucepan over low heat. Remove Crescentoli from oven and place on 4 individual serving plates. Spoon pizza sauce over and serve immediately. These can be made up to 1 hour before baking, but keep covered in refrigerator. *My family loves them as a main dish with a good tossed salad, or as a side dish with veal cutlets.*
Mary Sims

BROCCOLI, ZUCCHINI AND NOODLES

2 cups fresh broccoli, chopped
2 cups fresh zucchini, sliced or chopped
½ cup onion, chopped
1 clove garlic, minced
2 tablespoons butter or margarine
3 tablespoons snipped parsley
½ teaspoon salt
½ teaspoon dried oregano
¾ cup milk
1½ cups cream style cottage cheese (or Ricotta)
2 tablespoons all-purpose flour
8-ounces spinach noodles, cooked, drained and buttered (regular noodles can be used)

Cook vegetables in salt water until tender-crisp. In a sauce pan, cook onions and garlic in butter or margarine until tender, but not brown. Blend in flour, parsley, salt and oregano; add milk at once. Cook and stir until thickened and bubbly. Add cheese, cook and stir until cheese is nearly melted. Stir in vegetables. Heat through and serve over hot noodles.
Ginny Keltner
Betz Spacek

SPINACH-STUFFED SHELLS

1 (12-ounce) package jumbo macaroni shells
2 (9-ounce) packages frozen creamed spinach in cooking pouches
1 (15-ounce) container ricotta cheese
1 (8-ounce) package shredded mozzarella cheese
¼ teaspoon pepper
1 (32-ounce) jar spaghetti sauce

Cook and drain shells according to package directions. Cook spinach according to package directions and turn into a large bowl. Add ricotta, mozzarella and pepper; stir to mix. Stuff each macaroni shell with spinach mixture; arrange in casserole dish. Pour desired amount of spaghetti sauce over shells. May be frozen at this point if desired. Thaw 1 hour then bake as usual. Bake 50 minutes at 350 degrees. Yield: 6 to 8 servings.
Karen West

JUMBO STUFFED SHELLS

1 (12 or 16-ounce) package jumbo shell macaroni (approximately 40 shells)
2 pounds ricotta cheese
1 (8-ounce) package mozzarella cheese, diced
2 eggs, slightly beaten
1 teaspoon parsley
¼ cup grated Parmesan cheese
Salt and pepper to taste
Marinara sauce

Cook shells in boiling water for 12 to 15 minutes; drain. Combine remaining ingredients in large bowl, except Parmesan and Marinara sauce, and use mixture to fill cooled shells. Spread a thin layer of marinara sauce in bottom of 15x10x2-inch baking pan. Layer stuffed shells over sauce. Top with more sauce and ¼ cup Parmesan cheese. Cover with aluminum foil and bake at 350 degrees for 25 to 30 minutes. Remove foil and continue baking for 10 minutes more. Yield: 10 to 12 servings.
Elaine Della Donna

ZUCCHINI FETTUCCINE

Sauce:

8-ounces mushrooms
1¼ pounds zucchini, cut into julienne strips
¾ cup butter
1 cup heavy cream

Melt ¼ cup butter in heavy skillet over medium heat. Add mushrooms and sauté several minutes. Add zucchini; sauté until just tender. Add cream and remaining butter; heat through, stirring occasionally.

Fettuccine:

1 pound fettuccine, cooked according to package directions
¾ cup grated Parmesan cheese
½ cup chopped parsley
Salt and pepper to taste
Parmesan cheese

Place cooked and drained noodles in warm bowl. Add Parmesan cheese and parsley; toss lightly. Add sauce and salt and pepper to taste; toss again. Garnish with additional grated Parmesan cheese. 1 (12-ounce) can mushrooms may be used if you wish to omit the zucchini from the sauce. Yield: 4 to 6 servings.
Eileen Barlock

SCALLOPS VONETO

3 tablespoons butter
½ clove garlic, minced
Dash of black pepper
1 pound bay scallops
3 tablespoons grated Romano cheese
Dash of salt
¼ cup heavy whipping cream
½ pound spinach fettuccine, preferably homemade
1 tablespoon olive oil

Combine first 3 ingredients in a saucepan. Cook over medium heat until butter is melted. Add scallops. Sauté for 4 minutes. Add Romano, salt and cream. Cook, stirring constantly, until sauce is heated through. Cook fettuccine in boiling, salted water for 3 to 4 minutes or until tender, if homemade. If packaged fettuccine is used, follow directions on the package. Drain. Mix with olive oil until lightly coated to prevent sticking. Mix with scallop mixture before serving. Yield: 2 servings.
Joe Santosuosso
Johnny's Tavern and Restaurant

LASAGNA ROLL-UPS

8 lasagna noodles
1 pound sweet Italian sausage
½ cup chopped onion
1 clove garlic, crushed
2 (6-ounce) cans tomato paste
1⅔ cups water
1 teaspoon oregano leaves
½ teaspoon basil leaves
1 (10-ounce) package frozen chopped spinach, cooked and drained
1 pint ricotta cheese
1 cup grated Parmesan cheese
1½ cups shredded mozzarella cheese
1 egg, slightly beaten
½ teaspoon salt
¼ teaspoon pepper

Cook and drain lasagna noodles according to package directions. Remove casings from sausage; brown sausage with onion and garlic; pour off fat. Add tomato paste, water, oregano and basil. Cover and boil gently 20 minutes. Combine spinach, ricotta, Parmesan and 1 cup mozzarella with egg, salt and pepper. Spread about ½ cup mixture on each noodle. Roll up and place seam-side down in 12x7x2-inch baking dish. Pour sauce over rolls. Top with remaining mozzarella cheese. Bake at 350 degrees 30 to 40 minutes, or until heated through. Roll-ups may be prepared in advance, covered and refrigerated overnight. To bake, cover and place in preheated 350-degree oven 30 minutes. Remove cover and bake 30 minutes longer. Yield: 6 to 8 servings.

For a crowd, double the amount of noodles and sausage, using 1 pound mild sausage and 1 pound hot sausage, 1 cup onion, 4 cloves garlic, 2 (12-ounce) cans tomato paste, 3⅓ cups water, 2 teaspoons oregano and 1 teaspoon basil. Cut noodles in ½ to get more rolls which are not as thick. The spinach and cheese mixture will be made in the same proportions as the original recipe. This makes 2 (13x9x2-inch) baking dishes, or 30 rolls. Don't place rolls too close together.
Lil Kobs

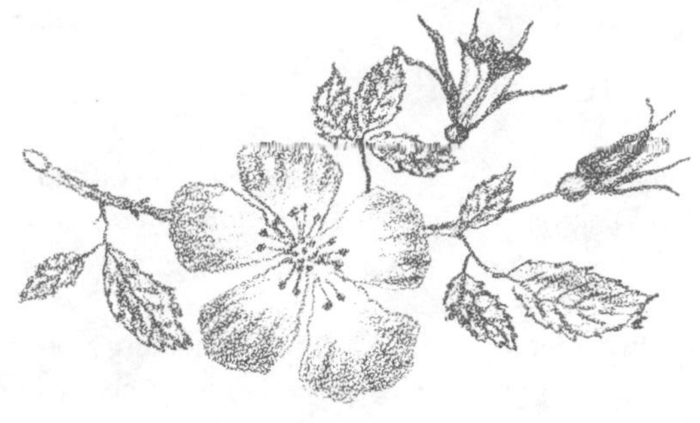

PEPPERONI FETTUCCINE

4 eggs
1/4 cup heavy cream
1/4 cup butter, melted
7-ounces pepperoni, sliced thin
1 pound fettuccine, cooked
1 cup grated Parmesan cheese
1/4 cup chopped parsley
Pepper to taste

Have eggs and cream at room temperature; combine in a bowl and beat until blended. Drain cooked fettuccini and turn into a baking dish. Toss with melted butter and pepperoni. Immediately pour egg mixture over hot pasta and toss. (Heat from pasta cooks eggs.) Sprinkle with fresh Parmesan cheese and parsley, add pepper to taste and toss to blend. Yield: 4 servings.
Eileen Barlock

PASTA SALAD PARMESAN

1/4 cup vegetable or olive oil
2 cups fresh broccoli florets
1/4 cup chopped green onions, with tops
1 clove garlic, minced
1/2 teaspoon fresh basil
1/2 teaspoon salt
1 (8-ounce) package pasta, cooked and drained
1/2 cup grated Parmesan cheese
1 cup cherry tomatoes, halved

Heat olive oil in large skillet over medium-high heat; add broccoli, onions, garlic, basil and salt. Sauté until broccoli is tender-crisp (about 4 minutes). Remove from heat and toss with pasta, cheese and tomatoes. Cover and chill thoroughly before serving. Yield: 4 servings.
Jean Croyle

M-M-GOOD BAKED RICE

1/3 cup butter or margarine
1(3 1/2-ounce) can mushroom stems and pieces
1 cup rice, uncooked
1 (10-ounce) can onion soup
1 (10-ounce) can beef consommé

Sauté mushrooms in butter in small skillet. Stir remaining ingredients together and add mushrooms. Pour into a greased 1 1/2-quart casserole and let stand for 10 minutes. Bake at 350 degrees for 1 hour. Yield: 4 to 6 servings.
Sister M. Claudia C.S.F.N.

SHRIMP AND RICE

1½ pound fresh shrimp
4 or 6 fresh medium size tomatoes or 1 (16-ounce) can tomatoes
3 tablespoons olive oil
4 tablespoons butter or margarine
1 tablespoon finely minced garlic
Salt and pepper to taste
1 tablespoon finely chopped parsley
1 teaspoon basil, optional
1 cup converted rice, prepared according to package directions

Shell and devein shrimp. Set aside. Peel and core fresh tomatoes or core canned tomatoes. Cut lengthwise and remove seeds. Cut into ½-inch cubes. Heat olive oil and 2 tablespoons butter in a large heavy skillet. Add garlic, salt and pepper to taste, and tomatoes. Cook over medium heat until tender, about 5 minutes. Add shrimp and parsley. Cook and stir an additional 5 minutes or until shrimp is pink. Serve over rice or vermicelli. Yield: 4 servings.
Jean Croyle

CRACKER BOTTOM SEAFOOD CASSEROLE

Saltine crackers
2 (15½-ounce) cans salmon
16 slices American cheese
6 eggs
1 (10¾-ounce) can cream of mushroom soup
1 soup can milk

Grease a 13x9x2-inch baking dish or pan and line bottom with crackers. Flake 1 can salmon over crackers. Lay 8 slices cheese over salmon. Flake remaining can salmon over cheese, then layer remaining cheese on top. Beat eggs well and blend with soup and milk; pour mixture over salmon and cheese. Cover with aluminum foil and refrigerate overnight. Bake at 350 degrees for 1 hour before serving. Remove from oven and let set 5 or 10 minutes before cutting into squares. Tuna may be substituted for salmon, if desired. Yield: 8 to 10 servings.
Gail Lynn

HINCKLEY PIKE

1 fresh pike, scaled and cleaned
1 large onion, chopped
1 tablespoon butter
½-ounce slivered almonds
Salt to taste
Pepper to taste

Place pike in foil. Add onion, butter, almonds and seasoning. Fold over edges and seal. Cook over an open fire until outer foil burns and fish steams. This can also be baked at 400 degrees for 15 minutes or until the fish flakes. Yield: 1 serving.
Gary Breckenridge

ORANGE ROUGHY WITH SHRIMP SAUCE

4 orange roughy fillets
3 tablespoons butter or margarine, melted
3 tablespoons fresh lemon juice
Salt and pepper to taste
1 pound baby shrimp
4 (1-ounce) slices Monterey Jack cheese

Arrange fillets in a greased 13x9x2-inch baking dish. Combine butter or margarine and lemon juice and spoon over fish. Season with salt and pepper. Sprinkle shrimp over fish. Place 1 slice cheese over each fillet. Bake at 325 degrees for about 8 minutes or until fish flakes easily and cheese is melted. Make sauce while fish is baking.

White Sauce:

½ cup heavy cream
1 tablespoon lemon juice
Dash of tumeric
Dash of white pepper
3 tablespoons butter or margarine
½ teaspoon Worcestershire sauce
¼ cup fish stock or chicken broth
3 tablespoons cornstarch
¼ cup cold water

Combine cream, lemon juice, tumeric, pepper, butter, Worcestershire sauce, broth or stock in saucepan and bring to a boil, stirring. Blend cornstarch with water until smooth. Stir into sauce, cooking and stirring until thickened. Remove from heat and immediately pour over hot fish fillets and shrimp. Return to oven for 5 minutes. Garnish with chopped parsley and a wedge of lemon or a fresh sprig of dill before serving. Yield: 4 servings.
Chef Terry Lawrence Clarke

FRIED SOLE IN BEER BATTER

2 pounds sole fillets, cut in servings size pieces
1½ teaspoons lemon juice
1½ teaspoon salt, sprinkle on fillets
¾ cup beer
2½ cups all-purpose flour
1½ teaspoons salt
1½ teaspoons paprika

Sprinkle fillets with lemon juice and salt; set aside. Pour beer into a bowl. Sift ½ cup of flour, salt and paprika and add to beer in bowl, mixing until batter is light and foamy. In remaining flour, dredge fillets and dip into beer batter. Fry fillets in oil in a heavy skillet or deep fryer, heated to 375 degrees, until golden brown. Yield: 4 to 6 servings.
Thomas More Program

SALMON ONION LOAF

1 (15½-ounce) can salmon
¼ cup salmon liquid
2 eggs, beaten
2 teaspoons lemon juice
½ teaspoon salt, optional
Dash of pepper
4 to 5 tablespoons milk
1 (2.8-ounce) can French fried onion rings

Sauce:

1 cup dairy sour cream
2 tablespoons white horseradish
1 teaspoon prepared mustard

Drain salmon, reserving ¼ cup of the liquid. Remove skin and bones. Break salmon into chunks and add liquid, eggs, lemon juice, salt, pepper, milk and onion rings. Lightly butter a 1½-quart baking dish. Place mixture in dish and shape into loaf. Bake at 400 degrees for 20 minutes or until firm. Mix ingredients for sauce and serve with salmon loaf. Yield: 4 to 6 servings.
Gloria Rosenbush

"SAMMY" CYLINDERS

¼ cup rice
¾ cup water
1 (15½-ounce) can pink salmon, drained
1 egg
1 tablespoon chopped parsley
1 tablespoon minced onion (optional)
Salt and pepper to taste
3 tablespoons vegetable shortening
1 cup fine dry breadcrumbs

Add rice to water in small saucepan; bring to a boil. Cover and simmer 15 minutes, until rice is cooked and water absorbed. Meanwhile, prepare salmon by removing any skin and bones. Flake salmon and add egg, parsley, salt, pepper and onion. Mix well with a wooden spoon. Stir in cooked, drained rice. Heat shortening in a heavy skillet. Place a heaping tablespoonful of crumbs in palm of one hand. Scoop a heaping spoonful of salmon mixture and place over crumbs. With both hands roll into a cylindrical shape, coating all sides with crumbs. Repeat with remaining salmon mixture. Place cylinders in hot shortening and brown on both sides, about 10 minutes. Yield: 4 servings.
Anna Jesenko

SWORDFISH IN WINE AND CREAM SAUCE

2 pounds swordfish steaks
1/3 cup butter or margarine
1 1/2 tablespoons all-purpose flour
1/4 teaspoon salt
Few drops of hot sauce
3/4 cup white wine
3/4 cup whipping cream
1 tablespoon lemon juice
Sugar to taste

In a skillet melt 1/4 cup butter. Add swordfish and brown on both sides. Lower heat and cook, covered, for 15 minutes or until fish flakes easily. In a saucepan, melt remaining butter, stir in flour, salt and hot sauce; add wine and cream. Cook over low heat for 5 minutes until thickened, stirring occasionally. Remove from heat and stir in lemon juice and sugar to taste. Serve over swordfish steaks.
Thomas More Program

GRILLED SWORDFISH STEAKS

Swordfish steaks, 1-inch thick
1 cup vegetable oil
1 tablespoon oregano, crushed
1 tablespoon bay leaf, crushed
Juice of 1 lemon
4 cloves garlic, chopped
2 tablespoons basil, crumbled
1 teaspoon celery salt
Pepper to taste
Melted butter

In a bowl, combine oil, spices, lemon juice and garlic. Brush both sides of swordfish steaks with marinade mixture and refrigerate for 2 to 3 hours in marinade, turning once or twice during this time. Remove from refrigerator and grill steaks over hot charcoal for 5 to 7 minutes on each side, basting with remaining marinade. When browned, serve with melted butter.
Thomas More Program

ORANGE ROUGHY MACADAMIA

1 pound orange roughy fillets
1/4 cup melted butter or margarine
1 tablespoon lemon juice
1/2 teaspoon garlic powder
1/4 teaspoon salt
Pepper to taste
1/4 teaspoon paprika
1/2 cup macadamia nuts, slivered or chopped

Place roughy fillets in broiler pan. Combine melted butter or margarine and lemon juice. Brush fillets with butter mixture. Season with garlic powder, salt, pepper and paprika. Broil 15 minutes. Sprinkle with nuts and broil 5 minutes longer. Yield: 4 servings.
Claire Kopit

CURRIED PERCH BAKE

1 (16-ounce) package frozen perch fillets, thawed slightly
Salt and pepper
½ teaspoon curry powder
1 tablespoon lemon juice
¼ teaspoon Worcestershire sauce
3 thin slices onion
2 tomatoes, cut into sixths
1 (4-ounce) can sliced mushrooms, drained
3 tablespoons chopped green pepper
2 tablespoons butter or margarine

Cut slightly thawed fillets into 3 equal portions. Place each portion on a square of heavy aluminum foil. Sprinkle with salt and pepper, curry, lemon juice and Worcestershire sauce. Divide vegetables equally among fish portions. Place a little butter or margarine on each one. Bring up ends of foil and double-fold ends tightly (to make a drugstore wrap). Be sure package is airtight. Place on baking sheet. Bake at 450 degrees for 30 minutes. Remove from oven. Turn back foil on top and bake for 10 minutes more. Yield: 3 to 4 servings.
Lissa Keller

HALIBUT STEAKS WITH MUSHROOM STUFFING

¼ pound fresh mushrooms
1 (4-ounce) can mushroom pieces, drained
6 tablespoons butter or margarine, divided
⅓ cup minced onion
½ cup seasoned dry breadcrumbs
¾ teaspoon salt
2 tablespoons lemon juice
1 egg, slightly beaten
2 halibut steaks, 1¼ pounds each

Chop fresh mushrooms or drain canned mushrooms and set aside. In a medium saucepan, melt 4 tablespoons butter. Add mushrooms and onions and sauté 5 minutes. Stir in breadcrumbs, salt, lemon juice and egg. Place 1 steak on an 12x8x2-inch greased baking sheet. Spread stuffing over fish. Top with second steak. Dot with remaining butter. Bake in a 400 degree preheated oven for 40 minutes. Garnish with lemon and parsley. Yield: 6 servings.
Char McQuilkin

SOLE STUFFED WITH CRABMEAT DRESSING

4½ cups breadcrumbs
Milk
6 tablespoons chopped onions
½ cup chopped mushrooms
3 tablespoons butter or margarine
1½ tablespoons chopped green onions
¼ cup white wine
1 tablespoon chopped parsley
2 eggs, slightly beaten
½ teaspoon salt
¼ teaspoon pepper
¼ teaspoon ground nutmeg
1 (6½-ounce) bag tiny frozen shrimp
1 (6½-ounce) package frozen crabmeat, drained
6 fillets of sole
Melted butter

Place breadcrumbs in large bowl and add just enough milk to make a loose dressing. Set aside. Melt butter in large skillet; sauté onions and mushrooms. Add these to breadcrumbs in bowl. Return skillet to heat and cook green onions in white wine until all moisture has evaporated; add to breadcrumb mixture. Stir in parsley, eggs, salt, pepper and nutmeg and blend well. Fold in shrimp and crabmeat. Wash sole fillets and salt and pepper well on both sides. Place 3 fillets skin side down in a greased glass baking dish. Spoon breadcrumb stuffing over fillets; cover with remaining 3 fillets, skin side up. Fasten stuffed fillets together, using about 3 toothpicks per stuffed fillet. Bake in preheated 350 degree oven for 30 to 45 minutes or until fish flakes easily with a fork. Baste frequently while baking with melted butter. Yield: 3 servings.
Hollis Hura, Registered Dietitian, Parmadale

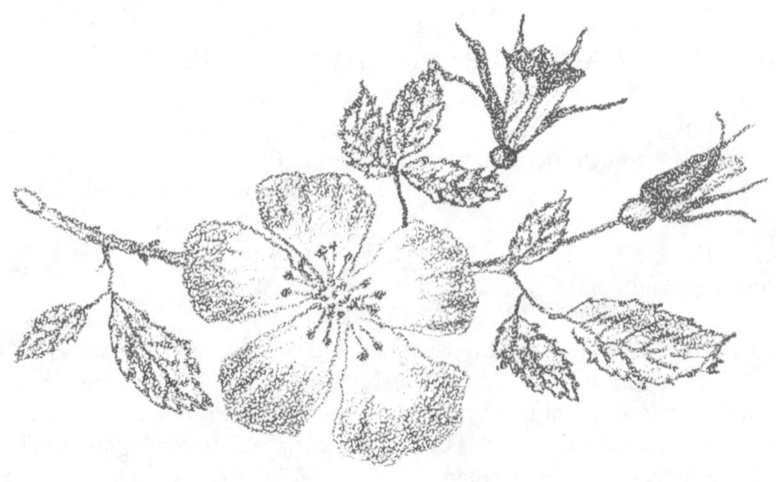

BAKED TUNA LOAVES WITH CAPER SAUCE

6 tablespoons butter or margarine
¾ cup chopped onion
¾ cup chopped celery
3 tablespoons chopped parsley
1 cup dried breadcrumbs, moistened with ¼ cup water
⅔ cup evaporated milk
2 hard-cooked eggs, chopped
3 tablespoons lemon juice
2 eggs, beaten
1 teaspoon salt
¼ teaspoon pepper
3 (7-ounce) cans tuna, drained and flaked

In 4 tablespoons butter or margarine, sauté onions, celery and parsley about 5 minutes, until onions are golden brown. Turn mixture into a large bowl; add breadcrumbs, chopped eggs, milk, lemon juice, beaten eggs, tuna and seasonings; mix thoroughly. On a lightly greased baking sheet shape tuna mixture into 8 loaves, using about ¾ cup for each. Melt remaining butter and brush over loaves. Bake at 350 degrees about 25 minutes, or until lightly browned. Serve with Caper Sauce. Yield: 8 servings.

Caper Sauce:

3 tablespoons butter or margarine
3 tablespoons all-purpose flour
¾ teaspoon salt
¼ teaspoon paprika
Dash hot pepper sauce
2 cups milk
1 tablespoon bottled capers, drained

Melt butter in medium saucepan over low heat. Remove from heat and add flour, salt and paprika, stirring until smooth. Return to heat and add pepper sauce, then milk, a little at a time, stirring constantly. Bring to a boil over medium heat, continuing to stir. Reduce heat, add capers and simmer 1 minute. Yield: 2 cups.
Jean Croyle

CHIPS TOPPED FISH FILLETS

Dip in Ranch dressing & sprinkle with potatoe chips

2 pounds fish fillets (haddock, scrod or perch)
1 cup crushed potato chips
½ cup shredded Cheddar cheese
1 to 1½ cups creamy Italian salad dressing

Wash fish fillets and pat dry. Combine potato chips and cheese in a small bowl. Pour salad dressing into a shallow dish and dredge fish in dressing, 1 piece at a time. Place, skin side down, into a buttered 13x9x2-inch glass baking dish. Sprinkle with chip/cheese mixture. Bake at 500 degrees for 12 minutes or until fish flakes easily with a fork. Yield: 6 servings.
Lissa Keller

SHRIMP CREOLE

1/4 cup butter or margarine
1 1/2 cups chopped onion
1 cup finely chopped celery
2 medium-sized green pepper, finely chopped
2 cloves garlic, minced
1 (15-ounce) can tomato sauce
1 cup water
2 teaspoons parsley, snipped
1 teaspoon salt
1/8 teaspoon red pepper
2 bay leaves, crushed
1 (14 to 16-ounce) package frozen shrimp (or fresh if available)
3 cups cooked rice

Melt butter in large skillet and sauté onion, celery, green pepper and garlic until tender but not browned. Remove from heat and stir in tomato sauce, water and seasonings. Return to heat. Simmer, uncovered, for 10 minutes, adding more water if needed. Stir in shrimp and heat to boiling. Cover and cook over medium heat for 10 to 12 minutes or until shrimp is tender and pink. Serve hot over rice. Yield: 6 servings.
Rita Grennan

POOR MAN'S CRABMEAT CASSEROLE

1 pound fresh fish fillets, (if using frozen, thaw and drain)

Crab Mix:

2/3 cup butter, melted
1 cup crushed herb seasoned stuffing mix
1 (6-ounce) package frozen crabmeat, thawed or "sealegs" shredded
1 (4-ounce) can mushrooms
1 egg
2 tablespoons chopped parsley
1/4 teaspoon salt
2 tablespoons lemon juice
1/4 teaspoon hot pepper

Topping:

1/2 cup crushed herb stuffing
2 tablespoons melted butter

Place fish fillets in bottom of an 8-inch square ungreased baking dish. Combine crab mix ingredients and spread over fish fillets. In same bowl combine topping ingredients. Sprinkle over crab mix. Do not cover. Bake at 375 degrees for 30 to 35 minutes, or until fish flakes with a fork. Yield: 4 servings.
Jean Croyle
Rita Grennan

BAKED CLAMS

1 cup butter or margarine
5 stalks celery, diced
2 large onions, diced
3 (6½-ounce) cans minced clams
1 (10½-ounce) can red clam sauce
1 small thin-sliced loaf white bread, diced (about 14 slices)
1 teaspoon oregano
½ teaspoon garlic powder
½ teaspoon onion powder
1 teaspoon basil
Salt and pepper to taste
½ cup grated Parmesan cheese
Seasoned breadcrumbs

Melt butter or margarine in saucepan; sauté celery and onions until tender. Drain 2 cans clams and add to saucepan; add remaining can of clams, with liquid, and red clam sauce to saucepan. Stir to blend. Stir in diced bread, seasonings and cheese; blend well with wire whisk. Fill clam shells with mixture; garnish with breadcrumbs and more Parmesan. Bake at 350 degrees for 20 minutes. Yield: 35 to 40 clams.
Chicky Weiner

CRABMEAT COQUILLE

2 tablespoons butter
Salt to taste
Pepper to taste
1 tablespoon all-purpose flour
½ pound (8-ounces) American processed cheese food
2 tablespoons sherry
1 cup milk
2 (6-ounce) packages frozen crabmeat, thawed and drained

Melt butter in a saucepan. Add flour, salt and pepper slowly, stirring gently over low heat. Gradually add milk, stirring constantly, until white sauce is thick and smooth. Add sherry and cheese to sauce mixture, stirring until cheese is melted. Fold in crabmeat. Serve over pastry shells, toast points or rice. *Great as a luncheon dish!* Yield: 3 to 4 servings.
Nancy Kumin

CONNIE'S CURRY

1 (10¾-ounce) can shrimp soup
Milk
1 pound cooked shrimp, peeled and deveined
2 tablespoons curry powder
4 servings of rice, prepared according to package directions

In large sauce pan, warm soup as directed on can, adding ½ can of milk. Add shrimp to soup; stir, add curry powder; stir. Pour over cooked rice and serve. Takes about 20 minutes. Yield: 4 servings.
Connie Allerton

CHICKEN, SHRIMP AND SCALLOP PROVENCAL

½ cup vegetable oil
½ pound shelled and deveined shrimp
¼ pound bay scallops
6 chicken breast halves, skinned and boned
2 large onions, sliced
2 green peppers, sliced into rings
2 red peppers, sliced into rings
1 cup chicken broth
⅔ cup canned plum tomatoes, drained and seeded
3 tablespoons tomato paste
6 cloves garlic, minced finely
1¼ teaspoons salt
¼ teaspoon pepper
¼ teaspoon basil
Dash of oregano

Heat oil in a 12-inch skillet over medium-high heat. Sauté shrimp just until pink and scallops just until firm. Remove with slotted spoon. Set aside. Add chicken to skillet and sauté until cooked through but still tender. Remove with slotted spoon and set aside. Add onions and peppers to skillet; sauté until soft but not browned. Stir in remaining ingredients and bring to a boil. Simmer over low heat for a few minutes. Cut chicken into 5 to 6 strips per breast and add to sauce. Stir in shrimp and scallops just before serving. Serve over rice or vermicelli with hot garlic bread and a bottle of crisp white wine. Yield: 8 servings.
Rita Grennan

SCALLOPS IN WINESAUCE

2 tablespoons unsalted butter
1 large shallot, chopped
2-ounces dry white wine
Salt, ground white pepper, garlic to taste
2 pounds fresh scallops
½ pound sliced fresh mushrooms

Heat butter in large skillet over medium heat; add shallot and sauté lightly. Stir in wine and scallops and simmer gently. Season to taste with salt, white pepper and garlic. Add mushrooms. Cook, stirring occasionally, for 10 to 15 minutes or until scallops are tender. Spoon into ovenproof serving dish. Sprinkle with seasoned Italian breadcrumbs and broil for a minute or two, just until lightly-browned. Serve immediately. Yield: 4 servings.
Stancato's Restaurant

GOURMET SEASHORE DELIGHT

½ pound lobster meat
½ pound cooked shrimp
½ pound crabmeat
1 tablespoon onion, minced
¼ cup butter or margarine
3 tablespoons butter or margarine
3 tablespoons all-purpose flour
1½ cups milk
2 teaspoon prepared mustard
1 tablespoon Worcestershire sauce
1 tablespoon onion, minced
Dash of hot pepper sauce
Salt and pepper to taste
2 tablespoons dry or cream sherry
Breadcrumbs as desired
Parmesan cheese as desired

In a medium-sized skillet, sauté lobster, shrimp, crabmeat and 1 tablespoon onion in ¼ cup of melted butter. Set aside. In a large saucepan melt 3 tablespoons butter; stir in flour; gradually add milk, stirring until smooth. Cook over medium heat until thickened. Fold seafood mixture into sauce. Add mustard, Worcestershire sauce, 1 tablespoon onion, hot pepper sauce, salt, pepper and sherry. Place mixture in a 2½-quart buttered casserole. Garnish with desired amount of breadcrumbs and cheese. Bake in a 400 degree preheated oven for 15 minutes.
Peg Woodburn

PHYLLIS' SEAFOOD MARINARA

2 tablespoons olive oil
1 large clove garlic, minced
1 medium onion, chopped
1 (32-ounce) can tomatoes, chopped
½ can water
1½ dozen clams
1½ dozen shrimp
1½ pounds crab legs
4 medium white fish fillets

Gently sauté garlic in olive oil in large heavy soup pot or Dutch oven. Do not brown garlic. Add onion and sauté until tender. Stir in tomatoes and water, breaking up tomatoes with spoon. Cover and simmer 45 minutes. Remove lid, turn up heat and bring mixture to a rolling boil; drop in clams; reduce heat and add shrimp and crab legs. Place fish fillets on top. Reduce heat to simmer, cover and continue cooking for 20 minutes, or until fish flakes easily with a fork. Serve with crusty bread or spooned over thin spaghetti *Wonderful!* Yield: 6 to 8 servings.
Phyllis Mazzella

MILLIONAIRE'S SEAFOOD EXTRAORDINAIRE

10 tablespoons butter or margarine
2/3 cup all-purpose flour
1 teaspoon salt
1/2 teaspoon paprika
3 to 3 1/2 cups half and half milk
1 1/2 cups dry white wine
3 to 4 lobster tails, cooked and cut into bite-sized pieces
1 1/2 to 2 pounds shrimp, cleaned and cooked
2 (6-ounce) packages frozen crabmeat, thawed and well-drained
1/2 to 2/3 cup cooked rice per serving

Melt butter or margarine in large skillet; add flour and stir to brown. Slowly add half and half, salt and paprika. Blend and cook, stirring constantly, until sauce is thick and smooth. Place seafood in large heavy saucepan or kettle; add wine. Pour white sauce over seafood/wine mixture and blend gently. Heat over medium heat until piping hot. Serve over rice. *This is an elegant dinner party dish.* Yield: 8 to 10 servings.
Mary Sims

SEAFOOD BAKE

1 (10 1/2-ounce) can of cream of celery soup
1/4 cup milk
1 egg, beaten
1/4 cup grated Parmesan cheese
1 (7 1/2-ounce) frozen or fresh crabmeat, drained and flaked with cartilage removed
1 (4 1/4-ounce) can shrimp, drained
1 (3-ounce) can sliced mushrooms, drained
3 tablespoons fine dry breadcrumbs
1 tablespoon butter, melted
4 pastry shells

Combine soup, milk, egg and 1/2 of the grated cheese in a medium saucepan. Stir over low heat until cheese is melted and mixture is hot. Stir in crabmeat, shrimp and mushrooms. Spoon into baking shells and put on cookie sheet. Mix breadcrumbs with remaining cheese and stir into melted butter. Sprinkle crumbs over shells. Bake in 375 degree oven for 20 minutes. Garnish with parsley or lemon twists. *This is a terrific luncheon dish.* Yield: 4 servings.
Sue Polacek

DO-AHEAD ELEGANT BEEF BURGUNDY

3 pounds rump roast, sirloin tip, or other good beef cut
Red wine to nearly cover meat
1 bay leaf
1 onion, studded with 2 cloves
1 clove garlic
6-ounces salt pork or thick bacon, cut into 1x½-inch pieces
5 tablespoons butter or margarine
3 tablespoons all-purpose flour
1 teaspoon thyme
1 leek
1 sprig parsley
1½ cups beef stock or bouillon
Salt and freshly ground pepper to taste
18 small white onions
3 tablespoons butter or margarine
1 teaspoons sugar
18 mushrooms caps
4 tablespoons butter

Cut meat into 2x2-inch pieces; place in large container. Add bay leaf, onion and garlic; cover with wine and let marinate several hours or overnight. Blanch pork or bacon in boiling water for 10 minutes. Remove and dry on paper towels. Melt 2 tablespoons margarine in a heavy pan. Sauté pork until brown but not crisp; remove to absorbent paper. Remove beef from marinade; drain and dry well. Add 3 tablespoons margarine to braising pan. Dust beef with flour and brown in margarine and pork fat. Turn meat often. Add thyme, leek, parsley, stock, salt, pepper and just enough marinade with onion and garlic to cover meat. Bring to a boil; reduce heat and simmer gently 1½ to 2 hours. Meat should be tender, not dry and stringy. Cook white onions in margarine in skillet. Sprinkle with sugar to glaze and color evenly. Cover pan and steam onions until tender but still crisp. Add mushrooms and sauté. Add pork or bacon. When meat is tender, remove with slotted spoon to warm plate. Reduce sauce if necessary and thicken with flour and water paste. Return meat to sauce; add mushrooms, onions and pork. Taste to correct seasoning. Serve with boiled potatoes or rice. May be made 1 or 2 days in advance, and may easily be multiplied for a crowd. Yield: 8 to 10 servings.
Sue Mahon

CORNED BEEF

4 pounds corned beef brisket
1 medium onion, chopped
2 cloves garlic, minced
1 bay leaf
6 medium potatoes
6 carrots, pared
1 medium head cabbage

Place corned beef in Dutch oven and cover with water. Add onion, garlic and bay leaf. Cover and simmer 3 hours. Scrub potatoes and carrots (don't peel potatoes), cut in half and add to meat. Simmer, covered, for 30 minutes. Add cabbage, which has been cut into 6 wedges. Simmer, covered, for 30 minutes longer. Yield: 6 servings.
Eileen Barlock

POT ROAST WITH RAVIOLI

3 to 4 pound seven-blade chuck roast
1 large onion, diced
3 tablespoons olive oil
1 clove garlic, minced
3 tablespoons all-purpose flour
4 (8-ounce) cans tomato sauce
4 (8-ounce) cans water
½ teaspoon rosemary
3 large bay leaves
1 cup sliced, fresh mushrooms, optional
Salt and pepper to taste
1 (48-count) box frozen ravioli
Grated Parmesan cheese

Heat olive oil in large Dutch oven and sauté onion and garlic until lightly browned. Add meat and braise on both sides. Remove meat to platter. Add flour to pan drippings and brown. Stir in tomato sauce and water. Cook, stirring, until smooth. Add salt and pepper to taste. Stir in rosemary, bay leaves and mushrooms. Return meat to Dutch oven and cover. Cook over low heat until tender (about 2 hours and 15 minutes). Meanwhile, cook ravioli according to package directions and drain. Stir gently into meat and sauce. Remove to serving dish and serve immediately, sprinkled with cheese. *This is great with sourdough French bread to dunk into the tomato gravy-yum! yum!* Yield: 6 to 8 servings.
Betz Spacek

ROUND STEAK NEAPOLITAN

2 pounds (½-inch thick) round steak, cut into serving pieces
Salt, pepper and garlic powder or salt to taste
¼ cup olive oil
1 onion, sliced thin
All-purpose flour
1 (16-ounce) can French-style green beans, drained
1 (8-ounce) can water chestnuts, drained and sliced
1 (32½-ounce) jar spaghetti sauce with mushrooms

Lightly sprinkle steak with seasonings. Sauté onion in olive oil until tender. Flour meat and fry until golden brown. Add beans, water chestnuts and spaghetti sauce; simmer about 15 minutes. Yield: 6 servings.
Darlene Zembala

AUNTIE DOT'S SWISS STEAK

2 pounds beef round steak
1/4 cup all-purpose flour
1 teaspoon salt
2 to 3 tablespoons vegetable oil
1 (16-ounce) can stewed tomatoes
1/2 cup chopped celery
1/2 cup chopped carrot
2 1/2 tablespoons chopped onion
1/2 teaspoon Worcestershire sauce
Shredded Swiss or Cheddar cheese

Divide meat into 4 portions. Combine flour and salt in small bowl; pound into meat on both sides. (Reserve remaining flour.) Heat oil in skillet until hot, and brown meat quickly on both sides. Remove meat from skillet and place in a greased 13x9x2-inch baking dish. Stir remaining flour mixture into pan drippings; add remaining ingredients (except cheese) and simmer until bubbly. Pour over meat. Cover dish tightly with aluminum foil and bake at 350 degrees for 2 hours or until tender. Sprinkle with cheese and return to oven for 2 or 3 minutes to slightly melt it. Serve immediately. Yield: 4 servings.
Dorothy Hunter

BEEF BURGUNDY

3 tablespoons vegetable oil
2 pounds beef chuck, cubed
2 tablespoons all-purpose flour
1 teaspoon salt
1/4 teaspoon pepper
1/4 teaspoon thyme
1 cup beef broth or bouillon
1 cup Burgundy wine
1 (3-ounce) can mushrooms, drained
1 (8-ounce) can pearl onions, drained

Heat oil in a 3-quart Dutch oven and brown meat well on all sides. Stir in flour, salt, pepper and thyme. Mix well, scraping bottom of pan. Pour beef broth or bouillon and wine over meat and stir. Bake, covered, at 325 degrees for 2 1/2 hours. Cool slightly and refrigerate overnight. Remove from refrigerator about 1 hour before serving time. Preheat oven to 325 degrees. Remove cover from beef and add more broth and wine, if necessary (in equal parts). Stir in mushrooms and onions. Cover and bake for 35 minutes. Serve over wide, flat noodles. *Beef Burgundy doesn't have to be made overnight, but this allows flavors to develop and it is really better.* Yield: 4 to 6 servings.
Sue Polacek

QUICK BEEF STROGANOFF

1½ to 2 pounds round steak, cut into 1½-inch strips
1 envelope meat marinade
3 tablespoons butter or margarine
1 onion, sliced thin
1 tablespoon all-purpose flour
1 cup beef bouillon
1 teaspoon prepared mustard
½ cup dairy sour cream
Salt and pepper to taste
Buttered cooked noodles (about 3 cups)

Tenderize meat according to marinade package directions. Heat 2 tablespoons butter or margarine in skillet until sizzling; add steak strips and brown quickly. Remove to hot platter. Sauté onions in steak drippings and spoon over meat. Melt remaining tablespoon butter in skillet; gradually stir in flour until smooth. Stir in bouillon and continue cooking over low heat, stirring constantly, until smooth and thickened. Bring to a boil; reduce heat and stir in mustard and sour cream. Heat through but do not boil. Season to taste with salt and pepper and pour over beef and onions. Serve immediately over hot buttered noodles. Sliced mushrooms may be added with onions. If more sauce is desired, double sauce ingredients. Yield: 6 servings.
Kathy Scali

KAY'S BEEF STROGANOFF

1½ pounds round steak, cut into ¼-inch cubes
1 teaspoon salt
⅛ teaspoon pepper
1 teaspoon garlic salt
¼ cup all-purpose flour
3 tablespoons butter or margarine
1 cup canned tomatoes with juice
1 cup dairy sour cream
2 tablespoons all-purpose flour
4 cups cooked noodles

Combine salt, pepper, garlic salt and ¼ cup flour in clean, heavy brown paper bag; shake steak cubes in mixture until well-coated. Melt butter or margarine in heavy skillet and brown meat slowly. Add tomatoes and stir well. Cover tightly and simmer for 2½ hours or until tender. Stir frequently and add water if necessary. After meat is cooked, combine 2 tablespoons flour with sour cream and stir until smooth. Add to meat mixture; cook and stir until thickened. *Do not boil.* Serve hot over noodles. Yield: 4 to 6 servings.
Kay McGorray

BEEF "IT'S SO GOOD IT SHOULD BE ILLEGAL" TERIYAKI

1 (2 pound) sirloin steak, cut 1½ to 2-inches thick

Place steak in a non-metal pan large enough for steak to lie flat. Pour over marinade until steak is nearly covered with the sauce. Sprinkle wtih garlic and onion powder. Cover and marinate in refrigerator for 12 hours. Turn and marinate an additional 12 hours. Grill over an extremely hot grill. Grill meat 5 to 7-inches from the fire for 8 to 10 minutes per side. Steak will be black and crisp on the outside and rare on the inside. Yield: 4 to 6 servings.

Secret Marinade Sauce:

4 cloves garlic, crushed or finely chopped
2 large onions, chopped
2 (10-ounce) bottles soy sauce
2 cups water
2 tablespoons sugar
1 teaspoon ground ginger

Combine ingredients in a jar with a tight fitting lid. Cover and shake until well-blended. Pour over steak until almost covered. If more marinade is needed, add proportionate quantities of soy sauce and water. *This is the last Teriyaki recipe you'll ever need!*
Bill Mengerink

ALL-IN-A-PACKAGE STEAK SUPPER

Aluminum foil, 2½-foot length on 18-inch wide foil
1½ pounds lean chuck steak, 1-inch thick
1 envelope dry onion soup mix
3 medium carrots, quartered
2 stalks celery, cut into sticks
2 or 3 medium potatoes, pared and sliced ½-inch thick
2 tablespoons butter or margarine
½ teaspoon salt

Place foil on baking sheet. Place meat in center; sprinkle with onion soup mix; cover with vegetables. Dot vegetables with butter and sprinkle with salt. Fold foil over and seal securely (drug store wrap) to hold in juices. Bake in very hot oven at 450 degrees for 1 to 1½ hours or until tender. For individual servings, ingredients may be divided and put into 4 separate foil packages then baked in a 400 degree oven for equal time. Yield: 4 servings.
Rosemary Corcoran

BEEF WELLINGTON

Pastry (recipe follows)
1 whole beef tenderloin, 3 to 5 pounds
Garlic powder
Salt and pepper
6 to 7 tablespoons melted butter or margarine
Chicken Liver Pâté or Mushroom Filling (recipes follow)
1 egg, slightly beaten

Prepare pastry as directed. Refrigerate. Preheat oven to 450 degrees. Sprinkle beef tenderloin lightly with garlic powder, salt and pepper. Place tenderloin on rack in shallow roasting pan and brush with melted butter or margarine. Insert meat thermometer into thickest part of tenderloin and roast for about 25 to 30 minutes or until thermometer reaches 150 degrees for rare beef, 160 degrees for medium or 170 degrees for well done. Brush several more times with melted butter or margarine during roasting. (If desired, place on aluminum foil "tent" over roast while baking to prevent splashing over in oven). Cool meat slightly at room temperature, then refrigerate until final preparation time. About 1 hour before serving time, preheat oven to 425 degrees and prepare Wellington as follows.

Roll prepared pastry dough into a rectangle about 18x12x⅛-inch thick. The pastry should be about 3-inches longer than the tenderloin, adjust as necessary. Remove beef from refrigerator. Cover top and sides of tenderloin with pâté, placing more pâté on top than on sides. Place tenderloin onto pastry, top side down. Fold pastry over bottom of meat and seal seam with water all around. Spray baking sheet with non-stick cooking spray and place tenderloin on sheet very carefully, sealed side down. Cut decorative shapes, such as flowers/leaves, from pastry trimmings and decorate top of Wellington. Brush all over with beaten egg. Bake for about 30 minutes, or until pastry is cooked and lightly-browned. Remove carefully to serving platter, using two large spatulas. Cut into 1 to 2-inch thick slices, crosswise, to serve. Serve with Madeira Sauce if desired. Yield: 10 to 12 servings.

Pastry:

5 cups all-purpose flour
1 teaspoon salt
¾ cup butter or margarine
¾ cup vegetable shortening
1 egg, slightly beaten
½ cup ice water (approximately)

Combine flour, salt, butter or margarine and shortening in mixing bowl using pastry blender or fingers to form crumbs size of coarsely ground cornmeal. Add egg and enough ice water to form a smooth dough. Roll dough into a ball and refrigerate until well chilled, at least 1 hour. Use as directed for Beef Wellington. (Amount of dough might have to be adjusted, depending upon size of beef tenderloin.)

Chicken Liver Pâté:

4 tablespoons butter or margarine
2 tablespoons chopped green onions
1 clove garlic, finely chopped
½ pound chicken livers, washed and drained
2 tablespoons cognac
2 thin slices ham, diced
½ pound fresh mushrooms, finely minced

Melt butter or margarine in skillet over medium heat; sauté onions and garlic until tender but not browned. Remove from skillet and set aside. Raise heat to medium-high and sauté chicken livers until all pink is gone. Remove from skillet and stir in cognac. Stir cognac to remove browned particles from bottom of skillet. Add ham and simmer about 2 minutes. Turn ham out into livers, onions and garlic, and put all through a meat grinder or food processor. Sauté mushrooms in about 1 tablespoon butter or margarine, drain, and blend into liver mixture. Cool. Use a directed for Beef Wellington.

Sauce Madeira:

2 tablespoons butter or margarine
2 tablespoons finely chopped green onions or shallots
1½ cups canned beef gravy
2 tablespoons lemon juice
¼ cup Madeira wine

Melt butter or margarine in small saucepan over low heat. Add shallots and sauté until tender but not browned. Stir in gravy and lemon juice and bring to a boil. Reduce heat, stir in Madeira and heat through. Yield: about 1½ cups sauce. Serve over Beef Wellington, if desired.

Mushroom Filling: (May be used in place of Chicken Liver Pâté). In medium skillet, cook and stir 1 pound fresh mushrooms, finely chopped, ½ cup chopped onion, ½ cup dry sherry, ¼ cup butter and ¼ cup snipped parsley until onion is tender and all liquid absorbed.
Hollis Hura, Registered Dietitian, Parmadale

PEPPER STEAK ON RICE
(FLIP STEAKS)

2 pounds sirloin tip steaks, cut into 2-inch long slices
3 tablespoons vegetable oil
1 clove garlic, minced
½ pound fresh mushrooms, sliced
3 cups celery, sliced diagonally
2 cups green pepper, cut into thin strips
1 cup beef broth or bouillon
¾ cup diced green onions
2 tablespoons soy sauce
1 tablespoon Worcestershire sauce
4 tablespoons cornstarch
½ cup water
½ teaspoon seasoned salt
1 teaspoon brown sugar
2 or 3 fresh tomato wedges

Sauté meat and garlic in hot oil in large skillet quickly. Add mushrooms and sauté. Remove meat and mushrooms from skillet to warm platter and set aside. Clean skillet; place celery, green peppers, onions, soy sauce, broth and Worcestershire sauce in skillet and cook until vegetables are just tender. Combine cornstarch with water until smooth; add to vegetables and cook until thickened. Gently fold in meat and mushrooms; season with salt and brown sugar. Heat through and add tomato wedges. Serve immediately over hot, cooked rice. Yield: 4 to 6 servings.
Florence Schall

WALK THE PLANK STEAK

½ cup vegetable oil
¼ cup chopped onion
1 clove garlic, minced
¼ cup honey
¼ cup catsup
¼ cup vinegar
3 tablespoons Worcestershire sauce
1 tablespoon dry mustard
1 teaspoon soy sauce
Pepper to taste
1 (1 to 1½-pound) flank steak

Combine all ingredients, except steak, in a large bowl. Add steak, turn once, and cover tightly with plastic wrap. Refrigerate overnight, turning once or twice if steak is not completely covered with marinade. To serve, broil in oven or over hot charcoal until desired doneness is reached (rare or medium-rare is best). Yield: 3 or 4 servings.
Florence Schall

BRACIOLA

3 eggs
3/4 to 1 1/2 cups breadcrumbs
1/2 cup grated Parmesan cheese
2 thin round steaks (about 1 pound)

Combine 3/4 cup crumbs with cheese. Add eggs 1 at a time until mixture is pasty. Add more crumbs if too moist, or a little milk if too dry. Spread mixture on salted and peppered steaks; dot with butter. Roll and tie with string. Brown in olive oil. Place in spaghetti sauce while it is cooking (1 to 2 hours). To serve, let cool slightly, then gently untie or cut string. Cut into slices and serve with spaghetti sauce, spaghetti and meatballs.
Gloria Scali

DELICIOUS TWO-MEAT STEW

1 (16-ounce) package bulk pork sausage links
1 pound top round steak, cut into bite-size chunks
1 medium apple, cored
1 (24-ounce) can vegetable juice cocktail
3 carrots, pared and thickly sliced
4 medium potatoes, cut into sixths
1 medium onion, thinly sliced

In a skillet, brown sausages. Remove and drain on paper towel. Add round steak to drippings in skillet; brown. Remove and drain on paper towel. Place meats and remaining ingredients in a Dutch oven. Cook over medium heat for about 60 minutes or until vegetables are tender. Yield: 4 to 5 servings.
Barb McGinty

FLANK STEAK TERIYAKI

3 pounds flank steak
1/4 cup sherry
1/4 cup soy sauce
1/4 cup olive oil
1 or 2 cloves garlic, minced
1/4 teaspoon ground ginger
Dash of pepper

Trim excess fat from steak; score both sides of meat into diamond shapes, cutting about 1/4-inch deep. Place steak in glass baking dish. Combine remaining ingredients in small bowl and pour over steak. Marinate for at least 1 hour. Remove meat from marinade and place on broiler pan. Broil quickly in preheated oven for 3 to 5 minutes, at least 3-inches from heat. Turn over and broil 5 minutes longer. Slice into thin diagonal strips to serve. Serve hot. Yield: 6 servings.
Lynne Della Donna
Amina Kapla

BARBECUE MARINADE SHORT RIBS

4 pounds well trimmed beef short ribs cut into 2½-inch pieces
½ cup soy sauce
½ cup water
¼ cup sliced green onions with tops
2 tablespoons sesame seeds
2 tablespoons sugar
2 cloves garlic, minced
½ teaspoon pepper

Keeping bone side down, dice cut beef this way: cutting halfway down to bone every ½-inch in one direction, at right angles cut every ½-inch but only ½-inch deep. Using a large baking pan, combine soy sauce, water, green onion, sesame seed, sugar, garlic and pepper to make the marinade. Put scored pieces of meat into marinade and chill, covered, in refrigerator for 4 to 5 hours. Place meat, bone side down, on barbecue grill over high heat. When brown, turn and cook on meat side. Lift and turn meat throughout cooking time (about 15 minutes) to expose all surfaces to the heat. Cook until crisply brown. *Provide plenty of napkins as the meat can be eaten out of hand—very tasty!* Yield: 4 main dish servings or 10 to 12 appetizers.
Tom Balchak

BARBECUE SPARERIBS

2 pounds pork spareribs
3 tablespoons honey or dark brown sugar
3 tablespoons vinegar
2 tablespoons sugar
3 tablespoons soy sauce
1 clove garlic, crushed
1 tablespoon dry sherry
½ cup chicken broth

Separate meat into 3 or 4 rib sections, cutting between bones with a sharp knife. Combine remaining ingredients and pour over meat in a bowl. Cover and refrigerate for 10 to 12 hours or overnight. Place meat on a rack in a shallow pan and baste with marinade mixture. Bake, uncovered, in a 325 degree oven for 1½ to 2 hours, basting occasionally with marinade. Turn once during baking time. Yield: 4 servings.
Patti Lovejoy

RIBS OF BEEF A LA BOUQUETIERE

2 ribs of beef (prime) per serving
Salt
Freshly ground pepper
Minced garlic
Butter

Cut 1 thick slice (2 ribs) of beef off a trimmed rib of beef per person being served. Season to taste with salt, pepper and garlic. Cook quickly in a sauté pan in clarified butter until desired doneness is reached (rare or medium-rare). Drain and serve immediately garnished with carrots and turnips. Serve with your choice of the following vegetables: French beans, artichoke hearts stuffed with garden peas, new potatoes or florets of cauliflower cooked in butter. Dilute pan juices with madeira wine and pour over rib of beef just before serving.
William D. Lemaster, Executive Chef, de cuisine

BETTY'S BARBECUE BEEF

1 pound beef stew
1 pound cubed pork
1 medium onion, diced
3 stalks celery, chopped
1 clove garlic, minced
1 (10¾-ounce) can tomato soup
¼ cup sugar
⅓ cup Worcestershire sauce
⅓ cup vinegar
1 cup water
Salt and pepper to taste

Place meat in a large bowl; add onion, celery, and garlic. Blend together. Place in Dutch oven or 13x9x2-inch baking pan. Combine tomato soup, sugar, Worcestershire sauce, vinegar and water; pour over meat. Salt and pepper to taste. Bake at 350 degrees, uncovered, for 3 hours. Mash with a potato masher until thick. Serve on buns. *This is terrific!*
Betty Jamiol

MA WHISTLER'S STROGANOFF

1½ pounds round steak, cut into ½-inch strips
¾ pound mushrooms, cleaned
1 onion, chopped
½ teaspoon grated nutmeg
Salt and pepper to taste
1 cup dairy sour cream
¾ cup chopped dill pickles

Combine meat, mushrooms, onions, nutmeg, salt and pepper in large bowl. Spread in greased 2½-quart baking dish, cover and bake at 325 to 350 degrees for 2 to 3 hours, or until meat is tender. Stir every 30 to 45 minutes. Do not add water. This makes its own gravy. Remove from oven and stir in sour cream and dill pickles just before serving. Serve hot over rice or noodles. Yield: 6 servings.
Lynn Malo

BAKED STUFFED PUMPKIN

1 small whole pumpkin or Hubbard squash
2 tablespoons vegetable oil
2 pounds ground chuck
6-ounces ground smoked ham
2½ cups finely chopped onions
1 green pepper, finely chopped
2½ teaspoons salt
2 teaspoons olive oil
2 teaspoons oregano
1 teaspoon vinegar
1 teaspoon ground black pepper
Dash crushed dried red pepper
2 large cloves garlic, mashed
¾ cup golden raisins
⅓ cup pimento-stuffed green olives, chopped
2 teaspoons capers, drained and minced
1 (8-ounce) can tomato sauce
3 eggs, beaten

With a sharp knife, cut a circular top out of the pumpkin. Save top for lid. Scoop out seeds; scrape inside of pumpkin clean. Place pumpkin in a large pan and cover with salted water. Cover pan and bring water to a boil, simmering until pumpkin meat is almost tender when pierced with a fork, 10 to 30 minutes. Some pumpkins cook faster than others. Do not over cook. Remove pumpkin from hot water, drain well, and dry the outside. Sprinkle inside with a little salt. Heat oil in a large frying pan. Add beef, ham, onion, and green pepper. Cook over high heat until meat is browned and crumbly; remove from heat. Mix together salt, olive oil, oregano, vinegar, black pepper, red pepper and garlic. Add to meat along with raisins, olives, capers, and tomato sauce. Mix well. Cover pan and cook over low heat for 15 minutes, stirring occasionally. Remove from heat and allow to cool slightly; then mix in the eggs thoroughly. Fill cooked pumpkin with the meat stuffing, pressing the stuffing slightly to pack it firmly. Cover with pumpkin lid. Place pumpkin in shallow, greased baking pan and bake in 350 degree oven for 1 hour. Cool 10 minutes before serving. At serving time, garnish with clean fall leaves or flowers, if desired. To serve, slice pumpkin from top to bottom in fat wedges. Lift each serving onto dinner plate and spoon more meat filling over top. Yield: 8 servings.
Joan Gullett

FRIED SWEETBREADS

1 pound sweetbreads
1½ cups crushed cornflakes
1 egg, beaten
½ teaspoon salt
⅛ teaspoon pepper
⅛ teaspoon ground ginger
Mustard Sauce

Parboil sweetbreads in a saucepan. Drain and roll in cornflakes; then in beaten egg and again in cornflake crumbs. Fry until golden brown in hot deep shortening. Drain on paper towels. Sprinkle with salt, pepper and ginger. Serve hot with mustard sauce. Yields: 4 servings.
Mike Pitroski

SWEET AND SOUR MEATBALL WITH SPECULA

Sauce:

1 tablespoon lemon juice
2 tablespoons sugar
¾ cup water
1½ cups tomato purée or sauce

Using a medium saucepan, combine ingredients well and simmer while preparing meatballs. Stir occasionally.

Meatballs:

1 pound lean ground beef
2 tablespoons grated onion
1 egg, slightly beaten
Dash of oregano
Salt and pepper to taste

Combine all ingredients, in order listed, in small bowl. Shape into marble-sized meatballs and set aside. Pour hot sauce into a 2-quart casserole dish and add meatballs. Cover and bake for 1 hour at 350 degrees. Serve over Specula.

Specula (dumplings):

2 eggs, beaten
1 cup water
1½ teaspoons salt
All-purpose flour

Combine eggs, water and salt in medium mixing bowl; mix in flour until dough forms threads. Fill a 3-quart saucepan with water (about ¾'s full) and add salt. Drop dough by teaspoons, scraped off of a knife, into rapidly boiling water. Cook dumplings for about 5 minutes or until they float to top of water. Remove with slotted spoon to colander and drain. Place speculas on serving platter; pour meatballs and sauce over all. Sprinkle with grated cheese, if desired. Yield: 4 servings.
Betz Spacek

INSIDE-OUT CABBAGE ROLLS

1 pound lean ground beef
¼ cup raw rice
2 cups finely shredded cabbage
1 medium onion, chopped
2 (10½-ounce) cans tomato soup
2 soup cans of water
Salt and pepper to taste

Mix together thoroughly meat, rice, onion and cabbage. Salt and pepper to taste. Roll into 1-inch balls. Place meatballs in large skillet. Blend tomato soup and water well and pour over meat. Simmer for 1½ hours. Yield: 4 servings.
Kay Holman

OLIVE MEATLOAF

2 pounds lean ground beef
½ cup chopped onion
1 clove garlic, minced
¼ teaspoon pepper
½ teaspoon oregano
½ teaspoon basil
½ teaspoon salt
1 (6-ounce) can pitted ripe olives, sliced
1 (8-ounce) can tomato sauce
3 slices bacon, halved

In a large bowl, thoroughly mix all ingredients together except olives, tomato sauce and bacon. Mix in olives, reserving a few for garnish. In a 13x9x2-inch baking pan, shape mixture into a 4x12-inch rounded loaf. Pour tomato sauce over loaf. Lay bacon slices across loaf. Bake in a 350 degree preheated oven for 1 hour and 15 minutes. Garnish with reserved olives. Slice to serve hot or cold. Yield: 8 servings.
Rosemary Corcoran

HAMBURGER CHOW MEIN

1½ pounds ground beef
¼ cup chopped onion
1 (16-ounce) can Chinese vegetables, drained
1 (10¾-ounce) can chicken with rice soup
1 (10¾-ounce) can cream of mushroom soup
1 cup cooked rice
⅛ teaspoon pepper
1 tablespoon soy sauce
¼ cup sherry
1 (3-ounce) can chow mein noodles

Brown meat and onion in medium-sized skillet until onion is tender and meat is no longer pink; drain off fat. Stir in vegetables, rice, soups and seasonings and mix well. Pour into a greased 2-quart casserole dish. Spread chow mein noodles over top. Bake, uncovered, at 350 degrees for 30 minutes or until hot and bubbly. Yield: 6 to 8 servings.
Rosemary Corcoran

RICE-STUFFED MEAT LOAF

1½ pounds ground beef
¼ cup onion, minced
⅔ cup breadcrumbs
2 eggs, slightly beaten
½ cup milk
1½ teaspoons salt
½ teaspoon sage
⅛ teaspoon pepper

Stuffing:

1½ cups cooked rice
1 egg, beaten
¾ teaspoon salt
¼ teaspoon pepper
¼ cup milk
¼ teaspoon thyme

Combine ingredients for meat loaf and place ½ of the mixture in a loaf pan. Combine ingredients for the stuffing and spread on meat mixture. Top with remaining meat mixture. Bake at 350 degrees for 1 hour and 15 minutes. Let stand in pan for 15 minutes before serving. Garnish with favorite tomato sauce. Yield: 6 servings.
Kay Kelly

BASQUE POTATO PIE

3 large baking potatoes
2 tablespoons butter or margarine
¼ teaspoon salt
½ cup chopped onions
1 pound lean ground beef
¾ cup tomato sauce
¾ cup shredded Monterey Jack cheese
⅓ cup sliced pitted ripe olives

Pare potatoes; slice crosswise as thin as possible, using food processor or sharp knife. In large skillet, melt butter; add salt and toss potatoes in butter to coat evenly. Line bottom and sides of a 9 inch pie plate with potato slices, reserving 8 slices for garnish. In the same skillet, sauté onion until golden. Add beef; cook until browned, breaking up with fork as it cooks. Drain off fat. Add tomato sauce, cheese and black olives; mix well. Spoon meat mixture into potato-lined pie shell. Garnish with reserved potato slices. Bake in preheated 350 degree oven for 35 to 40 minutes or until potatoes are soft and edges lightly browned. Allow pie to stand 5 minutes or more before serving so it will cut easily. Yield: 6 servings.
Ruth Abbott

SLOVAK HOLUBKY (STUFFED CABBAGE)

1 small onion, chopped
1 teaspoon vegetable shortening
1 pound ground beef
1 pound ground pork
½ cup raw rice
¼ teaspoon pepper
1 large head cabbage
1 (27-ounce) can sauerkraut, undrained
1 (16-ounce) can tomato juice

In a small skillet, sauté onion in shortening until golden brown. In a large mixing bowl, combine onion with beef, pork, rice and pepper. In a large kettle, parboil cabbage in water to cover until leaves soften. Holding cabbage firmly with a fork, carefully cut off outer leaves as they soften. Drain on paper towel. Trim off thick center vein. Spoon meat mixture into the center of each leaf, roll up and tuck in ends. In the bottom of a large, heavy kettle or saucepan, spread ½ of the sauerkraut. Arrange cabbage rolls on top. Cover with remaining sauerkraut. Pour tomato juice over all. Cover and cook slowly for 1½ hours. Yield: 8 to 10 servings.
Ann Vavrek

CHEDDAR FILLED BEEF ROLL

1½ pounds lean ground beef
¼ cup dry breadcrumbs
2 tablespoons barbecue sauce
1 egg
½ teaspoon salt
1 cup (4-ounces) shredded Cheddar cheese
¼ cup dry breadcrumbs
¼ cup chopped green pepper
2 tablespoons water

Combine meat, ¼ cup breadcrumbs, barbecue sauce, egg and salt; mix well. Pat meat mixture into 14x8-inch rectangle on foil or waxed paper. In a bowl, combine Cheddar cheese, ¼ cup breadcrumbs, green pepper and water. Pat cheese mixture over meat. Roll up meat like jellyroll. Cover and chill several hours. Place in shallow pan and bake at 350 degrees for 25 to 30 minutes. Slice and serve. Yield: 4 to 6 servings.
Karen Collins

HAMBURGER STROGANOFF

¼ cup butter or margarine
½ cup minced onion
1 pound mushrooms, sliced
1½ pounds lean ground beef
1 tablespoon all-purpose flour
1 teaspoon salt
¼ teaspoon pepper
¼ teaspoon paprika
1 (10½-ounce) can cream of chicken soup
1 cup dairy sour cream

Sauté onions and mushrooms in butter in a large skillet. Remove and set aside. Brown ground beef until pink is gone. Spoon off excess fat. Return onions and mushrooms to skillet and mix well. Sprinkle flour over mixture; add salt, pepper and paprika. Stir in chicken soup and blend thoroughly. Simmer for 15 minutes. Add sour cream and cook until mixture is heated through. Serve over noodles, rice, mashed potatoes or toast. Yield: 4 to 5 servings.
Rosemary Corcoran

JOE'S SPECIAL

1 pound lean ground sirloin
8-ounces mushrooms, chopped
1 medium onion, chopped
1 clove garlic, chopped
2 tablespoons red wine
Pinch of oregano
Pinch of pepper
Dash of salt
2 to 3 eggs, beaten
1 (10-ounce) package frozen, chopped spinach, thawed and drained
½ cup grated Parmesan cheese

Brown sirloin; drain. Add mushrooms, onions, garlic and wine; sauté until limp. Add seasonings and eggs. Stir in well-drained spinach and mix thoroughly. Add Parmesan cheese and stir to blend. This will turn out like a frittata. Serve with French or garlic bread. Yield: 4 servings.
Paula Knight

LEFTOVER HAM SURPRISE

1 (16-ounce) jar processed cheese spread
1 (10½-ounce) can cream of mushroom soup
1 (16-ounce) package chopped broccoli, thawed and drained
2 to 3 cups leftover diced cooked ham

In a 1½-quart buttered casserole, mix cheese and mushroom soup. Add broccoli and ham. Bake in preheated 350 degree oven for 30 minutes or until broccoli is tender. Serve over baked pastry shells or toasted English muffins. *This makes a nice luncheon dish served with a fruit salad.* Yield: 6 servings.
Peg O'Shea

STUFFED CABBAGE ROLLS, GREEK STYLE

1 large head cabbage, about 3 pounds
1 pound ground pork
½ cup raw rice
¼ cup chopped green onion
3 tablespoons catsup
1 tablespoon dried dill weed
½ teaspoon salt
Dash of pepper
1 egg, slightly beaten
1 (10¾-ounce) can chicken broth
2 tablespoons vegetable oil
1 tablespoon all-purpose flour
1 tablespoon lemon juice
1 small lemon, cut into wedges, optional

In large kettle, bring 3 quarts water to boiling. Add cabbage. Simmer 2 or 3 minutes or until leaves are pliable. Remove cabbage and drain. Carefully remove 12 large leaves from cabbage. Trim thick rib. If leaves are not soft enough to roll, return to boiling water for a minute. In large bowl, combine pork, rice, green onion, catsup, dill, salt, pepper and egg. Mix with fork until well-blended. Place 2 slightly rounded tablespoons of meat mixture in hollow of each of the 12 cabbage leaves. Fold side leaf over stuffing; roll up from thick end of leaf. In 5 quart Dutch oven, place a few of the remaining cabbage leaves. Arrange rolls, seam side down on leaves. Pour chicken broth and vegetable oil over rolls. Bring to boiling over medium heat. Simmer, covered, for 45 minutes, basting occasionally with broth. To serve: arrange cabbage rolls in warm serving dish. Measure remaining broth; add water to make 1 cup. Return to Dutch oven. Gradually blend in flour. Add lemon juice and ½ teaspoon salt. Bring to boil; simmer 3 minutes; stir until smooth. Spoon over cabbage. Yield: 6 servings.
Ann Papadimoulis

HAM LOAF

1 (10¾-ounce) can cream of mushroom soup
2 pounds ground ham loaf mixture
½ cup breadcrumbs
½ cup chopped onion
2 eggs, slightly beaten
1 teaspoon dry mustard
½ cup dairy sour cream

Combine ⅓ cup soup, ham, breadcrumbs, onions, eggs and mustard in a large mixing bowl. Pat mixture into a greased baking pan and bake at 350 degrees for 1 hour and 15 minutes. Combine remaining soup with sour cream. Heat and serve along side of ham loaf as a sauce. Yield: 6 servings.
Nicky Cowan

PORK CHOPS IN CREAM SAUCE

1 carrot, thinly sliced
1 onion, thinly sliced
1 small bay leaf
1/4 teaspoon dried thyme
1/2 cup sauterne
2 tablespoons vinegar
2 tablespoons water
4 to 6 loin pork chops, 1-inch thick, trimmed
1/2 cup water or chicken bouillon
1/2 cup heavy cream
1 tablespoon cornstarch
2 tablespoons water
1 teaspoon salt
1/8 teaspoon pepper

Combine carrot, onion, bay leaf, thyme, sauterne and vinegar in medium bowl. Add chops, cover tightly with plastic wrap, and refrigerate overnight or several hours. About 1 hour before serving time, drain chops and pat dry with paper towels. Reserve vegetable marinade. In large skillet, which has been rubbed with fat trimmed from chops, brown chops on both sides until golden, about 15 minutes. Add vegetables and 1/4 cup marinade; cover, and reduce heat to low. Simmer for about 45 minutes or until chops are fork tender. Remove to heated platter and keep warm. Stir remaining marinade into skillet along with about 1/2 cup water. Bring to a boil and simmer for 5 minutes. Stir in cream and cornstarch combined with 2 tablespoons water. Continue cooking and stirring until thickened. Add salt and pepper. Pour sauce over chops and serve. Yield: 4 to 6 servings.
Sister M. Ancilla

POPULAR PORK CHOPS

4 pork chops (about 1 1/2 pounds), trimmed
2 tablespoons vegetable shortening
2 (8-ounce) cans tomato sauce
1/2 cup water
2 tablespoons firmly packed brown sugar
1/3 cup finely chopped celery
Juice of 1/2 lemon
1/2 teaspoon salt
1/8 teaspoon pepper
1/2 teaspoon dry mustard

Brown chops on both sides in melted shortening in medium-sized skillet. Place chops in a greased 8-inch baking pan. Combine tomato sauce, water, celery, brown sugar, lemon juice and seasonings in small bowl. Pour over chops, cover tightly with aluminum foil and bake at 350 degrees for 1 hour and 15 minutes or until chops are fork-tender. Yield: 4 servings.
Gloria DeLambo

PORK CHOPS BEDEVILED

4 tablespoons margarine
1 medium red cooking apple, cored and cut into wedges
1 pound mushrooms, sliced
¼ teaspoon pepper
½ teaspoon salt
4 butterflied pork loin chops (½-inch thick)
½ cup mayonnaise
⅓ cup soft breadcrumbs
1 tablespoon chopped watercress
1 tablespoon prepared mustard
⅛ teaspoon paprika

Melt 1 tablespoon margarine in a large skillet; add apples and cook 5 to 7 minutes, until apples are fork-tender, turning once. Remove to large platter; keep warm. In same skillet melt remaining margarine and add mushrooms, pepper and ¼ teaspoon salt. Cook 10 minutes or until mushrooms are tender. Remove mushrooms to platter with apple wedges. Preheat broiler. Place chops on rack and broil 10 minutes, turning once. Meanwhile, in a small bowl, mix with a fork the mayonnaise, crumbs, watercress, mustard, paprika and remaining ¼ teaspoon salt. When chops are done, spread with mayonnaise mixture and broil 1 minute longer until topping is hot and bubbly. To serve, arrange pork chops on platter surrounded by apples and mushrooms. Yield: 4 servings.
Jean Croyle

PORK AND VEGETABLE KEBABS

½ cup dry sherry
6 tablespoons soy sauce
6 tablespoons vegetable oil
1 teaspoon ground ginger
8 cloves garlic, minced
1 trimmed, boned pork shoulder, cut into 1-inch cubes
2 dozen medium mushrooms
2 large sweet red peppers, halved, seeded and cut into wedges
2 medium onions, cut into wedges
1 medium yellow squash, cut into 1-inch rounds

Stir together sherry, soy sauce, oil, ginger and garlic. Add pork, mushrooms, red pepper, onion and squash. Stir to coat well. Cover and refrigerate overnight, stirring once. Onto each of 6 long skewers thread 6 to 7 pork cubes alternating with 4 mushrooms, 4 pepper wedges, 2 onion wedges, and 1 squash round. Grill kebabs 6 inches from coals, turning once and basting with marinade, until pork is no longer pink and vegetables are tender, 15 to 25 minutes. Heat any remaining marinade and pass as dipping sauce. Use a small fork to slide pork and vegetables from skewers onto serving plates. Yield: 6 servings.
Peg O'Shea

CROWN ROAST OF PORK WITH APPLE STUFFING

5-pounds Crown Roast of pork

Have butcher "French" chops and cut through backbone for easier carving. Preheat oven to 325 degrees. Place roast in shallow roasting pan. Sprinkle with salt and pepper. Protect rib bones with foil caps to prevent overbrowning. Fill center of roast with crushed foil to keep shape during roasting. Roast uncovered 2½ hours.

Stuffing:

6 slices bacon
½ cup chopped celery
½ cup chopped onion
3 cups fresh white bread cubes
1 teaspoon salt
½ teaspoon pepper
¼ teaspoon dried thyme leaves
½ teaspoon poultry seasoning
1½ cups peeled, chopped apples
¼ cup margarine

Fry bacon until crisp; crumble and set aside. Pour off all but 2 tablespoons bacon drippings from skillet. Add celery and onions and sauté until tender, stirring, about 5 minutes. Remove from heat; add crumbled bacon and remaining ingredients. Toss lightly to combine. After 2½ hours remove meat from oven. Remove foil from center and fill with stuffing. Cover loosely with foil; return to oven. Continue roasting until internal temperature reaches 185 degrees on meat thermometer. Remove foil from rib bones. Serve on platter, garnished with crabapples and parsley sprigs. *A beautiful holiday feast.* Yield: 8 to 10 servings.
Sue Mahon

SCALLOPED PORK AND RICE

1 tablespoon vegetable shortening
1 onion, chopped
1 teaspoon paprika
1 pound pork, cubed
1 teaspoon salt
1 cup rice
1 (8-ounce) can sauerkraut, drained
1 cup dairy sour cream

Melt shortening; add onion and brown slightly. Stir in paprika, pork and salt. Cook over low heat until meat is tender, about 1 hour, adding water as necessary to keep meat from burning. Cook rice in boiling salted water. In a large casserole arrange a layer of meat mixture, a layer of rice, and a layer of sauerkraut. Repeat until all are used. Spread sour cream over top. Bake at 350 degrees for about 1 hour, until top is browned. Yield: 6 to 8 servings.
Evelyn Maroush

PORK CHOP SKILLET PARMIGIANA

6 center cut pork chops, about ½-inch thick
1 tablespoon vegetable oil
Salt and pepper to taste
1 medium onion, peeled and chopped
1 (15-ounce) can herb tomato sauce
1½ cups water
¾ cup raw rice
¼ cup chopped green pepper
½ teaspoon salt
6-ounces thin sliced mozzarella cheese (6 slices)
2 tablespoons grated Parmesan cheese

Brown chops in oil in large heavy skillet over medium heat. Sprinkle with salt and pepper as desired. Remove chops from skillet and set aside. Sauté onion in drippings until yellow, but not brown. Drain off any excess fat. Add 1⅓ cups tomato sauce (reserving the rest for later), water, rice, green pepper and ½ teaspoon salt. Bring to boil, return chops to skillet; cover and reduce heat. Simmer 25 to 30 minutes or until chops and rice are cooked. May be covered, and baked in a preheated 350 degree oven in skillet, if handle is ovenproof, or if casserole is used. The last 10 minutes, place slice of mozzarella cheese on each chop, top with remaining tomato sauce; sprinkle Parmesan cheese over all. Yield: 4 to 6 servings.
Rosemary Corcoran

HAWAIIAN SPARERIBS

4 to 6 pounds lean pork ribs, fat trimmed
¼ cup all-purpose flour
1 teaspoon salt
¼ cup soy sauce
4 to 6 tablespoons vegetable oil
¾ cup firmly packed brown sugar
⅔ cup wine vinegar
½ cup cold water
1 (20-ounce) can pineapple slices, drained and juice reserved
1 clove garlic, minced
1 teaspoon grated fresh ginger root or ½ teaspoon ground ginger

Wipe ribs clean and cut into about 2-inch wide strips. In a small bowl, combine flour, salt and soy sauce into a smooth paste; brush over ribs. Allow to stand for 10 minutes. Heat oil in large skillet and brown ribs on both sides; transfer as they are browned to a large heavy roasting pan. Pour fat from skillet. Add sugar, vinegar, water, reserved pineapple juice, garlic and ginger to skillet and heat, stirring to loosen brown bits from bottom of skillet. Pour sauce over ribs, cover roaster, and bake at 350 degrees for 1½ hours, turning ribs occasionally during baking. Place pineapple slices over ribs during last 10 minutes of baking time. For 6 pounds of ribs, double amounts of flour, salt and soy sauce. Yield: about 6 servings.
Lynne Della Donna

VEAL AU GRATIN PIE

1 tablespoon butter or margarine
1 cup finely chopped onions
1 pound ground veal
1 tablespoon all-purpose flour
1 cup milk
Salt and pepper to taste
2 tablespoons chopped parsley
3 eggs, separated
1 cup dairy sour cream
⅔ cup all-purpose flour
¼ teaspoon salt
¾ cup shredded Cheddar or American cheese (plus another ¾ cup, optional)

Melt butter or margarine in large skillet and sauté onions until tender. Add veal and 1 tablespoon flour. Simmer, stirring, until tender. Gradually stir in milk, salt and pepper to taste. Simmer for about 15 minutes or until thick, stirring occasionally. Remove from heat and stir in parsley. Set aside. Blend slightly beaten egg yolks with sour cream in large bowl. Stir in remaining flour and ¼ teaspoon salt. Beat egg whites in small bowl until soft peaks form. Fold in beaten egg whites. Spread ½ this mixture into a well-greased 10-inch pie pan. Top with ¾ cup cheese. Bake at 400 degrees for 10 minutes. Remove from oven and spread with veal mixture; spoon remaining egg mixture over top. (Additional ¾ cup cheese may be added at this time, if desired.) Return to oven and continue baking for 10 to 15 minutes or until browned. Serve hot. Yield: 6 servings.
A Friend

VEAL SCALLOPINI

2½ pounds boned veal shoulder
½ cup all-purpose flour
½ teaspoon salt
⅛ teaspoon pepper
½ cup vegetable oil
½ cup minced onions
¾ cup mushrooms
2¼ cups tomato juice
1 teaspoon salt
1 teaspoon sugar
⅛ teaspoon pepper
Hot fluffy rice

Preheat oven to 350 degrees. Cut veal into 1¼-inch cubes and roll lightly in flour combined with ½ teaspoon salt and ⅛ teaspoon pepper. Heat oil in skillet, sauté onions until tender; remove onions to a 2-quart greased casserole. Sauté veal in oil remaining in skillet until brown on all sides. Place veal in casserole along with mushrooms, tomatoes, sugar, salt and pepper. Bake, covered for 1½ hours, or until fork tender. Serve over rice. Yield: 5 to 6 servings.
Gloria DeLambo

SHERRIED VEAL STEAKS

1/4 cup all-purpose flour
1/2 teaspoon salt
1/8 teaspoon freshly ground pepper
2 pounds veal steaks or chops, 1/2-inch thick
4 tablespoons butter
1 tablespoon olive oil
1 cup water
1 chicken bouillon cube
2 tablespoons chopped green onion
1/2 teaspoon dried basil, crumbled
1 (12-ounce) package egg noodles, cooked al dente, drained and buttered

Sauce:

1 cup dairy sour cream
2 tablespoons dry sherry

Combine flour, salt and pepper in shallow dish. Dredge veal in flour mixture, shaking off excess. Melt butter with olive oil in large skillet over medium-high heat. Add veal and brown 3 minutes on each side. Set veal aside. Add water to skillet and bring to boil. Add bouillon cube and stir until dissolved. Mix in green onion and basil. Reduce heat to medium-low. Return veal to skillet. Cover skillet and simmer veal for 30 minutes. Arrange noodles on platter; top with veal. Stir sour cream and sherry into pan juices. Stir until heated through (do not boil). Spoon over veal and serve. Yield: 4 to 6 servings.
Peg O'Shea

VEAL BERTRAND

2 pounds veal round steak
1 (6-ounce) can whole mushrooms, drained
2/3 cup dry sherry
1/4 cup snipped parsley
Dash of garlic powder
6 tablespoons butter or margarine
3 slices Swiss cheese, halved

Cut veal into 6 serving portions; pound to 1/4-inch thickness. Slash fat edges to prevent curling during cooking. Place in a 13x9x2-inch dish. Combine mushrooms, sherry, parsley and garlic powder in small bowl, stirring well. Pour over meat. Marinate for 30 minutes, turning several times. Drain meat, reserving marinade. Melt 3 tablespoons butter or margarine in medium-sized skillet. Sauté 1/2 the veal in melted butter for 3 minutes on each side. Remove to warm platter. Sauté remaining meat. Return all meat to skillet; add marinade and bring to a boil. Reduce heat; place a cheese slice over each piece of meat, cover and heat until cheese melts (about 2 minutes). Transfer meat to warm platter and spoon sauce over all. Serve immediately. Yield: 4 to 6 servings.
Lynne Della Donna

VEAL AND PEPPERS

3 tablespoons olive oil
4 green peppers, cut into 1/4-inch strips
1 large onion, sliced
1 pound veal stew, cubed
1 large can tomatoes, chopped, approximately 4 cups
1/2 teaspoon garlic powder
1 teaspoon salt
Pepper

In a large, deep skillet heat oil. Add peppers and onions. Sauté until tender. Push to one side and add veal. Brown lightly on all sides. Add tomatoes and seasonings. Cover and cook over low heat about 1 hour or until veal is tender. Yield: 4 servings.
Jean Croyle

NEAPOLITAN VEAL

1 pound veal, thinly sliced
1/4 cup all-purpose flour
3 tablespoons butter or margarine
1/4 cup chopped parsley
1 cup fresh mushrooms, sliced
1/2 cup wine

Dredge veal in flour. Melt butter in medium skillet and sauté veal. Stir in parsley, mushrooms and wine. Cover and simmer for 45 minutes or until tender. (Bake in 350 degree oven for 45 minutes, if preferred.) Serve immediately. *This recipe was sent to the United States from Italy in 1880 and has been in use in our family ever since. Yield: 2 to 3 servings.*
Sally Della Donna

VEAL PAPRIKASH

2 pounds veal, cut in 2-inch cubes
4 tablespoons all-purpose flour
4 tablespoons margarine or vegetable shortening
1 medium onion, chopped
3 teaspoons paprika
2 cups water
1 cup dairy sour cream
Salt and pepper to taste

Flour meat. In a large skillet, brown onions until just tender. Add floured meat and paprika and brown. Slowly add water, stirring to blend. Simmer for about 1 hour or until tender. Season with salt and pepper to taste. Add sour cream and simmer for another 4 minutes. Serve over noodles if desired.
Eileen Barlock

VEAL AMELIO

2 pounds veal fillets, cut into 1½-ounce pieces
¼ to ½ cup all-purpose flour
Salt and pepper to taste
2 tablespoons olive oil
½ cup butter
6 tablespoons dry white wine
1 tablespoon lemon juice
1 pound fresh mushrooms, cleaned and sliced

Pound veal thin between two pieces of waxed paper. Sprinkle lightly with flour, salt and pepper. Sauté veal in melted butter and olive oil. Stir in wine, lemon juice and mushrooms and continue to sauté for about 6 minutes or until veal is done. Yield: 4 servings.
Chef Terry Lawrence Clarke

LAMB SHANKS A LA LEMON

3 tablespoons all-purpose flour
1 teaspoon salt
1 teaspoon paprika
½ teaspoon ground pepper
4 lamb shanks, cracked
2 tablespoons vegetable oil
2½ cups water, approximately
2 chicken bouillon cubes
1 bay leaf
6 peppercorns
2 to 3 tablespoons lemon juice
1 clove garlic

Gravy:

3 tablespoons all-purpose flour
¼ cup water

Mix together 3 tablespoons flour, salt, paprika and ground pepper. Coat lamb shanks with mixture. Brown in hot oil in Dutch oven or large skillet; drain off fat. Add 2½ cups water, bouillon cubes, bay leaf, peppercorns, lemon juice and garlic. Stir until cubes dissolve. Cover and simmer 1½ hours, or until meat is tender. (Add more water if necessary.) Remove shanks to serving dish; keep warm. Strain liquid into pint measure, skim off fat and reserve 1½ cups liquid, adding water if necessary to make this amount. To make gravy: blend 3 tablespoons flour and ¼ cup water in pan; stir in reserved liquid. Cook and stir until gravy thickens and boils 2 minutes. Pour over lamb shanks or pass gravy separately and serve at once. Garnish with lemon slices and parsley, if desired. Yield: 4 servings.
Lynne Della Donna

MOIST CRISPY CHICKEN

3 cups crisp rice cereal, crushed
1 teaspoon paprika
½ tablespoon salt
¼ teaspoon pepper
½ cup mayonnaise
1 broiler-fryer chicken, cut up

Combine cereal, paprika, salt and pepper. Brush chicken pieces with mayonnaise. Place crumb mixture in a small paper or plastic bag and add chicken pieces, 1 or 2 at a time, shaking to coat well. Place coated chicken pieces in a greased 13 x 9 x 2-inch baking dish and bake at 425 degrees 40 to 45 minutes, or until chicken is tender. Yield: 6 to 8 servings.
Michele Leahy

ROQUEFORT CHICKEN

1 (4 to 5 pound) chicken, cut into pieces
1 medium onion, chopped
1 teaspoon celery salt
⅛ teaspoon pepper
½ pound mushrooms, sliced
1 cup cooked rice
½ cup slivered almonds
2 tablespoons onion, minced

Place chicken, onion, celery salt and pepper in large kettle with 1 quart water. Bring to a boil over high heat, reduce heat and simmer until chicken is tender (about 45 minutes to 1 hour). Remove chicken from broth and cool. Skin, bone and cut into bite-sized pieces. Place chicken in bottom of a 13x9x2-inch baking dish which has been coated with non-stick cooking spray. Cool broth, skim off fat and reserve for cream sauce. Sauté mushrooms in a little butter in small skillet. Add to chicken, along with rice, almonds and minced onion. Make Cream Sauce. Pour over chicken and bake at 350 degrees for 40 minutes or until hot and bubbly, gently stirring as necessary. Yield: 6 servings.

Cream Sauce:

3 tablespoons butter or margarine
3 tablespoons all-purpose flour
1½ cups chicken broth
1 cup light cream
½ cup Roquefort cheese, cut into small pieces

Melt butter in medium saucepan over low heat and blend in flour with wire whisk. Add broth and cream, stirring constantly. Cook over medium heat until smooth and thickened. Slowly stir in cheese until melted.
Kay McGorray

CHICKEN N' SPINACH

1 chicken breast, halved and skinned
Salt to taste
Pepper to taste
6 tablespoons butter or margarine, divided
1 lemon, quartered
1 clove garlic, chopped
2 tablespoons finely chopped onion
2 cups fresh mushrooms, cleaned and trimmed
White wine, optional
2 cups fresh spinach, washed and trimmed
½ ripe tomato, peeled and cored and cubed

Season chicken with salt and pepper. Arrange in skillet with 3 tablespoons butter. Squeeze lemon wedge over chicken. Cook over medium heat for 10 to 15 minutes or until partially cooked. Sauté garlic and onion in remaining butter until transparent. Slice one mushroom; set aside. Quarter remaining mushrooms and add to onion-garlic mixture. Continue cooking, stirring often, until mushrooms are tender. Turn chicken. Cook for 10 to 15 minutes more or until chicken is done. If pan dries out, splash in a little wine. Add spinach to onion-mushroom mixture. Toss lightly until spinach is wilted and heated through. Push spinach mixture to one side of the pan. Add tomato cubes and the sliced mushroom. Heat through. To serve, mound the spinach on 2 warm plates. Place chicken in the center of each; spoon on mushrooms and tomato cubes. Place lemon wedge on plate for garnish. *This recipe can easily be doubled or tripled.* Yield: 2 servings.
Sue Mahon

SIMPLE CHICKEN STEW

1 (4 to 5 pound) chicken, cut up and skinned
1 (10¾-ounce) can cream of chicken soup
1 cup water
1 cup sliced celery
1 medium-sized onion, chopped
1 teaspoon salt
⅛ teaspoon pepper
½ teaspoon poultry seasoning
4 medium-sized carrots, pared and thickly sliced
¼ cup all-purpose flour
½ cup water

Place first 8 ingredients in a 6 to 8-quart pan. Cover and simmer chicken for 1 hour, stirring occasionally. Add potatoes and carrots. Simmer for an additional 45 minutes or until chicken and vegetables are just tender. To thicken, blend ¼ cup flour and ½ cup water; stir slowly and carefully into the stew. Cook for 10 minutes or until thickened, stirring occasionally. Serve with fresh fruit and crescent dinner rolls. Yield: 4 to 6 servings.
Rosemary Corcoran

KENTUCKY STYLE FRIED CHICKEN

3 pounds chicken pieces
2 packages dry Italian salad dressing mix
3 tablespoons all-purpose flour
2 teaspoons salt
¼ cup lemon juice
2 teaspoons margarine, softened
1 cup vegetable oil
1 cup milk
1½ cups pancake mix
1 teaspoon paprika
½ teaspoon sage
¼ teaspoon pepper

Wipe chicken dry. Make paste out of first 5 ingredients, then brush chicken to coat evenly. Place pieces in bowl, cover and refrigerate for several hours. Heat ½ of oil in large skillet. Combine pancake mix with paprika, sage and pepper. Dip chicken in milk then in the pancake combination, coat well. Dust off excess. Lightly brown each piece about 4 minutes on each side. Place chicken in single layer in shallow pans. Spoon remaining milk over chicken, cover pans with foil. Bake 1 hour at 350 degrees. Uncover and bake 10 minutes more at 400 degrees until crisp. Baste with pan drippings. Yield: 8 servings.
Frances Willson

CHICKEN DIVAN

3 (10-ounce) packages frozen broccoli, thawed
6 whole chicken breasts, cooked, skinned, and boned
3 (10¾-ounce) cans cream of chicken soup
1½ cups mayonnaise
2 tablespoons lemon juice
6 tablespoons sherry
¾ cup shredded sharp Cheddar cheese
¾ cup breadcrumbs
2 tablespoons melted butter or margarine

Cover bottom of 15x10x2-inch baking pan, which has been coated with non-stick cooking spray, with broccoli. Cut chicken into bite-sized pieces and layer over broccoli. Blend soup, mayonnaise, lemon juice and sherry in medium bowl; pour over chicken. Sprinkle with cheese, then breadcrumbs. Drizzle butter or margarine over all. Bake at 350 degrees for 1 hour. Serve hot. *Wonderful!* Yield: 10 to 12 servings.
Betz Spacek

CHICKEN KIEV

3 whole chicken breasts, halved, boned and skinned
6 tablespoons chilled butter
Salt and pepper
2 tablespoons freeze-dried chopped chives
All-purpose flour
1 egg, beaten
½ cup breadcrumbs
Oil for deep-frying

Place each breast half between pieces of waxed paper or plastic wrap; pound with mallet until ¼-inch thick. Sprinkle with salt and pepper to taste, then with chives. Place 1 pat butter in center of each piece. Fold ends in and roll into tight rolls. Dust each roll lightly with flour, then dip into beaten egg and roll in crumbs until evenly coated. Arrange rolls, seam side down, on a baking sheet, cover and refrigerate for 1 hour or more so that coating will adhere well. Heat oil in a deep skillet. Fry rolls, a few at a time, until golden brown and crisp. Place on baking sheet. Bake for 20 minutes at 325 degrees, or cover and refrigerate for baking up to 24 hours later. *This makes an elegant meal.* Yield: 6 servings.
Ursula Bartosik

PECAN CHICKEN WITH DIJON SAUCE

2 whole chicken breasts, halved, skinned and boned
¾ cup butter or margarine, divided
4 tablespoons Dijon mustard, divided
6-ounces pecans, finely ground
2 tablespoons safflower oil
⅔ cup dairy sour cream
1 teaspoon salt
¼ teaspoon freshly ground pepper

Place chicken between sheets of waxed paper. Pound until ¼-inch in thickness. In a small saucepan, melt ½ cup butter over a medium heat. Add 3 tablespoons mustard. Beat with wire whisk until well-blended. Dip chicken into butter-mustard mixture. Dredge in pecans to coat both sides. Place remaining butter in a 10-inch skillet. Add oil. Sauté chicken for 3 minutes per side or until well-browned. Place in a 12x8x2-inch baking dish. Bake at 350 degrees for 20 minutes or until chicken is fork tender. While chicken is baking, stir sour cream into greased skillet, scraping brown particles from the bottom and sides. Add remaining Dijon, salt and pepper. To serve, cover each piece of chicken with ¼ of sour cream sauce. Yield: 4 servings.
Peg O'Shea

CHICKEN AND ARTICHOKE CASSEROLE

4 whole chicken breasts (8 halves)
½ cup all-purpose flour
¼ cup vegetable oil
1 (10¾-ounce) can golden mushroom soup
½ cup sherry
1 tablespoon Worcestershire sauce
½ cup milk
1 (4-ounce) can sliced mushrooms, drained
1 (4½-ounce) can whole artichoke hearts, drained and quartered
1 (16-ounce) can whole tomatoes, drained and quartered
6 or 8 ripe olives
1 (2-ounce) jar diced pimento
¼ cup grated Parmesan cheese
2 or 3 tablespoons parsley, fresh or dried

Separate chicken breasts into halves, wash and pat dry. Dredge in flour and brown in hot oil in large skillet. Remove chicken pieces as they brown and transfer to a greased 13x9x2-inch baking dish. Combine soup, sherry, Worcestershire sauce and milk in small bowl; spoon over chicken breasts. Layer remaining ingredients over sauce in order listed, ending with cheese and parsley. Cover and bake at 350 degrees for 1½ hours, or until hot and bubbly and chicken is tender. *Fabulous!* Yield: 8 servings.
Nicky Cowan

OVEN-FRIED CHICKEN ELEGANT

⅓ cup corn flakes, crushed
2 teaspoons salt
2 teaspoons paprika
¾ teaspoon dried dill weed
2 teaspoons chopped, fresh thyme leaves or ¼ teaspoon dried thyme, crumbled
6 chicken breasts, split in half
2 tablespoons butter
2 tablespoons vegetable oil
¾ cup Riesling or Chenin Blanc wine

Combine first 5 ingredients in a medium-sized plastic bag. Add chicken, one breast at a time, and toss until well coated. Melt butter with oil and place in a 13x9x2-inch glass baking dish. Arrange seasoned chicken, skin side down, in a single layer. Bake, uncovered, for 30 minutes. Turn chicken, add wine and continue baking for 25 to 30 minutes or until the chicken is tender. Serve warm or cold. Yield: 6 servings.
Rosemary Corcoran

LEMONY PAPRIKA CHICKEN

2 pounds chicken breast, skinned, boned and cut in cubes
2/3 cups all-purpose flour
1 teaspoon paprika
1/2 teaspoon onion powder
Salt to taste
Pepper to taste
6 tablespoons butter
Juice of 1 whole lemon

Place flour, paprika, onion powder, salt and pepper into a paper bag. Put cubed chicken into the bag and shake until well-coated. Melt butter in skillet and brown chicken well. Add lemon juice and cook an additional 10 minutes. Serve over rice or noodles. Yield: 4 servings.
Lynne Della Donna

CHICKEN REUBEN

4 chicken breasts, boned, skinned and halved
1 cup French or Thousand Island dressing
1 (16-ounce) can sauerkraut, drained
8 slices Swiss cheese

Place chicken breasts in a 13x9x2-inch baking pan. Pour dressing over chicken. Top with sauerkraut and Swiss cheese. Cover and bake at 350 degrees for 1 hour. Yield: 4 to 6 servings.
Sally Della Donna

GLAZED CHICKEN

12 pieces chicken
Garlic powder (do not use garlic salt)
1 (8-ounce) jar Russian dressing
1 (8-ounce) jar apricot preserves
1 envelope dry onion soup mix

Wash chicken pieces and pat dry; lay flat, skin side up, in baking dish. Sprinkle lightly with garlic powder. Combine remaining ingredients and brush over chicken. Bake at 400 degrees until chicken begins to brown; lower temperature to 325 degrees and bake 1 to 1½ hours, or until tender. Yield: 8 to 10 servings.
Darlene Zembala

CRABMEAT-STUFFED CHICKEN BREASTS

4 chicken breasts, boned and halved
¼ pound mushrooms, chopped
½ cup sliced onions
¼ cup margarine
2 tablespoons all-purpose flour
¼ teaspoon thyme
1 cup chicken broth
½ cup dry sherry
1 (6-ounce) package frozen crabmeat
⅓ cup dry breadcrumbs
⅓ cup chopped parsley
1½ cups shredded Swiss cheese

Pound chicken between waxed paper until ¼-inch in thickness. Sauté mushrooms and onions in margarine until tender. Blend in flour and thyme. Gradually, add broth. Cook over low to medium heat, stirring constantly, until mixture thickens. Combine ¼ cup sauce with crabmeat, breadcrumbs and parsley. Mix lightly. Spread filling on each chicken breast; roll up jellyroll style and place seam side down on a lightly greased 12x8x2-inch pan. Fold cheese into remaining sauce mixture, over low heat, until cheese is melted. Important: Do not stir as sauce will become paste-like. Pour over chicken breasts. Cover and bake at 350 degrees for 15 minutes; uncover and bake an additional 15 minutes or until chicken is fork tender. *This dish has a wonderful flavor and is great to serve for company.* Yield: 4 to 6 servings.
Rita Grennan

EASY CHICKEN PAPRIKA

½ cup all-purpose flour
1 teaspoon salt
⅛ teaspoon pepper
1 (2½ pound) chicken, cut into serving pieces
3 tablespoons vegetable oil
1 tablespoon paprika
1 medium-sized onion, chopped
2 (12-ounce) jars chicken gravy
1 cup diary sour cream
1 (8-ounce) package egg noodles, cooked according to package directions

Combine first 3 ingredients in a shallow bowl. Coat each chicken piece in flour. Fry in oil heated to 375 degrees until browned; turn as necessary. Remove chicken from skillet. Stir paprika, onion and gravy into the pan with drippings. Return chicken to skillet, cover and simmer for 1½ hours. Remove chicken and set aside. Let sauce cool. Blend in sour cream. Return chicken to skillet and heat gently. Serve over freshly cooked noodles. *This dish is great. Has a wonderful flavor!* Yield: 6 servings.
Judy Braun

TASTY CHICKEN PARMESAN

1 envelope onion soup mix
1 (10¾-ounce) can cream of mushroom soup
1 (10¾-ounce) can milk
1¼ cups rice, uncooked
1 soup can white wine
12 pieces of chicken, skinned
Salt to taste
Pepper to taste
¼ cup butter or margarine
Parmesan cheese

Combine first 5 ingredients in a medium-sized bowl. Place in the bottom of a greased 13x9x2-inch baking dish. Arrange chicken over the rice mixture. Salt and pepper to taste. Place a dot of butter on each piece of chicken. Bake at 325 degrees for 1 hour. Sprinkle with Parmesan cheese. Bake an additional 15 to 20 minutes. *Very Tasty!* Yield: 4 to 6.
Betz Spacek

CHEESE-GARLIC OVEN FRIED CHICKEN

½ cup breadcrumbs
¼ cup grated Parmesan cheese
2 tablespoons chopped parsley
1 teaspoon seasoned salt
¼ teaspoon thyme
⅛ teaspoon garlic powder
½ cup butter or margarine, melted
2½ to 3 pounds chicken, cut into serving pieces

Combine the first 6 ingredients in a shallow baking dish. Place butter in separate dish and dip chicken pieces into the butter and then into the crumbs. Arrange in a 13x9x2-inch baking pan. Bake at 375 degrees for 45 minutes. Yield: 4 servings.
Dottie Vanek

CASHEW CHICKEN DELISH

4 whole chicken breasts, boned and skinned
1 (10½-ounce) can cream of chicken soup
2 tablespoons brandy
⅓ cup dairy sour cream
2 green onions, chopped
½ teaspoon paprika
Pepper to taste
¼ cup whole cashews
Fresh chopped parsley

Preheat oven to 400 degrees. Arrange chicken in 13x9x2-inch baking dish. Add a small amount of water to create steam. Cover baking dish with foil and bake 35 minutes. Stir remaining ingredients together in a bowl and pour over chicken. Cover and bake 20 minutes longer. Yield: 6 to 8 servings.
Nicki Cowan

CHICKEN KELLY

6 boneless chicken breasts, cut into bite-sized pieces
2 to 3 eggs, beaten
2 cups breadcrumbs
1 teaspoon salt
1 tablespoon chopped parsley
½ teaspoon garlic powder
Vegetable oil
1 (8-ounce) package fresh mushrooms
6 slices Muenster cheese
1 cup chicken broth

Marinate chicken in the eggs for 2 hours in the refrigerator. Combine breadcrumbs, salt, parsley and garlic powder in a plastic bag. Shake chicken in breadcrumbs and brown in oil. Drain and place chicken in 13x9x2-inch baking dish. Cover with a layer of mushrooms, layer of cheese and top with chicken broth. Bake, covered, at 350 degrees for 45 minutes. This can be made up ahead of time, but do not pour chicken broth on until just before baking. Yield: 6 servings.
Mary Sims

BEAN-DRESSED CHICKEN

4 whole chicken breasts
2 (10-ounce) packages frozen green beans
1 (16-ounce) package bread stuffing mix, crumbled
2 (10¾-ounce) cans cream of celery soup
1 soup can milk

Bake chicken breasts in a pan with sufficient milk to cover bottom of pan for 1 hour, or until tender, at 350 degrees. Cool chicken; remove skin and bones and chop into small pieces. Cook beans until almost tender. Prepare stuffing mix according to package directions. Place ½ the stuffing mixture in the bottom of a greased 13x9x2-inch baking pan, patting mixture down lightly. Arrange chicken over dressing layer. Combine soup with milk and pour over chicken. Spread beans over soup mixture and spread remaining dressing mix over all. Bake at 350 degrees for 45 minutes. May be made 24 hours ahead and refrigerated. Allow a little more baking time. Yield: 8 to 10 servings.
Kathy Pilny

CHICKEN AND BRIE MORNAY

4 boneless chicken breast halves, skinned and slightly flattened
4 wedges Brie cheese, rind removed
4 whole canned artichoke hearts, well drained
Mornay Sauce (recipe follows)

Wrap a wedge of cheese around each artichoke heart. Place this in center of each flattened chicken breast and wrap chicken around it. Place chicken breast, seam side down, in a baking dish which has been coated with non-stick cooking spray. Pour Mornay Sauce over chicken, cover, and bake at 350 degrees for about 25 minutes. Uncover and continue baking for 20 to 30 minutes, or until chicken is fork-tender. Yield: 4 servings

Mornay Sauce:

2 tablespoons butter or margarine
2 tablespoons all-purpose flour
1 cup milk
3 tablespoons heavy cream
1-2 tablespoons white wine
Salt and pepper
2 - 3 tablespoons grated Swiss cheese

Melt butter or margarine in saucepan over low heat. Blend in flour using small wire whisk. Remove from heat and slowly add milk, blending until sauce is smooth. Return to heat and stir in cream and wine. Cook slowly, over low heat, stirring constantly, until sauce is smooth and thick. Remove from heat and gently fold in cheese. Salt and pepper to taste. Do not beat sauce after cheese is added or it will become a thick paste.
Paula Knight

LEMON ROAST CHICKEN

12 chicken pieces
Salt and pepper
2 tablespoons butter
1 teaspoon dried oregano
2 cloves garlic, minced
1/4 cup water
3 tablespoons lemon juice

Season chicken with salt and pepper; brown in butter and arrange in crockery slow-cooker. Sprinkle oregano and garlic over top. Stir water into drippings in skillet and add to cooker. Cover and cook on low heat setting 8 hours, adding lemon juice for final hour. Yield: 6 to 8 servings.
Beth Spacek

GOLDIE'S GOURMET CHICKEN

6 chicken breasts, boned and skinned
Garlic powder
Onion powder
Salt and pepper
6 stalks fresh broccoli
6 slices mozzarella cheese
2 cups packaged stuffing crumbs
½ cup margarine, melted
1 (10¾-ounce) can cream of chicken soup
Parsley

Preheat oven to 350 degrees. Sprinkle chicken breasts with garlic powder, onion powder, salt and pepper to taste. Wrap each chicken breast around a broccoli stalk and secure with wooden picks. Arrange in baking dish, laying a slice of cheese over each breast. Combine crumbs with melted margarine and spread mixture over cheese slices. Mix soup with ½ to ¾ cup water and pour over chicken. Cover dish with foil, making a few small slits in the foil. Bake 1 hour. Uncover dish and bake 10 minutes longer. Sprinkle with parsley. *A nice company dish to prepare ahead of time.* Yield: 6 servings.
Loe Goldwasser

STUFFING TOPPED CHICKEN

4 boneless chicken breasts, skinned and halved
8 slices Swiss cheese
½ pound fresh mushrooms, sliced (optional)
1 (10¾-ounce) can cream of chicken soup, undiluted
¼ cup dry white wine
1 (8-ounce) package herb-seasoned stuffing mix, prepared according to package directions
¼ cup butter or margarine

Place chicken breasts in a buttered 13x9x2-inch baking dish. Top with cheese and mushrooms. Combine soup and wine; blend well. Spoon mixture evenly over the chicken. Spread prepared stuffing over the soup. Drizzle with butter. Bake at 350 degrees for 45 to 55 minutes. Yield: 8 servings.
Kay Kelly

CHICKEN TORTILLA CASSEROLE

4 chicken breasts, skinned
½ cup water
½ teaspoon salt
¼ teaspoon pepper
1 cup chicken broth
1 (10¾-ounce) can cream of mushroom soup, undiluted
2 (7-ounce) cans green chili salsa
1 cup milk
1 (12-ounce) package corn tortillas
1 (6¼-ounce) can pitted ripe olives, sliced
1 pound Cheddar cheese, shredded
1 tablespoon finely chopped onion

Place first 4 ingredients in a large skillet or Dutch oven with a tight-fitting lid. Cover and bring to a boil over medium heat. Reduce heat and simmer for 1 hour or until tender. Remove chicken and reserve the broth, adding water as needed to make 1 cup. Cut chicken into bite-sized pieces. Combine reserved broth, soup, salsa, and milk. Mix until well blended. Cut tortillas into 2-inch squares. Arrange in the bottom of a 13x9x2-inch buttered casserole dish. Spread ½ chicken over tortillas followed by a layer of ½ the olives. Repeat layering. Pour soup mixture evenly over the casserole. Top with cheese and onion. Refrigerate for several hours or overnight. Bake at 350 degrees for 1 hour. Yield: 8 to 10 servings.
Thomas More Program

CHAUTAUQUA CHICKEN LUSH

3 cups chicken breast, cooked, boned, skinned and chopped
1 cup mayonnaise
1 (10¾-ounce) can cream of mushroom soup
½ teaspoon curry powder
1 (8-ounce) can water chestnuts, drained and chopped
1 cup butter breadcrumbs or crushed potato chips
Sprinkle of paprika
¼ cup slivered almonds

Thoroughly mix the first 5 ingredients and spread evenly in a greased, 1½-quart baking dish. Scatter crumbs or chips over the chicken mixture. Sprinkle lightly with paprika and top with almonds. Bake at 350 degrees for 45 minutes. Yield: 4 to 6 servings.
Ruth Hilovsky

CHICKEN CACCIATORE

1 (2½ to 3 pound) fryer, cut into serving pieces
Salt to taste
Pepper to taste
Flour
¼ cup vegetable or olive oil
1 clove garlic, finely chopped
1 large onion, chopped
2 green bell peppers, seeded and cut into 1-inch strips
2 cups tomatoes, juice strained
1 pimento, chopped
½ cup white wine
½ teaspoon oregano
1 cup sliced mushrooms

Lightly dust chicken pieces with seasoned flour. Brown chicken in oil over medium-high heat for 10 minutes or until well-browned on all sides. Add garlic, onion and green pepper. Cook for 5 minutes or until vegetables are browned. Add tomatoes, pimento, wine and oregano. Reduce heat and simmer, covered, for 45 minutes or until chicken is tender. Add mushrooms and simmer for an additional 30 minutes or until sauce has thickened. Serve over rice or thin spaghetti. Yield: 4 to 6 servings.
Rosemary Corcoran

CHICKEN AND WILD RICE

5 tablespoons butter or margarine, divided
1 (6¾-ounce) package wild/long grain rice with seasonings
2 chicken breasts, split
1 small onion, chopped
4 stalks celery, sliced
4 carrots, peeled and sliced
1 (13¾-ounce) can chicken broth
Garlic powder to taste
Pepper to taste

Sauté wild rice in 3 tablespoons butter over medium heat for 10 to 15 minutes. Sauté chicken breasts in remaining butter for 10 minutes or until well-browned on all sides. Add onion, celery and carrots. Sauté until partially cooked. A small amount of water or chicken broth may be added, if needed. Remove chicken, cool, debone and cut into bite-sized pieces. Return to skillet. Add rice. Sprinkle with seasoning packet from rice. Pour chicken broth over entire mixture. Cover and simmer over low to medium heat for 20 to 25 minutes or until liquid is absorbed. More water can be added if rice is not tender. Yield: 4 servings.
Lill Hanlon

SWEET AND SOUR PORK

1 pound pork shoulder, cut in bite-size pieces
1 large egg
¾ cup water
1 cup all-purpose flour
½ teaspoon salt
2 cups vegetable oil, for frying

In a bowl, combine egg and water; beat in flour and salt until batter is smooth. Set aside for 1 hour. In a wok, heat oil to 400 degrees. Dip pork pieces into batter and place in hot oil. Cook for 5 minutes, until cooked through and golden brown. Remove to paper toweling to drain. Keep warm, but do not cover.

Sweet and Sour Sauce:

1 large onion, cut into 8 wedges and separated
1 carrot, sliced into ⅛-inch slices
2 green peppers, cut into 1-inch squares
2 tablespoons sugar
2 tablespoons soy sauce
2 tablespoons dry sherry
2 tablespoons vinegar
1 tablespoon cornstarch in 2 tablespoons cold water
1 cup cubed canned pineapple, well-drained

In wok, stir-fry onion, carrot slices and green peppers in small amount of oil for 2 to 3 minutes. In a bowl, combine remaining ingredients, except pineapple, and blend well. Add to vegetables in wok. Add pineapple chunks and heat until sauce boils and is thick. Pour over pork and serve at once. Yield: 4 servings.
Patti Lovejoy

STIR-FRIED PORK

⅔ pound pork loin
1 teaspoon minced garlic
1 tablespoon soy sauce
½ tablespoon sugar
1 tablespoon rice wine
1 tablespoon cornstarch
2 tablespoons soy sauce
1 teaspoon sugar
¼ teaspoon monosodium glutamate
½ cup 2-inch sections green onion

Remove any fat from pork; cut into ⅓-inch thick slices. With the blunt edge of a cleaver, pound lightly to tenderize. Toss with garlic, soy sauce, sugar, wine and cornstarch; set aside for 30 minutes. Heat wok or skillet and 3 tablespoons oil. Fry pork on both sides until golden brown, adding more oil if necessary. Stir in soy sauce, sugar, MSG and green onion. Toss to combine and serve. Yield: 4 servings.
Mrs. Joe Wolf

BEEF CHOW MEIN

1/4 pound beef, cut into 1/4-inch strips
2 teaspoons soy sauce
2 teaspoons cornstarch
1 celery stalk, sliced
1 cup bean sprouts
1/2 pound noodles (may use very thin spaghetti)
1 tablespoon cornstarch dissolved in 2 tablespoons cold water
1/2 cup water or beef broth

Marinate beef in combined soy sauce and cornstarch for 15 to 20 minutes. Set aside. Cook noodles or spaghetti in boiling, salted water until done and rinse with cold water. After draining noodles, place in paper towel to absorb excess water. Heat 1 tablespoon oil in wok and stir-fry noodles until golden brown. Remove from wok. Stir-fry celery and bean sprouts in 1 tablespoon heated oil for 2 minutes and remove from wok. Stir-fry beef in 1 tablespoon heated oil for 3 minutes or until done. Add cornstarch mixture and water or beef broth to beef. Heat and stir until sauce is thickened. Add vegetables and noodles to beef and mix well. This recipe can also be Chicken Chow Mein, using 1/4 pound chicken, cut into 1/4-inch strips and using 1/2 cup water or chicken broth. Yield: 2 servings.
A Friend

STEAK-VEGETABLE POCKETS

3/4 pounds top round steak
1 1/2 cups thinly sliced broccoli
1 small carrot, thinly sliced
1 small onion, sliced
1/2 green pepper, cut into strips
3 tablespoons vegetable oil
8 pea pods, halved crosswise
6 fresh mushrooms, sliced
1 small tomato, chopped
3 tablespoons soy sauce
1 1/2 teaspoons cornstarch
4 pita bread rounds, halved
1/2 cup shredded Cheddar cheese

Thinly slice beef across the grain into bite-sized strips; set aside. Stir-fry broccoli, carrot, onion and green pepper in wok with 1 tablespoon hot oil for 7 minutes. Add pea pods, mushrooms and tomato; stir-fry for 2 minutes. Remove vegetables. Add beef and remaining oil. Stir-fry for 3 minutes. Combine 1/4 cup cold water and soy sauce. Blend in cornstarch. Add to wok. Cook, stirring constantly, for 5 to 8 minutes or until bubbly. Return vegetables to wok; heat through. Spoon mixture into pita bread. Top with cheese. Yield: 4 servings.
Patti Lovejoy

BEEF WITH SNOW PEA PODS AND MUSHROOMS

½ pound steak, sliced in thin strips
4 teaspoons soy sauce, divided
1 tablespoon plus 2 teaspoons cornstarch, divided
½ cup canned mushrooms or ¼ pound fresh mushrooms, cut in T-shape
2 tablespoons vegetable oil, divided
1 small onion, thinly sliced
8 snow pea pods, strings removed
½ cup chicken broth
2 tablespoons water

Marinate steak in 2 teaspoons soy sauce with 2 teaspoons cornstarch for 10 to 15 minutes; set aside. If using fresh mushrooms, boil whole for 2 to 3 minutes before slicing. Heat 1 tablespoon oil to 375 degrees in wok. Add onion, mushrooms and pea pods; stir-fry for 3 minutes or until pea pods become bright green. Remove from oil; set aside. Stir-fry steak in 1 tablespoon oil for 3 minutes. Add soy sauce, broth, water and cornstarch mixed with water. Heat until sauce is thickened. Return vegetables to wok. Mix well and heat through. Serve over steamed rice. Yield: 4 servings.
Michele Cotner

BEEF SUBGUM

½ pound beef, thinly sliced
2 teaspoons soy sauce
2 teaspoons cornstarch
1 small onion, sliced
1 small green pepper, sliced
½ cup water chestnuts, sliced
½ cup mushrooms, sliced
1 celery stalk, sliced
1 carrot, cut into matchstick size
2 tablespoons vegetable oil
1 tablespoon cornstarch dissolved in ¾ cup water or beef broth
1 teaspoon salt

Marinate beef in combined soy sauce and cornstarch for 15 minutes. Set aside. Stir-fry vegetables in 1 tablespoon of oil for 3 minutes. Remove from wok. Heat 1 tablespoon oil in wok and stir-fry beef for 3 minutes or until done. Add cornstarch mixture and salt. Cook until sauce is thickened. Add vegetables to wok and mix well. Yield: 2 servings.
Michele Cotner

CHINESE CHICKEN AND BEAN SPROUTS

2/3 pound chicken meat
1/2 teaspoon salt
1/2 teaspoon rice wine
1 egg white
2 teaspoons cornstarch
1/2 pound bean sprouts
3 cups vegetable oil
1 teaspoon rice wine
1/2 teaspoon salt
1/4 teaspoon monosodium glutamate
1/4 teaspoon sugar
1/4 teaspoon black pepper
1/4 teaspoon sesame oil
1 1/2 tablespoons water
1 teaspoon cornstarch

Cut chicken into shreds and toss with salt, rice wine and egg white. Let stand 20 minutes. Add 2 teaspoons cornstarch. Remove discolored ends from sprouts and rinse; place in cold water. Heat oil in wok for deep frying. Fry chicken 1 minute over medium heat, until color changes, stirring to separate shreds. Remove and drain. Drain all but 1 tablespoon oil from wok. Drain sprouts and briefly stir-fry. Add chicken, wine, salt, MSG, sugar, pepper, sesame oil, water and cornstarch. Stir fry quickly and serve. Yield: 6 servings.
Mrs. Joe Wolf

ORIENTAL MUSHROOM CHICKEN

4 chicken breast halves, boned and cut into 1/2-inch cubes
1/4 cup dry white wine
1/2 teaspoon salt
2 scallions, cut into 1/2-inch slices
1/2 cup celery, cut into 1/2-inch cubes
1 tablespoon vegetable oil
12 snow pea pods, strings removed
1/4 pound mushrooms, sliced
6 water chestnuts, sliced
1/2 cup chicken broth
1 tablespoon cornstarch, dissolved in 2 tablespoons cold water
1/2 teaspoon salt
Whole, blanced almonds (optional)

Toss chicken cubes with wine and salt, set aside. Heat oil in wok, stir-fry scallions and celery 1 minute; push aside. Add snow peas; stir-fry 2 minutes and push aside. Add mushrooms and water chestnuts; stir-fry 1 to 2 minutes and push aside. Add chicken and wine; stir-fry 2 to 3 minutes or until chicken is tender. Stir to mix chicken and vegetables. Stir together broth, cornstarch mixture and salt. Add slowly to mixture in wok and heat until thickened and clear. Serve over rice, sprinkling almonds over top. Yield: 4 servings.
Patti Lovejoy
Michele Cotner

EGG FOO YOUNG

4 eggs
1 tablespoon water
½ teaspoon salt
1 teaspoon soy sauce
4 cups bean sprouts
2 green onions, cut into 1-inch length
2 cups vegetable oil

Sauce:

1 cup chicken broth
1½ tablespoons cornstarch
½ teaspoon sugar
1 tablespoon soy sauce

Preheat oil in wok or frying pan (use enough oil to cover bottom of pan or a little more). Beat eggs with water, salt and soy sauce. Add bean sprouts and green onion, then chop in bowl. Fry egg mixture like an omelet, until both sides are golden brown. Keep warm in oven until sauce is made. To make sauce, combine ingredients in small sauce pan. Heat and stir until sauce is thickened. Spoon over egg foo young. Yield: 4 to 6 servings.
Michele Cotner

ALMOND DING CHICKEN

2 chicken breasts, halved, boned, thinly sliced
2 teaspoons soy sauce
2 teaspoons cornstarch
2 tablespoons vegetable oil
2 celery stalks, cut into ½-inch cubes
2 bok choy stalks, cut into ½-inch cubes
1 carrot, cut into ½-inch cubes
1 teaspoon salt
½ cup water or chicken broth
1 tablespoon cornstarch dissolved in 2 tablespoons water
½ cup water
¼ cup of whole almonds

Marinate chicken in combined soy sauce and cornstarch for 10 to 15 minutes. Set aside. Heat 1 tablespoon oil in wok and add vegetables. Stir-fry for 3 minutes, then add salt, ½ cup of water or chicken broth and cook, covered for 3 more minutes. Remove vegetables from wok. Stir-fry chicken in 1 tablespoon oil in wok, until brown. Add cornstarch mixture and water. Heat and stir until sauce thickens. Return vegetables to wok and mix well. Garnish with almonds. Yield: 4 to 6 servings.
Michele Cotner

ZUCCHINI SHRIMP

1½ tablespoons butter
1 tablespoon vegetable oil
1 cup chopped zucchini
1 cup minced onion
½ pound fresh baby shrimp
1 clove garlic, crushed

Melt butter and oil in wok or electric skillet. Add zucchini, onion and garlic. Cook, stirring frequently, until tender, 4 to 5 minutes. Remove garlic. Add shrimp and cook 3 to 5 minutes, or until shrimp are pink. Serve over rice pilaf. Yield: 4 servings.
Maureen May

ITALIAN SAUSAGE AND ZUCCHINI STIR-FRY

1 pound sweet Italian sausage, sliced into ¾-inch pieces
½ cup chopped onion
4 cups shredded, unpared zucchini
1 teaspoon lemon juice
¼ teaspoon salt
¼ teaspoon hot liquid pepper
¼ cup grated Parmesan cheese

Brown sausage over medium heat, stirring occasionally. Pour off excess fat. Add onions, cover and cook over low heat for 5 minutes. Add remaining ingredients, except cheese. Cook, uncovered, for 5 minutes, stirring occasionally. Sprinkle with Parmesan cheese before serving. *This makes a meal with salad and garlic bread.* Yield: 4 to 5 servings.
Rosemary Corcoran

HAM FRIED RICE

3 cups cold boiled rice (prepared 1 day ahead and chilled)
½ cup cooked ham, cut into matchstick size
1 egg omelet, cut into matchstick size
1 tablespoon soy sauce
1 tablespoon vegetable oil
1 green onion minced

Heat 1 tablespoon oil in wok and stir-fry rice for 5 minutes. Add ham and egg and continue to stir-fry until hot. Add salt and soy sauce. Garnish with green onion. Yield: 4 to 6 servings.
Kate Martin

THE SIDE CAR

Dinner Accompaniments

ASPARAGUS IN AMBUSH

2 pounds asparagus
2 to 4 thin slices of ham or dried beef
¼ cup butter
¼ cup all-purpose flour
¼ teaspoon salt
¼ teaspoon pepper
1 cup milk
¼ teaspoon dry mustard
½ cup Cheddar cheese

Remove stalks from asparagus as far down as they snap easily. Wash well, tie whole stalks in a bundle with string and cook upright in a narrow, deep pan or coffee pot. Cook, covered, in 1-inch boiling, salted water for 10 to 20 minutes or until tender. Catch string with fork when lifting out of water. Roll cooked stalks in ham - 2 to 3 stalks for each piece of ham. Broil until browned. Melt butter over low heat in a heavy saucepan. Blend flour and seasonings. Cook over low heat, stirring constantly, until the mixture is smooth and bubbly. Remove from heat and stir in milk. Add cheese. Bring to a boil, stirring constantly, and boil for 1 minute. Pour over broiled servings of asparagus and ham. Yield: 2 to 4 servings.
Lenore Sims

CARROT, APPLE AND RAISIN CASSEROLE

¾ cup raisins
¼ cup honey
¾ teaspoon ground cinnamon
½ teaspoon salt
1 lemon
1 large apple, thinly sliced
3 cups carrots, thinly sliced
Butter or margarine
Chopped parsley

Combine raisins, honey, cinnamon and salt in large bowl. Cut lemon into halves and add juice from ½ lemon to mixture in bowl. Slice remaining lemon half and set aside. Add apples and carrots to mixture and toss to mix well. Spoon into greased 2-quart casserole. Arrange sliced lemon over top, cover, and bake at 400 degrees for 1 hour or until carrots are just tender. Dot with butter and sprinkle with parsley immediately upon removing from oven. Serve. Any leftover casserole may be refrigerated and served cold as a relish the next day. Yield: 6 servings.
Rita Grennan

CABBAGE AND SPATZLE

Spatzle:

4 eggs, beaten
$1/2$ cup milk
$1/2$ cup water
$2 1/2$ cups all-purpose flour
1 teaspoon salt

Combine ingredients in a medium-sized mixing bowl. Beat with a wooden spoon until bubbly. Do not use an electric mixer. Fill a large saucepan about $1/2$ full of water. Bring to a boil over high heat. Salt lightly and reduce heat until water simmers. Spread a small portion of batter over a salad plate. Cut small shreds of batter using quick strokes with the point of a butter knife or the side of a teaspoon. Let shreds drop into simmering water. Dip knife or spoon into the hot water after several strokes to keep the blade clean. As spatzle come to the surface, they are done. Skim spatzle from the pan into a colander to drain.

Cabbage:

$1/2$ cup butter or margarine
1 medium-sized head of cabbage, shredded
1 medium-sized onion, chopped (optional)
Salt to taste
Pepper to taste

In a large skillet, melt butter or margarine over low heat. Add cabbage and onion to butter. Cook over medium heat until tender and slightly browned, stirring occasionally. Add drained spatzle and mix together. Season with salt and pepper to taste. Yield: 6 to 8 servings.
Eileen Barlock

HONEY CARROTS WITH BACON

$3/4$ cups water
$3 1/2$ cups sliced carrots
$1 1/2$ tablespoons butter
4 slices bacon, cooked and crumbled
2 tablespoons sliced scallions
1 tablespoon honey
1 tablespoon lemon juice
1 teaspoon bay leaves
$1/2$ teaspoon pepper

Bring water to a boil over medium-high heat. Add carrots, simmer, stirring occasionally, for 10 to 12 minutes or until crisp and tender. Drain. Melt butter. Add carrots and remaining ingredients. Mix until well-blended. Cook, covered, over medium heat for 5 to 7 minutes or until heated through. This recipe has about 100 calories per servings. Yield: 6 servings.
Jeanette Lazzaro

SKILLET GREEN BEAN PIE

1/4 cup chopped onion
2 tablespoons vegetable oil
2 (10-ounce) packages frozen French-style green beans, thawed and well-drained
1 (15-ounce) can tomato sauce
2 tablespoons sliced green onions
1 teaspoon salt
1/8 teaspoon pepper
6 eggs, beaten
1 cup shredded sharp Cheddar cheese (8-ounces)
2 tablespoons chopped parsley

In large heavy skillet, sauté chopped onion in oil until tender. Add beans and tomato sauce. Cover and cook 5 minutes, stirring occasionally. Add green onion, salt and pepper to beaten eggs. Set aside. When cooking time is completed for beans and sauce, uncover and sprinkle cheese over bean mixture. Pour egg mixture over cheese in skillet. Cover and cook 10 minutes or until eggs are firm. Uncover. Let stand 10 minutes before serving. Sprinkle with parsley. Serve from skillet. Yield: 4 servings.
Kay McGorray

CRUNCHY HERBED BEANS

1 pound green beans
1/2 cup water
1/2 teaspoon basil
1/2 teaspoon marjoram
1/2 teaspoon chervil
1 tablespoon chopped fresh parsley
2 teaspoon chopped chives
1/8 teaspoon savory
1/8 teaspoon thyme
1 small onion, chopped
1 clove garlic, minced
2 tablespoons vegetable oil
1/2 cup sunflower seeds
1/2 teaspoon salt
1/4 teaspoon pepper

Cook beans in water 10 minutes, covered, until tender-crisp. Combine herbs in a small bowl. Sauté onion and garlic in oil. Add herbs and sunflower seeds. Add beans, salt and pepper and toss lightly. Yield: 4 to 6 servings.
Nicki Cowan

SUNSHINE CARROTS

3 pounds carrots
1 cup peach preserves
2 tablespoons butter or margarine, melted

Pare, slice and cook carrots; drain. Place in large skillet. Combine preserves and melted butter; spoon evenly over carrots. Cook gently 15 minutes, or until heated through (carrots may be baked at 350 degree oven for 15 minutes). Yield: 12 servings.
Ursula Bartosik

HUNGARIAN GREEN BEANS

2 (17-ounce) cans green beans, drained
2 cups medium white sauce
1 small onion, chopped
2 tablespoons minced parsely
¼ teaspoon paprika
Salt to taste
Pepper to taste
2 egg yolks, slightly beaten
1 (4-ounce) can mushrooms with liquid
Buttered breadcrumbs

Spread drained green beans in a 2-quart baking dish. Mix white sauce with the next 7 ingredients and pour over the beans. Top with breadcrumbs. Bake, uncovered, at 350 degrees for 30 minutes. Yield: 6 servings.
Mary Sims

BROCCOLI DISH

1 (8-ounce) package stuffing mix
½ cup butter
2 (10-ounce) packages frozen, chopped broccoli, parboiled
1 (6-ounce) can French fried onion rings
1 cup grated Cheddar cheese
2 (10¾-ounce) cans cream of mushroom soup
Almonds, if desired

Combine stuffing and butter. In a greased, 1½ quart casserole, layer ½ of the ingredients in the following order: broccoli, onion rings, cheese, stuffing mixture and mushroom soup. Repeat layers reversing the soup and stuffing mix layer. Top with almonds, if desired. Bake at 325 degrees for 45 minutes. Yield: 6 to 8 servings.
Kathy Cocco

SESAME CAULIFLOWER

2 tablespoons butter or margarine
2 tablespoons all-purpose flour
1 cup chicken broth or bouillon
2 teaspoons lemon juice
1 large head cauliflower, boiled in lemon water
2 tablespoons sesame seeds

Melt butter in a small saucepan over medium heat. Slowly, add the flour, stirring constantly, until well-mixed. Gradually, add broth and lemon juice. Cook and stir until mixture thickens. Pour over cooked cauliflower. Sprinkle with sesame seeds. Yield: 6 to 8 servings.
Lucille Phillips

SAVORY BROCCOLI CASSEROLE

1 bunch fresh broccoli or 2 (10-ounce) packages frozen chopped broccoli
2 eggs
½ cup milk
1 (10¾-ounce) can cream of celery soup, undiluted
1 cup mayonnaise or salad dressing
1 cup shredded sharp Cheddar cheese
Buttered cracker crumbs

Cut broccoli into 1-inch pieces. Cook according to package directions for 10 minutes or until tender. Drain. Combine next 5 ingredients and stir into cooked broccoli. Pour mixture into a greased, 2-quart casserole and sprinkle with cracker crumbs. Bake at 350 degrees for 30 to 40 minutes or until golden brown. Let cool 15 minutes before serving. Yield: 6 to 8 servings.
Lynne Della Donna

MUSHROOM AND CHEESE STUFFED PEPPERS

4 tablespoons vegetable oil
1 pint fresh mushrooms, cleaned and sliced
¼ pound grated Parmesan cheese (½ cup)
3 eggs, slightly beaten
1 pound shredded Swiss cheese
¼ cup snipped parsley
½ cup finely chopped celery
6 large green peppers

Sauté mushrooms in 2 tablespoons oil until browned in small skillet. Beat eggs and add Parmesan cheese; stir to make a paste. Drain cooled mushrooms on paper toweling and add to egg mixture along with Swiss cheese, parsley and celery. Mix well. Slice green peppers into halves, length-wise; remove seeds and membranes and rinse well. Spoon cheese mixture into pepper halves and place in a greased 13x9x2-inch baking pan. Pour in ½ cup water mixed with remaining 2 tablespoons oil. Cover with aluminum foil and bake at 350 degrees for 35 minutes. Yield: 6 servings.
Rosemary Corcoran

POTATOES IN OLIVE SAUCE

6 pared medium potatoes, cooked and drained
2 cups dairy sour cream
¼ cup finely chopped onions
2 tablespoons finely chopped pimento-stuffed olives
1 teaspoon salt
½ teaspoon pepper
½ teaspoon paprika
1 tablespoon snipped parsley
4 pimento-stuffed olives, sliced

Cut cooled potatoes into ½-inch cubes. Combine potatoes, sour cream, onions, chopped olives, salt and pepper in skillet; heat over medium heat, stirring frequently, until cream bubbles and potatoes are heated through. Pour into serving dish, garnish with paprika, parsley and sliced olives. Yield: 6 servings.
Hollis Hura, Registered Dietitian, Parmadale

GOLDEN BAKED MUSHROOM CASSEROLE

1 pound mushrooms, coarsely chopped
2 small onions, chopped
3 tablespoons butter or margarine
2 eggs
⅔ cup fine dry breadcrumbs
¾ cup milk
¾ cup light cream
2 teaspoons salt
¼ teaspoon pepper

Sauté onions in butter until golden. In a 1½-quart casserole, beat eggs, then mix in crumbs, milk, cream, salt and pepper, until crumbs are liquified. Blend in mushrooms and onions. Bake, uncovered, at 350 degrees for 60 to 70 minutes, or until golden and set. Good as a vegetable with chicken or fish. Yield: 8 servings.
Lenore Sims
Mary Sims

RICE-MUSHROOM BAKE

4 tablespoons margarine
1 cup regular uncooked rice
1 (7-ounce) can mushrooms, drained
1 (10¾-ounce) can condensed beef bouillon
1 (10¾-ounce) can condensed onion soup

In a 1½-quart ovenproof dish, sauté rice and mushrooms in margarine until rice is browned. Add bouillon and soup; cover and bake at 350 degrees 50 minutes. Remove cover and stir. Bake, uncovered, 10 minutes longer. Yield: 6 servings.
Rosemary Balchak

PEROGIES

3 cups all-purpose flour
1 teaspoon salt
2 eggs
½ cup water
½ to ¾ cup dairy sour cream

Combine all ingredients in a bowl, blending well. Add sufficient sour cream to make a rollable dough. Roll out on floured surface to ½-inch thickness. Cut circles from dough with a large water glass. Fill center of each circle with about 1 tablespoon filling; fold edges over and pinch edges to seal (dip fingertip in water and touch to edges). Drop perogies into a large saucepot of boiling water. Perogies are done when they float to the surface. Remove with slotted spoon and drain in a colander. Serve with melted butter. To freeze, spread drained perogies on linen towels and allow to dry. Place in freezer bags or containers. To serve frozen perogie, drop into boiling water and allow to float to surface.

Filling:

6 medium potatoes, boiled and drained
1 cup processed cheese food, shredded

Mash potatoes and season with salt and pepper. Add cheese to hot potatoes; stir to blend.
Judy Porter
Eileen Barlock

POTATO PANCAKES

5 medium raw potatoes, grated
1 teaspoon salt
⅛ teaspoon pepper
⅛ teaspoon garlic powder
1 medium onion, minced
1 egg
3 teaspoons all-purpose flour

Combine all ingredients in a bowl. Batter darkens as it stands so it should be used promptly. Using about 2 tablespoons batter for each pancake, fry in hot shortening until crisp. Turn and fry other side until crisp. Serve hot with sour cream.
Eileen Barlock

CREAM POTATOES

8 to 10 medium-sized potatoes, parboiled and cooled
2 cups whipping cream
Seasoned salt

Chill and peel potatoes. Grate potatoes into a buttered, 13x9x2-inch baking dish to cover the bottom of the dish. Sprinkle with seasoned salt. Continue in this manner until all potatoes are used. Pour whipping cream over the potatoes, distributing evenly over the mixture. Refrigerate, covered, overnight. Bake, uncovered, at 350 degrees for about 45 minutes or until mixture is bubbling and browned on top. *These are so easy and wonderful!* Yield: 6 to 8 servings.
Mary Sims

SPECIAL POTATOES

2 (12-ounce) packages frozen hash-brown potatoes, thawed
1 (2.8-ounce) can fried onion rings
1/2 cup melted butter
1 teaspoon salt
1/8 teaspoon pepper
1 (10 3/4-ounce) can cream of mushroom soup
1/2 soup can milk

Combine all ingredients well in a 2-quart casserole. Bake, covered, at 375 degrees 25 minutes. Uncover and bake 5 minutes longer. Yield: 6 servings.
Dorothy Loebs

ONION CASSEROLE

2 tablespoons butter
2 tablespoons all-purpose flour
1 cup chicken broth
1 (5 1/3-ounce) can of evaporated milk
4 cups sweet onion wedges
1/2 cup slivered almonds
1/2 teaspoon salt
1/2 teaspoon pepper
1 cup or less breadcrumbs
1/2 cup grated Parmesan cheese

Melt butter in a saucepan. Stir in flour to form a paste. Gradually stir in broth and evaporated milk, stirring constantly. Continue to cook over medium heat while stirring constantly until mixture begins to thicken and becomes smooth. Add onions, almonds and seasonings. Pour into a buttered, 1 1/2-quart casserole. Cover with breadcrumbs and cheese. Bake at 375 degrees for 30 minutes. Yield: 6 to 8 servings.
B.J. Arth

POTATOES POCATELLO

8 to 10 potatoes, boiled and cooled
1 (16-ounce) processed cheese loaf
1 medium onion, chopped
1 (2-ounce) jar pimentoes, drained and chopped
2 slices bread, cubed
2 to 3 tablespoons parsley
Garlic salt to taste
¾ cup margarine, melted

Cube potatoes, leaving skins on. Arrange in bottom of a greased 13 x 9 x 2-inch baking dish. Cube cheese and arrange over potatoes. Scatter onions, then pimento, then bread cubes over cheese layer. Sprinkle with parsley and garlic salt. Drizzle margarine over all and cover baking dish with foil. Bake at 350 degrees 35 to 45 minutes, until cheese is melted and top is browned. Remove foil for final 15 minutes of baking time. Yield: 8 to 10 servings.
JoAnn Balchak

COTTAGE POTATOES

10 medium-sized potatoes
1 large onion, finely chopped
1 medium-sized green pepper, chopped
8 ounces American cheese, cubed
1 slice white bread, cubed
1 cup butter or margarine
2 tablespoons parsley
Milk
Corn flakes

Parboil potatoes in skins. Cool, peel and cube. Place in a 13x9x2-inch baking dish. Add next 6 ingredients, distributing them evenly over the potatoes. Add milk to fill ½ of the casserole. Top with crushed corn flakes. Bake at 350 degrees for 45 minutes or until browned. Yield: 10 to 12 servings.
Kathleen Holmes

POTATO CABBAGE FRY

2 tablespoons water
2 tablespoons teriyaki sauce
½ teaspoon all-purpose flour
⅓ cup onion, chopped
1 clove garlic, minced
2 tablespoons vegetable oil
3 cups cabbage, shredded
3 medium potatoes, cubed and boiled
1 tablespoon parsley, snipped

Combine first 3 ingredients; set aside. Sauté onion and garlic in oil until tender. Add cabbage and fry an additional 2 minutes. Add potatoes and continue to fry for 2 minutes. Add remaining ingredients and cook for an additional 1 to 2 minutes, stirring constantly. Yield: 6 to 8 servings.
Eileen Barlock

SQUASH BAKE

1 cup water
4 pounds zucchini or yellow summer squash, cut into 1/2 inch thick slices
3/4 cup chopped onion
1 clove garlic, minced
1/3 cup butter
1/3 cup all-purpose flour
1/8 teaspoon pepper
2 1/2 cups milk
2 tablespoons chicken flavor instant bouillon
1 teaspoon oregano
1 1/2 cups shredded Cheddar cheese
1 (3-ounce) can French fried onions, optional

Bring water to a boil over high heat. Add zucchini, cover and cook for 8 to 10 minutes or until tender. Drain. Melt butter in a saucepan. Add onion and garlic. Sauté, stirring constantly, until tender. Stir in flour and pepper. Slowly, add milk, bouillon and oregano, stirring constantly. Cook until thickened. Remove from heat and add 3/4 cup cheese, stirring to blend. Combine zucchini and hot sauce mixture in a bowl. Pour into a greased, 13x9x2-inch baking dish. Bake at 350 degrees for 25 minutes or until bubbly. Remove from oven and sprinkle with remaining cheese. Return to oven until cheese melts. Garnish with onion rings, if desired. Yield: 8 servings.
Eileen Barlock

WELSH RAREBIT SPINACH

1 (10-ounce) package frozen chopped spinach
1 (16-ounce) package frozen Welsh rarebit
8 slices bacon, cooked and crumbled
1/2 (16-ounce) can sliced water chestnuts
1/2 (6-ounce) can French fried onion rings

Cook spinach and Welsh rarebit according to package directions. Drain spinach. Layer ingredients in an 8 or 9-inch casserole in the following order: Welsh rarebit, spinach, bacon and water chestnuts. Top with onion rings. Bake at 325 degrees for 30 minutes. Yield: 6 to 8 servings.
Jean Haas

BAKED ACORN SQUASH FILLED WITH GREEN PEAS

4 medium sized acorn squash, approximately 3½ pounds
⅓ cup margarine, melted
¼ cup light brown sugar, packed
½ teaspoon salt
¼ teaspoon ground cinnamon
2 (10-ounce) packages frozen green peas
2 tablespoons butter or margarine

Cut squash in half lengthwise, remove seeds and stringy fiber and arrange cut side down in a shallow baking pan. Add ½ inch hot water. Bake, uncovered, at 375 degrees for 30 minutes. Pour off excess water, turn squash right side up. Combine margarine, brown sugar, salt and cinnamon; mix well. Spoon mixture into the center of the squash halves dividing evenly. Bake at 375 degrees for an additional 15 minutes, basting well with the sauce. Cook peas according to package directions, drain and toss with butter. Spoon into baked squash. Yield: 8 servings.
Peg O'Shea

ZUCCHINI ROUNDS

⅓ cup biscuit mix
¼ cup grated Parmesan or Romano cheese
⅛ teaspoon pepper
2 eggs, slightly beaten
2 cups shredded unpeeled zucchini
2 tablespoons chopped parsley
Butter or margarine for frying

Stir together biscuit mix, cheese and pepper. Stir in eggs just until mixture is moistened. Fold in zucchini and parsley. Drop by generous tablepoonsful into hot butter or margarine; fry 2 to 3 minutes on each side, or until golden brown. *A delicious side dish.* Yield: 4 to 6 servings.
Betz Spacek

ZUCCHINI BAKE

4 cups sliced zucchini, blanched
1 (10¾-ounce) can cream of chicken soup
1 cup dairy sour cream
1 (8-ounce) package herb stuffing mix
¼ cup butter or margarine

In large bowl, stir sour cream, soup and zucchini together gently. Melt butter in saucepan over medium heat; stir in seasonings and stuffing mix. Layer ½ the stuffing in bottom of a greased 1½-quart baking dish. Add zucchini mixture and top with remaining stuffing mixture. Bake at 350 degrees for 30 minutes or until hot and bubbly. Yield: 6 to 8 servings.
Betz Spacek

SWEET POTATO CASSEROLE

3 large sweet potatoes, peeled and boiled
½ cup butter
2 eggs, beaten
⅓ cup milk
1 cup sugar
1 tablespoon lemon juice

Combine ingredients in order listed. Blend with a mixer until the consistency of mashed potatoes. Pour into a greased 2-quart casserole dish. Sprinkle topping over the casserole. Bake at 350 degrees for 25 minutes. This can be made ahead and frozen before baked. Thaw and bake as above when ready to use. Yield: 6 to 8 servings.

Topping:

⅓ cup butter, melted
½ cup all-purpose flour
½ cup brown sugar
1 cup chopped pecans

Combine topping ingredients in order listed. Mix until well blended and crumbly. Sprinkle over casserole.
Judy Braun

BUTTERNUT BAKE

3 pounds butternut squash, halved and seeds removed
2 tablespoons butter
2 teaspoons brown sugar
¼ teaspoon salt
¼ cup golden raisins
2 tablespoons chopped pecans

Bake squash, cut side down, at 400 degrees for 45 minutes or until tender. Scoop out pulp. Add butter, brown sugar and salt. Beat until well-blended. Stir in raisins and 1 tablespoon pecans. Pour into a lightly greased 1-quart casserole. Drizzle topping over squash. Sprinkle with remaining pecans. Bake at 350 degrees for 25 minutes. Yield: 6 to 8 servings.

Topping:

1 tablespoon butter
1 tablespoon brown sugar
1 tablespoon light corn syrup

Combine ingredients and mix until well-blended.
Sister M. Claudia O.S.F.N.

SWEET POTATO-CASHEW BAKE

½ cup brown sugar, firmly packed
⅓ cup broken cashews
Salt to taste
⅛ teaspoon ground ginger
2 pounds sweet potatoes, cooked, peeled and cut into thick chunks
1 (8-ounce) can peach slices, well drained
3 tablespoons butter or margarine

Combine brown sugar, cashews, salt and ginger. Layer ½ sweet potatoes, ½ peach slices and ½ brown sugar mixture in a lightly greased 10x6x2-inch baking dish. Repeat layer. Dot with butter. Cover and bake at 350 degrees for 30 minutes. Spoon brown sugar syrup over potatoes before serving. Yield: 6 to 8 servings.
Colleen Karpac

FLORIDA SWEET POTATOES

2 pounds sweet potatoes
6 large oranges
¼ cup butter
½ cup golden raisins
6 large marshmallows
Milk

Cut sweet potatoes in half and cook in boiling water, about 20 minutes, or until tender. Meanwhile slice tops off oranges and scoop out pulp and save, discarding white membrane. Peel and mash sweet potatoes. Add orange fruit pulp and butter to sweet potatoes and blend well. A little milk may be added if mixture seems dry. Add raisins and spoon mixture into orange shells. Top each with a marshmallow. Bake at 350 degrees for about 20 minutes, or until golden brown on top. yield: 6 servings.
Paula Knight

SWEET POTATO PUFF

3 pounds sweet potatoes, cooked
⅓ cup melted butter or margarine
1 cup sugar
6 eggs, separated
1 tablespoon grated lemon rind
1 cup orange juice
¼ teaspoon ground cinnamon

Beat cooked sweet potatoes in large bowl of electric mixer until smooth. Stir in butter and ¾ cup sugar. Beat eggs yolks; add lemon rind, orange juice and cinnamon. Stir into potatoes. Beat egg whites in small bowl of electric mixer until stiff peaks form; fold into sweet potato mixture. Pour into a greased soufflé dish. Sprinkle top with remaining ¼ cup sugar. Bake at 350 degrees for 1 hour. Yield: 10 to 12 servings.
Chicky Weiner

TOMATOES WITH PESTO

2 tablespoons red wine vinegar
1/4 cup fresh basil leaves
1 cup minced garlic
1/4 teaspoon salt
1/4 teaspoon sugar
1/4 cup grated Parmesan cheese
1/3 cup olive or vegetable oil
3 large tomatoes

Place vinegar, basil, garlic, salt, sugar, cheese and oil in blender container; blend well and let stand 1 to 2 hours. Slice tomatoes, pour sauce over slices and grind black pepper over all. *Delicious!* Yield: 3 to 4 servings.
Karen West

VEGETABLES MORNAY SAUCE

1/4 cup butter or margarine
1/3 cup sifted all-purpose flour
2 cups liquid (drained from vegetables with cream added to make 2 cups)
1/4 cup grated Parmesan cheese
Pinch of ground nutmeg
Pinch of dried thyme
1/8 teaspoon garlic salt
2 tablespoons white wine
1 teaspoon salt

Melt butter in medium saucepan and stir in flour gradually with a wire whisk. Gradually whisk in liquid; place over low heat and cook until smooth and thickened. Add remaining ingredients and simmer for about 5 minutes more. Taste; adjust seasonings and use with vegetables.

Vegetables:

Cook *2 (10-ounce) packages frozen, mixed vegetables* in a tightly covered saucepan as directed on package, just until tender crisp. Remove from heat, drain (reserving liquid) and season with *2 tablespoons butter or margarine, 1 teaspoon salt, 1/2 teaspoon salt, 1/2 teaspoon garlic salt and pepper.* Spread cooked vegetables in greased 13x9x2-inch baking dish. Pour prepared Mornay Sauce over vegetables and cover with about 2 cups cubed bread. Pour 3 tablespoons melted butter over bread cubes and place in oven. Bake at 350 degrees for 30 minutes or until bread is brown and casserole is hot and bubbly. Yield: 6 to 8 servings.
Sharon Wiza

MOM'S SCALLOPED CABBAGE

1 large head cabbage, chopped, parboiled and drained
1 (10¾-ounce) can cream of mushroom soup
3-4 tablespoons butter or margarine
1 cup round butter cracker crumbs

Layer ½ of the ingredients in the following order: cabbage, soup, butter and crumbs in a lightly greased, 13x9x2-inch baking dish. Repeat layers. Cover and refrigerate until 1 hour before baking. Bake at 350 degrees for 45 minutes to 1 hour. Yield: 6 to 8 servings.
Blanche Archer

HOT CURRIED FRUIT

¼ cup margarine
¾ cup brown sugar, firmly packed
3 teaspoons curry powder
1 (20-ounce) can peaches
1 (20-ounce) can pears
1 (20-ounce) can pineapple tidbits
1 (16-ounce) can dark cherries

Melt margarine over low heat. Add brown sugar and curry powder; heat, stirring constantly, until well-blended. Drain fruit on paper towels. Arrange fruit in a single layer in a 13x9x2-inch ovenproof glass dish. Spread sugar mixture over the fruit. Bake, uncovered, at 350 degrees for 1 hour. Refrigerate overnight. Reheat at 325 degrees for 30 minutes before serving. Serve as a side dish with pork, ham or chicken. May also be spooned over vanilla ice cream as an elegant dessert. Yield: 6 to 8 servings.
Sue Mahon

HOT PINEAPPLE CASSEROLE

5 slices white bread, cubed
½ cup butter or margarine
2 (20-ounce) cans crushed pineapple
3 tablespoons all-purpose flour
1 cup sugar
2 eggs

Sauté bread cubes in butter or margarine until golden brown. Stir together flour and sugar and add to pineapple. Beat eggs well and stir into pineapple mixture. Turn into buttered casserole and top with bread cubes. Stir gently and bake at 350 degrees for 35 minutes or until set. *Nice with ham.* Yield: 8 servings.
Barb Radthe

CORNBREAD STUFFING

2 tablespoons butter, melted
1½ cups onion, chopped
1½ cups celery, chopped
½ cup parsley, chopped
1 cup chicken broth
4 eggs beaten
6 cups cornbread crumbs
Salt to taste
Pepper to taste

Combine butter and vegetables in a saucepan and cook over low heat for 5 to 8 minutes or until just wilted. Remove from heat; add broth, beaten eggs and cornbread crumbs. Stir until all ingredients are just moistened. Season to taste. Pour into a buttered, 2½ quart casserole dish and bake at 325 degrees for 45 minutes or until firm and golden brown. Yield: 8 to 10 servings.
Eileen Barlock

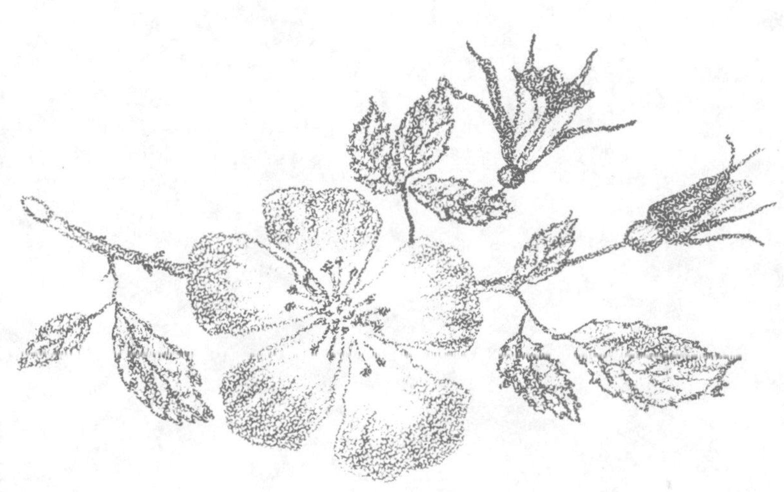

Happy
Birthday

THE GRAND FINALE

Tempting Desserts

BOCCONE DOLCE
(Sweet Mouthful)

4 egg whites
Pinch of salt
½ teaspoon cream of tartar
1 cup sugar

Combine egg whites, salt and cream of tartar. Beat until stiff. Gradually, beat in sugar and continue to beat until thick and glossy. Line baking sheets with waxed paper and trace 3 circles, 8 inches in diameter. Spread meringue 1¼-inches thick and bake at 250 degrees for 20 to 25 minutes or until meringue is a pale gold but still pliable. Remove from oven and peel paper from bottom. Place on cake racks to dry. To serve, place a meringue layer on a serving plate and spread with a thin coating of melted chocolate. Next, spread a layer ¾-inches thick of whipped cream. Top this with a layer of strawberries. Repeat layers and top with the third layer of meringue. Frost sides smoothly with remaining whipped cream. Decorate the top meringue layer using remaining melted chocolate squeezed through a pastry cone with a tiny, round opening or with whole ripe strawberries. Refrigerate for 2 hours before serving. Yield: 8 to 10 servings.

Filling:

1 (6-ounce) package semi-sweet chocolate morsels
3 tablespoons water
3 cups whipping cream
⅓ cup sugar
1 pint strawberries, cleaned, stemmed and sliced

Combine chocolate morsels and water in the top of a double boiler. Heat, stirring constantly, until chocolate is melted. Whip cream until it begins to thicken. Gradually, add the sugar and beat until very stiff. Assemble as directed.

Justin Baum

EASY BLINTZ CUPCAKES

16-ounces small-curd cottage cheese
3 tablespoons dairy sour cream
3 eggs
1 teaspoon vanilla extract
½ cup biscuit mix
3 tablespoons sugar
¼ cup melted butter or margarine

Preheat oven to 350 degrees. Line or grease a 12-cup muffin tin. Place all ingredients in a large bowl and beat with electric mixer until smooth. Fill muffin cups ½ full. Bake 35 to 40 minutes. Yield: 12 cupcakes.

Gloria Rosenbush

COLD CHOCOLATE SOUFFLÉ

5 (1-ounce) squares bitter or semi-sweet chocolate
1 cup milk
5 egg yolks
6 egg whites
1 cup sugar
1 envelope unflavored gelatin
½ cup cold water
1 tablespoon vanilla extract
½ cup boiling water
1 (9-ounce) container non-dairy frozen whipped topping, thawed

Combine chocolate with milk in saucepan and heat over low to medium heat, stirring, until chocolate is melted. Remove from heat and set aside to cool. Beat egg yolks with sugar until thick and lemon colored. Soak gelatin in cold water to soften. Blend chocolate mixture into egg yolks. Add boiling water to dissolved gelatin and then stir into chocolate mixture along with vanilla. Beat egg whites until stiff and gently fold into mixture. Spoon into glasses or soufflé dish and chill. To serve, garnish with whipped topping and shaved chocolate. To give a mocha flavor, add 1 tablespoon of strong coffee to melted chocolate before adding gelatin. Yield: 8 servings.
Chicky Weiner
Elaine Wolfe

GRASSHOPPER SOUFFLÉ

1 cup sugar
2 envelopes unflavored gelatin
2 cups water
4 eggs, separated
8-ounces cream cheese, softened
¼ cup crème de menthe
1 cup heavy cream, whipped
Additional whipped cream
Strawberries

Combine ¾ cup sugar and gelatin; gradually add water. Stir over low heat until dissolved; remove from heat. Blend in beaten egg yolks and return to heat; cook 2 to 3 minutes. Gradually add to cream cheese, stirring until well-blended. Stir in crème de menthe and chill until slightly thickened. Beat egg whites until soft peaks form. Gradually add remaining sugar and beat until stiff. Fold beaten whites and whipped cream into cream cheese mixture. Wrap a 3-inch foil collar around top of a 1½-quart soufflé dish and secure with tape. Pour mixture into prepared dish; chill until firm. To serve, remove foil collar and garnish with additional whipped cream and strawberries. May be served in individual stemmed glasses. Yield: 8 to 10 servings. *Delicious and elegant!*
Jane Boyd

PUDDIN'S FRUIT DESSERT

1 (8¾-ounce) can pineapple tidbits
1 (11-ounce) can mandarin oranges
1 (17-ounce) can fruit cocktail
½ cup coconut
2 tablespoons lemon juice
1 (3-ounce) package instant lemon pudding mix
2 bananas, peeled and chopped
Whipped topping

Combine drained canned fruit, coconut and lemon juice. Stir, then sprinkle dry pudding mix over fruit mixture. Cover and refrigerate until needed. Before serviing, stir in bananas. layer fruit and whipped topping in parfait glasses. Yield: 8 to 10 servings.
Kay Vicsi
Betz Spacek

ALASKAN BURNT CREME

1 pint whipping cream
4 egg yolks
½ cup sugar
1 tablespoon vanilla extract

Heat whipping cream over low heat until bubbles form around the edge of the pan. In a bowl, beat egg yolks and sugar until thick, about 3 minutes. Gradually, beat cream into yolks and stir in vanilla. Pour mixture into 6 six-ounce custard cups. Place custard cups in a baking pan that has about ½-inch of water. Bake at 350 degrees for 45 minutes or until set. Refrigerate until cool. Sprinkle tops with 2 teaspoons sugar, completely covering tops. (Use more if needed.) Place under broiler until topping is golden brown. Topping will burn easily, so watch carefully. Chill until very cold. Yield: 6 servings.
Thomas More Program

SO-EASY CHOCOLATE MOUSSE

1 (4-ounce) package German sweet chocolate
3 tablespoons water
1 teaspoon vanilla extract
2 cups frozen whipped topping, thawed

(All ingredients should be at room temperature.) Melt chocolate with water in top of double boiler. Cool to room temperature. Add vanilla and stir well. Place whipped topping in a large bowl. Gently fold in chocolate mixture until smooth and well-blended. Spoon into individual serving glasses and top with whipped topping and shaved chocolate, or may be used as frosting for a chocolate sheet cake. *This mousse is so delicious you would never believe it's so easy.* Yield: 6 to 8 servings.
Maureen May

DAISY HILL DATE PUDDING

1 egg
1 cup sugar
1 cup chopped dates
1 cup chopped walnuts
1 cup breadcrumbs
1 teaspoon baking powder
1 cup milk
1 teaspoon vanilla extract
2 tablespoons butter, melted

Beat egg in medium bowl of electric mixer until light and fluffy. Add sugar and beat to blend. Stir in dates, nuts, breadcrumbs and baking powder. Add milk, vanilla and butter. Mix well. Pour into a greased 1-quart mold and place in a pan of water. Bake at 325 degrees for 40 to 50 minutes, or until knife inserted in center of pudding comes out clean. Serve warm with the following sauce.

Sauce:

2 egg yolks
1 cup confectioners' sugar
2 tablespoons brandy
1 cup heavy cream, whipped

Beat egg yolks with sugar; add brandy and fold in whipped cream. Serve over date pudding.
Sally Zetl

GALA BREAD PUDDING

8 slices cinnamon-raisin bread
1 (13-ounce) can evaporated milk
3 large apples, peeled, cored and diced
½ cup sugar
1½ teaspoons ground nutmeg
1 tablespoon vanilla extract
⅔ cup raisins
2 eggs, well-beaten
½ cup butter or margarine, melted

Break bread into small bite-sized pieces. Place in a greased, 8-inch square baking dish. Pour evaporated milk over the bread and let stand for 5 to 10 minutes to soak. Add apples, sugar, nutmeg, vanilla and raisins. Mix well. Fold in eggs. Carefully, fold in melted butter. Bake at 375 degrees for 50 minutes. Cool 45 minutes before serving. Yield: 6 to 8 servings.
Shirley Zirm

PLUM PUDDING

2 eggs
½ cup butter or margarine, melted and cooled
½ cup orange juice
1 cup brown sugar, firmly packed
1 tablespoon grated orange rind
1 cup sifted all-purpose flour
1 teaspoon baking soda
2 cups pitted prunes, soaked overnight and cut into small pieces
Chopped nuts, optional

Combine ingredients in order listed. Mix until well-blended. Pour mixture into a covered pudding pan and place pan in a pot of boiling water so that ½ of the pan is emerged. Steam for 1½ hours. Serve hot with cold sauce on top. Yield: 12 to 15 servings.

Sauce:

1 egg white
5 tablespoons butter, melted and cooled
1½ cups powdered sugar
4 tablespoons rum
½ pint whipping cream, whipped

Beat egg white until stiff. Fold butter into beaten whites. Gently, fold in powdered sugar and rum. When thoroughly mixed, fold in whipped cream into mixture. Both the pudding and sauce may be made ahead and frozen until needed.
Sue Mahon

GRANDPA MOZZ'S BURNT SUGAR CUSTARD

1¾ cup sugar
½ cup water
1 teaspoon vanilla extract
6 eggs
1 quart milk

Place ¾ cup sugar and water in an 8-inch round pan. Cook over medium heat until mixture begins to scorch. Allow sugar to reach a deep golden brown. Remove from heat and turn pan to coat all sides. Keep turning until syrup stops moving. Allow to cool (as syrup cools, it will become glassy and will crack). Combine remaining sugar, vanilla eggs and milk; add to caramel-coated pan. Place pan in a larger pan containing 1 inch of water. Bake at 350 degrees for 1½ hours, or until knife inserted in center comes out clean. Cook and invert onto serving plate. Caramel will become syrupy during baking. If shell is cloudy and grainy, it was not cooked long enough in caramelizing stage. Shell may be made in advance and stored for weeks in a plastic bag. *This is a long-time family favorite.* Yield: 6 to 8 servings.
Betz Spacek

BAKED DEVILS FLOAT

1 cup all-purpose flour
¾ cup sugar
¼ teaspoon salt
2 teaspoons baking powder
1½ tablespoons cocoa (heaping)
½ cup milk
1 teaspoon vanilla extract
2 tablespoons melted butter
½ cup walnuts

Sauce:

½ cup sugar
½ cup firmly packed brown sugar
5 tablespoons cocoa
1½ cups hot water

Sift flour, sugar, salt, baking powder and cocoa together in small bowl. Combine milk, butter and vanilla in large cup and pour over dry ingredients. Add nuts. Blend Well. Pour batter into a greased 1-quart baking dish. Combine sauce ingredients in a small bowl in order given. Pour sauce over batter and bake at 350 degrees for 40 minutes. Serve like upside-down cake (sauce will be on bottom when float is cooked). Top with ice cream or whipped cream. Yield: 4 to 6 servings.
Sally Zetl

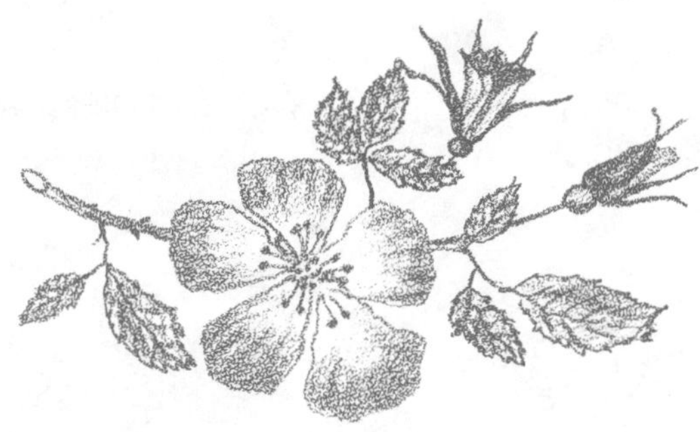

FROSTY STRAWBERRY BOMB

1 (8-ounce) package cream cheese
1 (7-ounce) jar marshmallow creme
2 cups strawberry halves or 10 ounces frozen strawberries, thawed
1 tablespoon lemon juice
1 cup heavy cream, whipped; or 1 cup non-dairy frozen whipped topping

Combine softened cream cheese and marshmallow creme. Beat in strawberries and lemon juice. Fold in non-dairy frozen topping or whipped cream. Mix all ingredients and pour into a 1½-quart pan or mold which has been lined with foil. Freeze until firm. Remove from freezer and place in refrigerator 30 minutes before serving. Garnish with fruit. Yield: 6 to 8 servings.
Elaine Wolfe

PUMPKIN ROLL

3 eggs
1 cup sugar
2/3 cup pumpkin
1 teaspoon lemon juice
3/4 cup all-purpose flour
1 teaspoon baking powder
2 teaspoons ground cinnamon
1 teaspoon ground ginger
1/2 teaspoon salt
1 cup walnuts, finely chopped

Beat eggs on high speed of electric mixer for 5 minutes. Stir in sugar. Fold in pumpkin. Add remaining ingredients, except walnuts. Beat well. Spread into a well-greased 15x10x1-inch jellyroll pan. Top with chopped nuts. Bake at 375 degrees for 12 to 15 minutes. Remove from oven and sprinkle with powdered sugar. Turn out onto a towel, sprinkle with more powdered sugar and roll like a jellyroll. Let cool completely. Unroll. Spread filling on and roll up again. Refrigerate until ready to use. This freezes well. Large 29-ounce can pumpkin makes 3 rolls. Filling amounts, and recipe as given, is for 1 roll. Yield: 1 roll.

Filling:

1 cup powdered sugar
1 (8-ounce) package cream cheese, softened
4 tablespoons butter, softened
1/2 teaspoon vanilla extract

Combine all ingredients in order listed and beat until smooth. Spread on cooled pumpkin roll.
Eileen Barlock

STRAWBERRIES A LA RITZ

1 quart fresh, ripe strawberries
1/2 to 1 cup sugar
1/4 cup anisette liqueur
1/3 cup all-purpose flour
1 cup sugar
4 eggs, slightly beaten
1 quart milk
1 cup heavy cream, whipped

Toss strawberries with 1/2 to 1 cup sugar (use enough to sweeten well). Pour anisette over berries, cover with plastic wrap and refrigerate for 2 hours, or until well-chilled. Blend remaining 1 cup sugar, flour and eggs together in 2-quart saucepan, using a wire whisk. Bring milk to a boil and gradually add to flour/egg mixture, whisking constantly. Return to heat, stirring constantly, until mixture boils and is smooth. Remove from heat and set aside to cool. When completely cooled, fold together strawberries, custard, whipped cream and enough red food coloring to just tint mixture pink. Serve in stemmed glasses or a compote, garnished with whole, fresh strawberries. Yield: 8 servings.
Sue Polacek

PISTACHIO DESSERT

1 cup all-purpose flour
½ cup butter or margarine
1 cup chopped nuts
1 (8-ounce) package cream cheese
1 cup powdered sugar
1 (8-ounce) container non-dairy whipped topping, thawed
2 (3-ounce) packages instant pistachio pudding mix
3 cups milk

Combine flour, margarine and nuts (reserve about 3 tablespoons for topping) in medium mixing bowl until crumbly. Press into bottom of 13x9x2-inch baking pan. Bake at 350 degrees for 20 minutes. Remove from oven and set aside to cool. Cream cheese with sugar in small mixing bowl and beat until light and fluffy. Fold in ½ the whipped topping and spread over cooled crust. Refrigerate. Beat the instant pudding mix with milk for 2 minutes. Spread over chilled cream cheese layer. Return to refrigerator for 30 minutes. Spread remaining whipped topping over pudding layer, sprinkle with a few chopped nuts and refrigerate for at least 2 hours before serving (overnight is best). Yield: 10 to 12 generous servings.
Peggy Vitteck

LUCY MILLER'S RHUBARB SHORTCAKE

2 cups all-purpose flour
3 teaspoons baking powder
1 teaspoon salt
½ cup sugar
¼ cup butter or margarine
1 egg
¾ cup milk
1 teaspoon vanilla extract
4 cups fresh or frozen rhubarb, cut into 1-inch slices
1 (3-ounce) package strawberry or raspberry-flavored gelatin mix

Combine flour, baking powder, salt, sugar, butter, egg, milk and vanilla; turn into a greased 14x11x2-inch baking pan. Arrange rhubarb slices over top, then sprinkle with dry gelatin mix.

Topping:

1½ cups sugar
6 tablespoons all-purpose flour
6 tablespoons butter or margarine

Combine all ingredients and crumble over top. Bake at 350 degrees for 40 minutes. Yield: 15 to 18 servings.
Betz Spacek

EASY STRUDEL

1 cup butter or margarine
2 cups all-purpose flour
4 egg yolks
2 tablespoons vinegar
¼ cup cold water
1 tablespoon flour
3 tablespoons sugar
½ teaspoon cinnamon
1 (21-ounce) can sliced pie apples or 6 fresh apples (pared and sliced)

Using a pastry blender or fingers, cut butter or margarine into flour until it is the consistency of cornmeal. Carefully stir in egg yolks, vinegar and enough ice water to blend lightly. Divide into 2 or 3 balls, wrap in waxed paper and chill at least 1 hour or overnight. Remove from refrigerator (working with only 1 ball at a time) and roll out on floured surface into a rectangle about ⅛-inch thick. Place ⅓ of the apples in center of dough and sprinkle with 1 tablespoon flour, 3 tablespoons sugar and ½ teaspoon ground cinnamon. Roll from long side as for jelly roll. Place on baking sheet seam side down which has been coated with non-stick cooking spray. Bake at 375 degrees until golden brown, about 25 to 30 minutes. Repeat with remaining dough and apples. Makes 2 or 3 strudels, depending upon size you choose to make.
Sally Vlasik

HUNGARIAN NUT CRESCENTS

2 cups all-purpose flour
⅛ teaspoon salt
1 cup butter or margarine, softened
⅔ cup dairy sour cream
1 egg yolk
½ teaspoon vanilla extract
⅔ cup chopped nuts
⅔ cup sugar
1 teaspoon ground cinnamon
1 egg white, slightly beaten

Combine flour and salt. Cut in butter with a pastry blender until mixture resembles coarse crumbs. Blend sour cream, egg and vanilla with a fork. Gradually add to flour mixture. Mix until well-blended. Chill for 3 to 4 hours or until firm enough to handle. Divide dough into 3 parts. On a lightly-floured board, roll each part into a 9- or 10-inch circle about ⅛ inch thick. Cut each circle into 12 wedges. Combine nuts, sugar and cinnamon. Sprinkle ¾ of the mixture over the wedges. Roll each wedge from the widest end to the point. Brush with egg white and sprinkle with remaining nut mixture. Bake on a greased 15x10x1-inch baking sheet at 350 degrees for 25 minutes. Yield: 3 dozen cookies.
Katie Murphy

SUE'S BLUEBERRY BUCKLE

1/4 cup butter or margarine
3/4 cup sugar
1 egg
2 cups all-purpose flour, sifted
2 teaspoons baking powder
1/2 teaspoon salt
1/2 cup milk
2 cups blueberries, washed and drained

Cream butter until smooth and soft. Gradually, add sugar and beat until mixture is fluffy and pale yellow. Add eggs. Beat well. Sift dry ingredients together. Add to creamed mixture, alternately, with milk, beating well after each addition. Stir berries in gently. Pour into a greased 9x9x2-inch pan. Sprinkle topping over mixture. Bake at 375 degrees for 35 minutes. Serve warm. Yield: 6 to 9 servings.

Topping:

1/2 cup sugar
1/2 cup all-purpose flour
1/2 teaspoon ground cinnamon
1/4 cup butter, softened

Combine all ingredients and cut with fork until crumbly. Sprinkle over batter.
Sue Robinson

THAT'S THE BERRIES COBBLER

2 pints strawberries, hulled and halved
1 pint fresh, or thawed frozen, blueberries
1/3 to 1/2 cup sugar
1/4 cup all-purpose flour
1 tablespoon butter or margarine
1 1/2 cups all-purpose flour
1/3 cup sugar
1 1/2 teaspoons baking powder
1/8 teaspoon ground cinnamon
1/8 teaspoon ground nutmeg
6 tablespoons butter or margarine
1/2 cup milk

Toss berries with sugar and flour. Arrange fruit mixture in ungreased 12x7x2-inch baking pan. Dot with butter. Mix remaining flour, sugar, butter, baking powder, cinnamon, nutmeg and butter until crumbly. Stir in milk to form dough and spoon over berries. Bake at 375 degrees 45 minutes. Yield: 8 to 12 servings.
Patti Lovejoy

EASY BLACKBERRY COBBLER

½ cup margarine
1 cup milk
1 cup sugar
1 cup sifted all-purpose flour
1 quart blackberries, cleaned and stemmed

Melt margarine in an 8-inch square pan. Add milk, but do not stir. Sift flour and sugar together. Add to the pan, but *do not stir.* Place blackberries on top of mixture in pan. Bake at 325 degrees for 25 minutes or until the top rises and turns brown. Yield: 6 to 8 servings.
Dolores Sygula

LAST MINUTE CINNAMON APPLE COBBLER

1 (21-ounce) can apple pie filling
1 can refrigerated quick cinnamon rolls

Pour apple pie filling into 9-inch pie pan or square cake pan. Separate dough into 8 rolls. Cut each roll in ½. Place on pie filling, cinnamon-side up. Bake at 350 degrees for 20 to 25 minutes. *This makes a great last minute dessert!* Yield: 8 to 10 servings.
Dolores Sygula

AMBROSIA

1 envelope unflavored gelatin
¼ cup sugar
½ cup cold water
1¼ cups orange juice
1 tablespoon lemon juice
2 medium oranges
1 medium banana
¼ cup flaked coconut

Combine gelatin with sugar and cold water in small saucepan; stir over low heat until gelatin and sugar are dissolved. Stir in orange and lemon juices. Pour into bowl and chill until partially set. Peel oranges and section. Cut sections into bite-sized pieces, leaving a few whole for garnish. Peel and slice banana. Remove gelatin mixture from refrigerator and fold in fruit and coconut. Spoon into a 4½-cup mold. Chill until firm. Unmold onto serving dish and garnish with reserved orange sections. *A gelatin variation of a Southern favorite. Serve with whipped cream.* Yield: 6 servings.
Mary Sims

LEMON AMBROSIA

6 eggs, separated
3/4 cup sugar
Juice and grated rind of 2 lemons
1 (3-ounce) package lemon-flavored gelatin
Scant cup boiling water
1/2 cup heavy cream
Vanilla extract
Toasted coconut
2 (9-ounce) packages lady fingers, split
3/4 cup sugar

Place egg yolks, sugar, lemon juice and rind in top of double boiler; cook, stirring constantly, until thick; cool. Meanwhile dissolve gelatin in boiling water; cool and add to yolk mixture. Beat egg whites with 3/4 cup sugar; fold into yolk mixture. Line bottom and sides of an 8-inch springform pan with ladyfingers. Pour lemon mixture into pan and refrigerate overnight. To serve, whip cream with vanilla to taste. Spread over ambrosia mixture and sprinkle with toasted coconut. Yield: 12 servings.
Barb Radthe

SCOTCH SQUARES (ELEPHANT EARS)

2 cups milk
4 tablespoons margarine
4 to 5 cups all-purpose flour
1 envelope active dry yeast
1 teaspoon salt
1 egg

Heat milk and margarine. Combine salt, yeast and flour. Make a well in dry ingredients; add egg and milk mixture. Stir together to make a sweet dough. Place in a large, greased bowl and let rise 20 to 30 minutes. Punch dough down and roll into a rectangle. Cut into 4-inch squares and allow to rise again. Fry squares in about 1 inch hot oil in a large skillet. Brown on one side, turn, and brown on other side. Drain and dip in a bowl of sugar; turn and dip other side. Serve warm.
Kathy Korzekwa

ZABAGLIONE

2 egg yolks
2 tablespoons sugar
2 tablespoons sweet golden sherry

Combine egg yolks, sugar and sherry in a small bowl. Place over a pan of hot (not boiling) water and whisk until the mixture is light and almost thick enough to leave a ribbon trail when the whisk is lifted. Pour into warm stemmed glasses. Serve at once. This is a popular Italian dessert. It can be served alone in stemmed glasses or as a sauce for cakes, ice cream or fruit. Although it is easy to make, it does not keep well and should be served within 15 minutes after making. Yield: 2 servings.
Lynne Della Donna

FRENCH VANILLA ICE CREAM

1½ cups sugar
4 tablespoons cornstarch
1½ quarts milk
4 eggs, separated
4 teaspoons vanilla extract
2 cups whipping cream, whipped

Combine sugar and cornstarch in large saucepan. Gradually add milk; beat in egg yolks until mixture is frothy. Add vanilla. Place over medium heat and bring to a boil, stirring constantly so mixture doesn't scorch. Remove immediately and cool to room temperature. Beat egg whites in small mixing bowl until soft peaks form; fold into cooled custard mixure. Pour into 2 baking pans and freeze until mushy, about 2 hours. Remove from freezer and place in large mixing bowl; beat until light and frothy. Fold in whipped cream, mix well and pour into baking pans again. Freeze until firm. Yield: 10 to 12 servings.
Patti Lovejoy

GINGERBREAD

½ cup sugar
½ cup butter
1 teaspoon ground ginger
1 teaspoon ground cinnamon
½ teaspoon salt
1 egg
1 cup dark molasses
1 cup sour milk
2 cups all-purpose flour
1 teaspoon baking soda

Combine sugar, butter, spices and salt in a medium-sized mixing bowl. Add egg and beat until fluffy. Add molasses and milk. Continue beating until well mixed. Sift flour with soda and add to the mixture; mix well. Pour into a lightly-greased and floured 8-inch baking pan. Bake at 325 degrees for 25 to 30 minutes or until a knife inserted in the center comes out clean. Yield: 6 to 8 servings.
Eileen Barlock

ANGEL ALEXANDER

1 baked angel food cake
½ cup crème de cacoa
2 tablespoons heavy cream
1 pint heavy whipping cream
¼ cup sugar
1 (6-ounce) package chocolate morsels

Place cake on serving plate and poke holes in top with a skewer. Stir crème de cacoa with 2 tablespoons heavy cream in small bowl. Pour over cake until all liquid is used up and it has been absorbed by cake. Whip remaining cream until soft peaks form; gradually beat in sugar until mixture is smooth and all sugar is dissolved. Frost cake with whipped cream and sprinkle with chocolate morsels. Keep refrigerated.
Lynne Della Donna

NO-BAKE CREAMY PINEAPPLE SURPRISE

1 angel food cake
1 (3-ounce) package cream cheese
3 cups milk, divided
2 (3¾-ounce) packages pineapple cream-flavored instant pudding mix
1 (20-ounce) can crushed pineapple
1 (8-ounce) container frozen whipped topping, thawed
½ cup ground nuts, optional

Shred cake into bottom of a 13x9x2-inch baking pan. Cream the cheese with ½ cup milk. Add remaining milk and beat well. With electric mixer at low speed, mix in pudding only until well-blended. Pour over shredded cake. Drain pineapple and spread over pudding layer. Frost with whipped topping; sprinkle with chopped nuts. Refrigerate at least 2 hours. Cut into squares to serve. Yield: 12 to 15 servings.
Jane Lesiak

SOUR CREAM KALACKY

1 cup butter
3 egg yolks
3 cups all-purpose flour
1 teaspoon baking powder
½ pint dairy sour cream
1 (20-ounce) can crushed pineapple, well drained
Powdered sugar

Cream butter and eggs until smooth. Sift dry ingredients and add to butter-egg mixture. mix until well-blended. Stir in sour cream. Roll out on a floured board until ⅛-inch thick. Place 1 teaspoon of crushed pineapple in the center of each square. Pinch together the opposite corners of the square. Place on ungreased baking sheet. Bake at 400 degrees for 15 minutes or until golden brown. When cool, sprinkle with powdered sugar. 1 (20-ounce) can strawberry pie filling may be substituted for the pineapple. Yield: 2 dozen.
Ann Vavrek

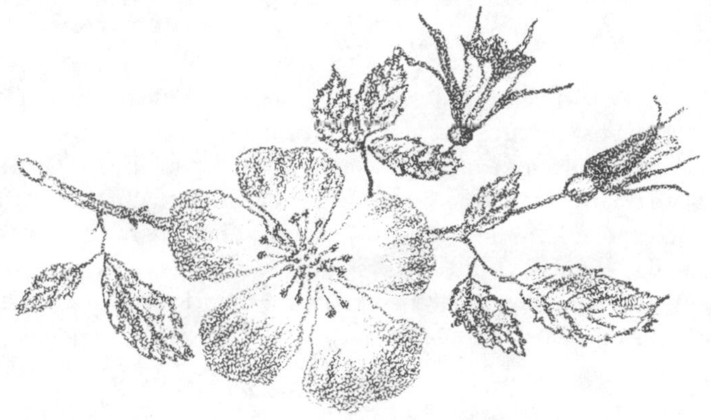

CHOCOLATE CHEESECAKE

1 (18.5-ounce) package dark chocolate cake mix with pudding
1 pound ricotta cheese
⅓ cup plus 1 tablespoon sugar
2 tablespoons vanilla extract

Prepare cake mix according to package directions. Pour batter into a greased and floured 13x9x2-inch baking pan. Combine cheese, sugar and vanilla; spoon over cake batter. Do not spread. Bake at 350 degrees 1 hour; cool completely before frosting.

Frosting:

1 (8-ounce) carton frozen whipped topping, thawed
1 (3-ounce) package instant chocolate pudding mix
1 cup milk

Combine ingredients and use to frost cake. Store cake in refrigerator. Yield: 12 servings.
Betz Spacek

CHEESECAKE DREAMS

⅓ cup brown sugar, firmly packed
1/cup unsifted all-purpose flour
½ cup chopped walnuts
⅓ cup margarine, melted
1 (8-ounce) package cream cheese, softened
¼ cup sugar
1 egg
2 tablespoons milk
1 tablespoon lemon juice
1 teaspoon vanilla extract

Preheat oven to 350 degrees. In a small bowl, mix brown sugar, flour and walnuts. Stir in melted margarine until well combined. Reserve ⅓ cup mixture; pat remainder gently into greased 8-inch square pan. Bake 12 minutes; remove from oven. Meanwhile, in small bowl with electric mixer at medium speed, beat cream cheese and sugar until smooth and creamy. Beat in remaining ingredients. Pour over crust and sprinkle with reserved crumb mixture. Bake 25 minutes longer, or until set. Cool on wire rack. Remove cooled cake from pan, cut into 2-inch squares, and cut each square diagonally in ½. Yield: 32.
Darlene Zembala

CHOCOLATE CHIP CHEESECAKE

1½ cups finely crushed creme-filled chocolate sandwich cookies (about 18)
¼ cup butter or margarine, melted
3 (8-ounce) packages cream cheese, softened
1 (14-ounce) can sweetened condensed milk
3 eggs
2 teaspoons vanilla extract
1 cup semi-sweet chocolate mini-morsels
1 teaspoon all-purpose flour

Preheat oven to 300 degrees. Combine crumbs and margarine; pat firmly into bottom of a 9-inch springform pan. In large mixing bowl, beat cream cheese until fluffy. Add milk and beat smooth. Add eggs and vanilla; mix well. In a small bowl, toss mini-morsels with flour to coat and stir into batter. Pour into prepared pan and sprinkle additional mini-morsels over top. Bake 1 hour or until cake springs back when lightly touched. Cool to room temperature; chill. Remove side from pan and garnish as desired. Store in refrigerator. Yield: 16 servings.
Sandy Jaffe

CHOCOLATE CHERRY CHEESECAKE CUPS

1 (16-ounce) roll refrigerated chocolate chip cookie dough
1 cup sugar
¼ cup all-purpose flour
2 (8-ounce) packages cream cheese, softened
½ cup margarine, softened
1 teaspoon vanilla extract
2 eggs
1 (21-ounce) can cherry pie filling

Line 24 muffin cups with paper baking cups. Slice well-chilled cookie dough into 24 slices and place 1 slice in the bottom of each muffin cup. Combine sugar, flour, cream cheese, margarine, vanilla and eggs. Beat with an electric mixer for 1 minute at medium speed. Top each cookie slice with cream cheese mixture, filling the cups ⅔ full. Bake at 350 degrees for 35 to 45 minutes or until tops are light golden brown. Top with pie filling. Yield: 24 cheesecakes.
Nicki Cowan

PEACH MOUSSE

1 cup mashed peaches, drained
1/2 cup sugar
1/2 pint heavy cream, whipped
2 egg whites
1/4 teaspoon almond extract

Fold peaches and sugar into whipped cream. In a separate bowl, beat egg whites until stiff. Fold into whipped cream mixture. Add flavoring. Cover and freeze. To serve, spoon into sherbet or parfait glasses. Yield: 6 to 8 servings.
Patti Lovejoy

CHEESECAKE TOASTIES

1 loaf thin-sliced party-type white bread
1 (8-ounce) package cream cheese
1 egg yolk
2 teaspoons sugar
1 cup butter or margarine, melted
1 cup sugar
1 teaspoon ground cinnamon

Remove crusts from bread slices and set aside. Combine cream cheese, egg yolk and sugar. Spread on 1/2 the bread slices and cover with remaining slices. Cut into triangles. Combine sugar and cinnamon. Dip triangles in melted butter, then into cinnamon-sugar mixture, taking care to coat thoroughly. Lay on ungreased cookie sheets and freeze overnight. To bake do not thaw first. Bake toasties at 350 degrees for 15 minutes. Serve warm.
Mary Kay Wise

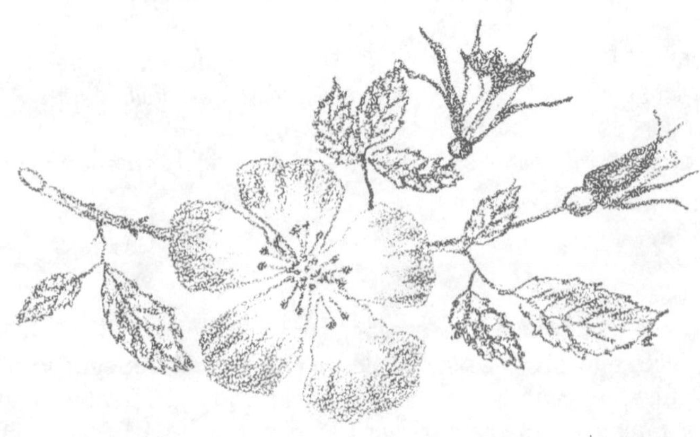

CAKE MIX CHEESECAKE

1 (18.5-ounce) package yellow cake mix
2 tablespoons vegetable oil
2 (8-ounce) packages cream cheese, softened
½ cup sugar
4 eggs
1½ cups milk
3 tablespoons lemon juice
3 teaspoons vanilla extract
1 (21-ounce) can cherry or blueberry pie filling

Reserve 1 cup dry cake mix. Combine remaining cake mix with oil and 1 egg. Press mixture evenly over bottom and ¾ way up sides of a greased 13x9x2-inch baking pan. In the same bowl blend cream cheese and sugar; add remaining eggs and reserved cake mix. Beat 1 minute at medium speed of electric mixer. Slowly add milk, juice and vanilla. Mix until smooth. Pour into prepared crust and bake at 300 degrees 40 to 45 minutes, until center is firm. Cool and top with pie filling (use any topping you like). Refrigerate. *Easy and delicious!* Yield: 12 servings.
Kay Kelly

OLD-FASHIONED CHEESECAKE

2 tablespoons butter or margarine
½ cup graham cracker crumbs
Pinch of ground cinnamon
1 tablespoon sugar
½ cup chopped pecans
4 eggs
1 cup sugar plus 4 tablespoons
1 teaspoon vanilla extract
1 teaspoon lemon juice
4 (8-ounce) packages cream cheese
1 pint dairy sour cream

Butter a 9-inch spring form pan and line well with graham cracker crumbs, which have been combined with cinnamon and 1 tablespoon sugar. Refrigerate crust for about 20 minutes. Press pecans gently into crust. Beat eggs in large mixing bowl with 1 cup sugar. Continue beating and add lemon juice. Blend in cream cheese, a little at a time. Mix well. Spoon into prepared crust and bake at 450 degrees for 25 minutes. Combine sour cream with 3 tablespoons sugar and vanilla. Spoon over top of baked cheesecake and return to oven and bake at 475 degrees for 8 to 10 minutes. (Leave oven door slightly open after baking first 5 minutes.) Remove from oven, cool and refrigerate overnight. Serve with your favorite topping, or plain. Yield: 8 to 10 servings.

HAWAIIAN PASTRY

½ cup butter or margarine
1½ cups all-purpose flour
1½ teaspoons baking powder
4 eggs, separated
4 tablespoons milk
1 teaspoon vanilla extract
1 (21-ounce) can prepared pineapple pie filling
½ cup sugar
1½ cups flaked coconut

Combine margarine, flour, baking powder, egg yolks, milk and vanilla in large mixing bowl; mix well. Spread into a greased 13x9x2-inch baking pan. Spread pineapple pie filling over batter. Beat egg whites until stiff; beat in sugar. Fold in coconut. Spread over pie filling in pan. Bake at 350 degrees for 35 minutes or until golden brown. Yield: 10 to 12 servings.
Jean Luther

NUT TORTE

8 eggs, separated
1 cup sugar
½ teaspoon vanilla extract
½ pound (8-ounces) ground walnuts
⅞ cup breadcrumbs

Beat egg yolks with sugar in large bowl of electric mixer for 2 minutes; fold in walnuts and breadcrumbs. Beat egg whites in separate bowl, add vanilla; fold into egg yolk mixture. Spread into 2 greased and floured 9-inch cake pans; bake at 350 degrees for 30 minutes. Remove to wire rack to cool. Cut each layer horizontally, into 2 equal layers (making 4 layers, totally) and spread filling between each layer.

Filling:

½ pound sweet butter
9 tablespoons sugar
2 cups milk
4 tablespoons all-purpose flour

Cream butter and sugar until it looks like cream cheese. Scald 1½ cups milk; set aside. Combine remaining ½ cup milk with flour to make paste; stir into scalded milk with wooden spoon or wire whisk. Cook and stir until thickened and smooth. Cool. Combine cooled mixture with creamed butter and vanilla and whip until smooth (mixture should look like whipped cream at this point). Use to fill torte layers.
Eileen Barlock

MOM'S DATE-NUT GRAHAM CRACKER ROLL

½ pound graham crackers, crushed, reserve some crumbs to roll mixture in
½ pound marshmallows, cut fine with scissors, or ½ pound miniatures
1 cup chopped nuts
1 (10-ounce) package dates, chopped fine
½ pint whipping cream

Combine all ingredients including whipping cream. Blend well. Roll mixture in reserved crumbs forming a roll. Wrap in foil and freeze overnight. Remove from freezer and allow to set ½ hour before slicing. Slice and top with whipped cream. *This has been an old family favorite for many years, usually made around the holidays.*
Blanche Archer

SOUR CHERRY CAKE WITH SAUCE

⅓ cup vegetable shortening
1½ cups sugar
2 eggs, well beaten
2¼ cups all-purpose flour
1½ teaspoons baking powder
½ teaspoon baking soda
½ teaspoon salt
1 cup milk
1 (20-ounce) can pitted sour cherries, drained and juice reserved
½ cup chopped nuts

Cream shortening and sugar in large bowl of electric mixer until light and fluffy; beat in eggs. Sift dry ingredients together and add to creamed mixture alternately with milk. Fold in cherries and nuts. Pour batter into a greased and floured 12x8x2-inch baking pan and bake at 350 degrees for 50 to 60 minutes, or until cake tests done. Remove from oven and cool in pan. Pour warm sauce over warm cake. Keep any leftovers stored in refrigerator. Yield: 10 to 12 servings.

Sauce:

½ cup sugar
Dash of salt
2 tablespoons cornstarch
Reserved cherry juice
Water
¼ teaspoon almond extract

Blend sugar, salt and cornstarch together in small saucepan. Add enough water to cherry juice in large cup to make 1¾ cups liquid. Stir into sugar mixture and place over medium heat. Bring to a boil stirring constantly. Reduce heat. Continue simmering until thickened, about 10 minutes, stirring occasionally. Remove from heat and blend in almond extract.
Sharon Wiza

PINEAPPLE UPSIDE-DOWN CAKE

1 (20-ounce) can sliced pineapple, drained and juice reserved
2 (4-ounce) packages instant vanilla pudding mix
½ cup firmly packed light brown sugar
1 (18.5-ounce) package yellow cake mix
4 eggs, slightly beaten
1 cup water
¼ cup vegetable oil
10 walnut halves

Arrange pineapple slices in a 13x9x2-inch baking pan which has been coated with non-stick cooking spray. Combine 1 box pudding mix with reserved pineapple juice; pour over pineapple in pan. Sprinkle with brown sugar. Combine cake mix, remaining pudding mix, eggs, water and oil in large bowl of electric mixer and beat, at medium speed, for 4 minutes, stopping to scrape down sides of bowl. Pour into pan over pineapple. Bake at 350 degrees for 55 to 60 minutes or until cake tests done. Do not underbake. Cool in pan for 5 minutes; invert onto platter and let stand for 1 minute. Remove pan and serve warm. (Deluxe cake mix is recommended.) Yield: 12 to 16 servings.
Sally Vlasik

PUMPKIN PIE CAKE

1 (18.5-ounce) package yellow cake mix
½ cup margarine, thoroughly softened

Reserve 1 cup dry cake mix. Combine remainder with margarine and press into 13x9x2-inch baking pan.

Filling:

1 (29-ounce) can pumpkin
3 eggs
⅔ cup evaporated milk
2 teaspoons ground cinnamon
1 cup sugar

Combine all ingredients well and pour over prepared crust.

Topping:

1 cup dry cake mix
½ cup sugar
¼ cup margarine, softened
1 cup chopped pecans

Combine reserved cake mix, sugar and margarine; mix until crumbly. Sprinkle over filling. Sprinkle pecans over top. Bake at 350 degrees for 1 hour, 15 minutes. Serve warm with whipped cream. Yield: 12 to 15 servings.
Kitty Morrisey

MOCHA CAKE

3 cups cake flour
3 teaspoons baking powder
1 teaspoon baking soda
1 teaspoon salt
1 cup butter or margarine
1 cup sugar
3 eggs
1 cups dairy sour cream

Sift flour, baking powder, soda and salt together. Set aside. Beat butter or margarine, and sugar together in large bowl of electric mixer until light and fluffy; add eggs, 1 at a time, beating after each addition. Add flour mixture alternately to batter with sour cream, beginning and ending with flour. Prepare filling.

Filling:

1 (6-ounce) package chocolate morsels
2 tablespoons instant coffee powder
½ cup firmly packed brown sugar

Combine chocolate morsels, coffee powder and brown sugar until crumbly. Spoon ⅓ cake batter into a greased 10-inch fluted tube pan. Sprinkle with ½ chocolate mixture. Cover chocolate morsels with ⅓ batter and sprinkle on other ½ chocolate filling. Cover with remaining ⅓ batter. Bake at 350 degrees for 1 hour. Remove from oven and cool in pan for 15 minutes. Turn cake out onto wire rack and cool completely. Drizzle with glaze.

Glaze:

2 tablespoons instant coffee powder
3 tablespoons boiling water
1¾ cups powdered sugar, sifted

Dissolve coffee in water. Beat with sugar in small bowl until smooth. Drizzle over prepared, cooled cake.
Nicki Cowan

RUBY'S HOT MILK BUTTER SPONGECAKE

½ cup milk
1 tablespoon butter
2 eggs
1 cup sugar
1 cup all-purpose flour
¼ teaspoon salt
1 teaspoon vanilla extract

Heat milk to almost boiling and stir in butter. Beat eggs with sugar in small mixing bowl; beat in milk/butter mixture, flour, salt and vanilla. Pour into a greased and floured 12x8x2-inch baking pan. Bake at 350 degrees for 30 minutes. Serve with favorite fruit. *A very good shortcake. This is a third generation family recipe.*
Betz Spacek

ORANGE NUT BUTTER CAKE

¾ cup butter, softened
1 cup sugar
1 tablespoon grated orange rind
1 teaspoon vanilla extract
3 eggs
1 cup orange marmalade
3 cups all-purpose flour
1½ teaspoons baking soda
1 teaspoon salt
½ cup orange juice
½ cup evaporated milk
1 cup chopped nuts

Cream butter thoroughly. Add sugar, orange rind and vanilla. Beat until mixture is light and fluffy. Add eggs, 1 at a time, beating well after each addition. Blend in marmalade. Sift together flour, soda and salt. Add to creamed mixture alternately with combined orange juice and evaporated milk. Stir in chopped nuts and blend. Turn into a well-buttered 10-inch tube pan. Bake in preheated 350 degree oven for 55 to 60 minutes. Cool in pan for 10 minutes; remove. Serve warm or cold. Cake is too rich for frosting but can be served with whipped cream or dairy topping. May be frozen if well wrapped.
Rosemary Corcoran

PINEAPPLE NUT CAKE

½ cup margarine or butter
1½ cups sugar
2 eggs
2 cups all-purpose flour
2 teaspoons vanilla extract
2 teaspoons baking soda
1 (20-ounce) can crushed pineapple with juice
½ cup chopped nuts

Cream butter or margarine with sugar and eggs in large bowl of eletric mixer until fluffy. Add flour, soda and vanilla; mix well. Stir in pineapple and nuts. Spread batter in a greased 13x9x2-inch baking pan. Bake at 350 degrees for 35 to 40 minutes or until cake tests done.

Frosting:

½ cup margarine or butter
1 (8-ounce) package cream cheese, softened
1¾ cups powdered sugar
1 teaspoon vanilla extract

Cream margarine in small bowl of electric mixer until fluffy; beat in cream cheese. Gradually add sifted powdered sugar, beating until smooth, light and fluffy. Beat in vanilla. Frost cake after it has cooled in pan.
Mary Gorbet
Nicki Cowan

DEE'S COCONUT CAKE

Topping:

2½ cups water
2 cups sugar

Bring sugar and water to a boil; set aside to cool while making cake.

Cake:

1½ cups margarine
1 cup sugar
7 eggs
1 teaspoon baking soda
2 teaspoons baking powder
1½ teaspoons vanilla extract
2 cups all-purpose flour
4 cups coconut (12-ounces)

Cream together margarine and sugar; add eggs, one at a time. Add vanilla and dry ingredients, blending well. Stir in coconut. Pour into 13x9x2-inch baking pan and bake at 350 degrees 45 to 50 minutes. Remove cake from oven and let cool 5 minutes. Cut into diamond shapes. Pour cooled syrup mixture over entire cake. If desired, diamond shapes may be placed in paper cupcake liners. Keeps well in refrigerator or may be frozen.
Betz Spacek

FATHER NOVAK'S CAKE

1⅔ cups all-purpose flour
1 teaspoon baking powder
½ cup butter
⅓ cup sugar
1 egg

Sift flour and baking powder into a bowl. Add remaining ingredients in the order given, making a smooth paste. Set aside.

Filling:

2 cups ground almonds
2 cups sugar
1 cup butter
4 eggs
2 teaspoons almond extract
Raspberry jam

Work almonds, sugar and butter together by hand; then beat in eggs with a wooden spoon, adding almond extract last. To assemble cake, roll out crust between layers of waxed paper and line 2 (9-inch) round cake pans with thin crusts. Spread raspberry jam ½-inch thick over crust, then add filling. Bake at 325 degrees for 1 hour. Filling should be risen but not soggy. Wooden pick will come out clean when cakes are done. Serve in tiny wedges. *Great with coffee!* Yield: 16 large or 32 small servings.
Father David Novak

MELODY'S MANDARIN ORANGE CAKE

1 (21-ounce) package yellow cake mix (butter flavor)
4 eggs, slightly beaten
1 (11-ounce) can mandarin oranges, drained
⅓ cup vegetable oil

Combine ingredients, in order listed, in large bowl of electric mixer. Beat well (about 3 or 4 minutes) scraping sides of bowl. Orange pieces should be broken up completely. Spread batter into three 8-inch baking pans which have been coated with non-stick cooking spray. Bake at 350 degrees for 20 to 25 minutes or until cake tests done. Frost.

Icing:

1 (20-ounce) can crushed pineapple with juice
1 (3-ounce) package instant vanilla pudding mix
1 cup flaked coconut
1 (9-ounce) container frozen non-dairy whipped topping, thawed

Beat undrained pineapple and pudding mix together in large mixing bowl. Fold in coconut and whipped topping. Use to fill between layers and on top and sides of cake.
Sister Patricia Ann, O.S.U.

GRANDMA'S OLD-FASHIONED CHOCOLATE CAKE

3 cups all-purpose flour
1 teaspoon baking powder
1 teaspoon salt
2 cups sugar
½ cup vegetable oil
2 eggs
½ cup unsweetened cocoa powder
1 cup sour milk
1 cup water
1 teaspoon baking soda
1 teaspoon vanilla extract

Sift together flour, baking powder and salt. Set aside. In a large bowl combine sugar, oil, cocoa and eggs. Add flour mixture alternately with sour milk, beating until smooth. Boil 1 cup water and add soda. Stir soda water and vanilla into batter; turn into 2 (9-inch) cake pans. Bake at 350 degrees 40 minutes. Yield: 16 servings.
Peggy Koch

GINGERBREAD FLAN CAKE

1/4 cup margarine
1/4 cup sugar
1 egg
1/2 cup molasses
1 1/4 cups all-purpose flour
1 teaspoon baking soda
1/4 teaspoon ground nutmeg
1/4 teaspoon ground ginger
1/4 teaspoon salt
1/2 cup hot water

Cream margarine, sugar and egg in large bowl until light and fluffy. Add molasses to blend. Sift dry ingredients together and add along with hot water; beat 1 minute. Pour into greased and floured flan pan. Bake at 375 degrees for 20 minutes or until flan tests done. Cool for 35 minutes in pan. Remove from pan and place on serving dish. Fill with 1 can prepared peaches. Top with whipped cream. (See recipe below.) Yield: 8 servings.

Whipped Cream With Gelatin:

1 cup heavy whipping cream
1/2 teaspoon unflavored gelatin
2 tablespoons sugar
1 tablespoon water
2 teaspoons vanilla extract

Soften 1/2 teaspoon unflavored gelatin in small metal cup containing 1 tablespoon of cold water. Set cup in pan of boiling water or over very low heat and stir until gelatin is dissolved. Beat dissolved gelatin into whipping cream just until it begins to thicken. Use as desired.
Hollis Hura, Registered Dietitian, Parmadale

BUTTERMILK CAKE

3/4 cup vegetable shortening
2 cups sugar
3 eggs, slightly beaten
1 teaspoon vanilla extract
3 cups all-purpose flour
1 1/2 teaspoons baking powder
1 teaspoon baking soda
1 teaspoon salt
1 1/2 cups buttermilk

Combine shortening, sugar and eggs in large bowl of electric mixer and beat until light and fluffy. Blend in vanilla. Sift together dry ingredients and add to batter, alternately, with buttermilk. Beat well. Spread batter into 2 greased and floured 9-inch baking pans. Bake at 350 degrees for 35 to 40 minutes. Cool before frosting with your favorite frosting.
Maryann Ustach

FLAN CAKES

A flan cake is a cake that has been baked in a special pan designed to hold puddings or mounds of berries or other fresh fruits. To bake this type of cake you must use a flan pan, available at most major department stores or cake and candy supply stores.

Basic Flan Cake Shell:

½ cup milk
2 tablespoons butter
2 eggs
1 cup sugar
½ teaspoon vanilla extract
1 cup sifted all-purpose flour
1 teaspoon baking powder
¼ teaspoon salt

Scald milk in small saucepan. Add butter and remove from heat. Using a large mixing bowl, beat eggs until thick and lemon colored; add sugar and vanilla, beating until light and fluffy. Sift together flour, baking powder and salt; fold into egg mixture. Combine with hot milk. Pour batter into a greased and floured flan pan. Bake at 350 degrees for 25 minutes or until cake tests done. Cool 5 minutes in pan, then turn out onto a serving plate. Fill with desired filling. Yield: 1 flan cake. *You may use your favorite cake mix for flan shell. 2-layer mix will make 2 flan cakes. Make sure cake and filling flavors complement one another.*

Cherry Custard Flan:

Prepare flan shell. Using 1½ cups milk, prepare a 3-ounce package of vanilla pudding mix according to package directions. Cool and pour into prepared flan shell. Spoon cherry pie filling over vanilla pudding. (Other fruit fillings may be substituted for cherry.) Must be refrigerated. Yield: 8 servings.
Hollis Hura, Registered Dietitian, Parmadale

APPLE CAKE

1¾ cups sugar
1 cup vegetable oil
3 eggs
1 teaspoon vanilla extract
2 cups all-purpose flour
1 teaspoon baking soda
1 teaspoon ground cinnamon
Pinch of salt
1 cup chopped nuts, optional
4 or 5 apples, sliced as for pie

In a mixing bowl, beat sugar, oil, eggs and vanilla. Add dry ingredients, beating well after each addition. Stir in nuts and apples with a wooden spoon. Pour into greased 13x9x2-inch pan and bake at 350 degrees for 1 hour. You may sprinkle nuts on top before baking if desired. Serve plain or with whipped cream. Yield: 15 to 20 servings.
Karen Collins

BLUEBERRY CRUMB CAKE

Topping:

1/2 cup sugar
1 teaspoon ground cinnamon
1/4 cup butter or margarine
1/3 cup sifted all-purpose flour
2 cups fresh blueberries, washed, drained and dried

Mix sugar, cinnamon and flour in small bowl; cut butter into dry ingredients until coarse crumbs form. Set aside.

Cake:

2 cups sifted all-purpose flour
2 teaspoons baking powder
1/2 teaspoon salt
1/4 cup butter
1 teaspoon vanilla extract
3/4 cup sugar
1 egg
1/2 cup milk
Finely grated rind of 1 lemon
1/2 cup chopped walnuts
Breadcrumbs (fine)

Sift flour, baking powder and salt together. Place blueberries in large bowl; sprinkle with 1 1/2 teaspoons sifted dry ingredients. Toss gently to coat blueberries with flour without crushing. Set aside. Cream butter and sugar in small bowl of electric mixer, beat in egg; add vanilla and beat for 1 minute. Add sifted dry ingredients, alternately, with milk, beginning and ending with dry ingredients. Stir in lemon rind. Gently fold in blueberries with a spatula. Spread batter (it will be stiff) into a 9-inch square baking pan which has been buttered and dusted with fine breadcrumbs. Sprinkle batter with chopped walnuts, then topping. Bake at 375 degrees for 50 minutes. Cool in pan for 1/2 hour. Cover top of pan with aluminum foil and invert cake onto foil, then invert again (original top side will be up) onto serving dish.
Betty Schadle

CAPE COD BLUEBERRY CAKE

1 cup vegetable shortening
2 1/2 cups sugar
3 eggs
1 cup milk
5 teaspoons baking powder
1 teaspoon salt
5 cups all-purpose flour
1 1/2 to 2 pints (3 or 4 cups) blueberries

Cream shortening and sugar in large bowl of electric mixer until light and fluffy. Beat in eggs, one at a time; add milk. Sift dry ingredients together and add to batter. Mix well. Stir in fresh blueberries. Spread in greased and floured 15x10x2-inch baking pan. Bake at 350 degrees for 40 to 50 minutes. *This is good plain or with whipped cream - great for a large group!*
Betz Spacek

RUM-RAISIN RING CAKE

1 (20-ounce) can crushed pineapple, drained (reserve juice)
1½ cups sugar
½ cup butter, softened
3 eggs
1 teaspoon vanilla extract
2½ cups all-purpose flour
1 teaspoon baking powder
1 teaspoon baking soda
1 teaspoon ground allspice
½ teaspoon salt
½ cup dark rum
1 cup raisins
1 cup chopped walnuts

Press out 1¼ cups pineapple juice, reserving ¼ cup for cake and 3 tablespoons for icing. Cream sugar and butter; beat in eggs and vanilla. Stir together flour, baking powder, soda, allspice and salt. Add to creamed mixture alternately with reserved ¼ cup pineapple juice and rum. Stir in pineapple, raisins and nuts. Spoon into greased 10-inch bundt pan and bake at 350 degrees 50 to 55 minutes, until wooden pick inserted in cake comes clean. Invert on wire rack to cool completely. *Wonderful!*

Rum Glaze:

3 tablespoons dark rum
3 tablespoons pineapple juice
2 tablespoons butter, softened
3 cups powdered sugar

Beat until blended; spoon over cooled cake. Yield: 16 servings.
Mary Kaminski

CHARLOTTE'S EASY CHOCOLATE CAKE

2½ cups all-purpose flour
1½ cups sugar
1 teaspoon salt
½ cup cocoa
2 teaspoons baking soda
⅔ cup butter or margarine
2 eggs, slightly beaten
*1 cup sour milk**
½ cup water
1 teaspoon vanilla extract

*Use 1 cup milk plus 1 tablespoon vinegar if sour milk isn't available.

Sift flour, sugar, salt, cocoa and soda into large mixing bowl. Add butter or margarine, eggs, milk, water and vanilla and beat at low speed for 3 minutes. (Batter will be lumpy from margarine.) Spread into two 8-inch baking pans which have been coated with non-stick cooking spray. Bake at 350 degrees for 30 to 35 minutes or until cake tests done. Frost with whipped cream frosting. *This is a very moist, heavy cake. You can bake it in a 13x9x2-inch pan and sprinkle cooled cake with sifted powdered sugar.*
Charlotte Rosko

GOLDEN FRUITCAKE

2 cups golden raisins
1 cup diced candied citron
1 cup diced candied lemon peel
1 cup diced candied orange peel
1 cup chopped pitted dates
1 cup chopped walnuts
2 cups candied red cherries, halved
½ cup all-purpose flour

Preheat oven to 300 degrees. Line a 10-inch tube pan with aluminum foil. In a large bowl, combine fruits and nuts. Toss lightly with ½ cup flour until well-coated. Set aside.

Batter:

1 cup butter or margarine, softened
2 cups sugar
3 cups all-purpose flour
2 teaspoons baking powder
½ teaspoon salt
6 eggs
1 teaspoon lemon extract
1 cup orange juice

In a large bowl, beat butter with sugar until light and fluffy, using medium speed of mixer. Add flour, baking powder, salt, eggs, lemon extract and orange juice. Beat at low speed until well-mixed, scraping sides of bowl. Continue beating for 4 minutes. Stir fruit mixture into batter and blend. Pour batter into pan and bake for 3 hours or until toothpick inserted in center comes out clean. Cool cake completely in pan. Remove when cool from pan and store in plastic container or wrap with foil.
Eileen Barlock

GRAHAM STREUSEL CAKE

2 cups fine graham cracker crumbs (24 square crackers, crushed)
¾ cup chopped nuts
¾ cup firmly packed brown sugar
1¼ teaspoons ground cinnamon
¾ cup butter or margarine, melted
1 (18.5-ounce) package yellow cake mix
1 cup water
⅓ cup vegetable oil
3 eggs, slightly beaten

Combine crumbs, nuts, brown sugar, cinnamon and butter in large mixing bowl. Set aside. In separate bowl, beat cake mix, water, oil and eggs together, on low speed, for about 2 minutes. Pour 2⅓ cups of batter into a greased 13x9x2-inch baking pan. Sprinkle with 2 cups reserved crumb mixture. Pour on remaining batter, then sprinkle with remaining crumb mixture. Bake at 350 degrees for 40 to 50 minutes. Remove from oven and cool in pan.
Marianne Gebura

FRUITCAKE

1 cup butter
½ cup brown sugar, firmly packed
6 eggs
2 cups all-purpose flour
½ teaspoon ground cinnamon
¼ teaspoon ground nutmeg
¼ teaspoon ground allspice
2½ teaspoons baking powder
1 cup raisins
1½ cups chopped walnuts
½ cup candied cherries
½ cup candied pineapple
½ cup orange juice
2 tablespoons honey
Rum, bourbon or brandy

Preheat oven to 275 degrees. Grease a bundt pan or 2 (9x5x3-inch) loaf pans. Cream butter and sugar until light and fluffy. Add eggs, one at a time, beating well after each addition. Sift together flour, cinnamon, nutmeg, allspice and baking powder. Combine raisins, cherries, pineapple, walnuts, orange juice and honey. Stir in ⅓ cup of the flour mixture. Fold remaining flour mixture into batter and stir in fruit mixture. Pack into prepared pans. Bake about 2¼ hours, or until a wooden pick inserted in center comes out clean. Wrap cooled cakes in cheesecloth soaked in rum, bourbon or brandy and store in airtight tins. *The longer it is kept, the better it gets!* Yield: 12 to 20 servings.
Pat Navin

LEMON-GLAZED POPPY SEED CAKE

¼ cup poppy seed
⅔ cup water
1 (18.5-ounce) package butter recipe yellow cake mix
½ cup butter or margarine, softened
3 eggs

Soak poppy seed in water about 30 minutes. Combine all ingredients and blend until moistened. Beat 4 minutes at medium speed. Pour into greased and floured 12-cup bundt pan and bake at 350 degrees 45 to 50 minutes, or until cake springs back when lightly touched with fingertip. Cool in pan 10 minutes, then remove and cool completely on wire rack. Drizzle cooled cake with glaze. Yield: 12 to 16 servings.

Lemon Glaze:

1 cup powdered sugar
1 tablespoon lemon juice
Water

Combine sugar and lemon juice, adding enough water to reach glaze consistency.
Ursula Bartosik

KAY'S POPPY SEED TORTE

1 pound poppy seed
3 cups milk
2 cups sugar
1 cup butter
2 tablespoons baking powder
2 tablespoons flour
1½ cups fine breadcrumbs
8 eggs

Combine poppy seed, milk and 1 cup sugar in saucepan and place over medium heat. Bring to a boil, stirring to dissolve sugar, and then remove from heat and set aside to cool. Cream butter, remaining 1 cup sugar until light and fluffy. Add baking powder, flour and breadcrumbs; beat well. Add eggs, one at a time, beating well after each addition. Stir in poppyseed mixture to blend. Spread in 2 greased 15x10x1-inch jellyroll baking pans. Bake at 325 degrees for about 45 minutes or until toothpick inserted near center comes out clean. Cut each cake in half to make 4 layers. Cool and frost each layer.

Frosting:

1 tablespoon butter
2 to 3 tablespoons boiling milk
Confectioners' sugar

Blend butter and milk in small bowl of electric mixer; beat in enough confectioners' sugar to reach spreading consistency. Beat until light and smooth. Use to frost torte.
Betz Spacek

POPPY SEED CAKE

1 (21-ounce) package yellow cake mix
1 (3-ounce) package vanilla pudding mix
4 eggs
1 cup dairy sour cream
½ cup vegetable oil
½ cup cream sherry
1 teaspoon butter-flavored extract
¼ cup poppy seed (scant)

Mix ingredients together in large bowl of electric mixer and beat for 3 or 4 minutes, scraping sides. Spread into a greased 10-inch fluted tube pan. Bake at 350 degrees for 45 to 50 minutes or until cake tests done. Cool in pan for 15 minutes; remove to wire rack to complete cooling.
Sue Robinson
Rene O'Day

MISSISSIPPI MUD CAKE

1 cup butter or margarine
3½ tablespoons cocoa
2 cups sugar
4 eggs, slightly beaten
1½ cups all-purpose flour
1 teaspoon vanilla extract
1½ cups shredded coconut
1½ cups chopped nuts
1 (7-ounce) jar marshmallow creme

Melt margarine; stir in cocoa and sugar. Beat in eggs, flour and vanilla. Mix well. Stir in coconut and nuts. Spread in a greased and floured 13x9x2-inch baking pan and bake at 350 degrees for 30 to 35 minutes. Remove from oven and spread with marshmallow creme. Cool slightly while making icing.

Icing:

½ cup butter or margarine
½ cup cocoa
½ cup milk
1 cup chopped nuts
1 (16-ounce) package powdered sugar

Cream margarine, cocoa and sugar. Blend in remaining ingredients and pour over warm cake. Let cool in refrigerator before cutting.
Shirley Holler
Peggy Rollins

RICE CAKE

1 cup long-grain rice
1 quart milk
¾ cup butter or margarine
5 eggs, separated
1 orange rind, grated
1 cup sugar
½ cup golden raisins
¼ cup cracker crumbs

Wash rice; place into 4-quart saucepan. Add water to cover and bring to a boil over high heat. Remove from heat; drain. Return to pan and stir in milk. Cook slowly, stirring occasionally, until rice is tender (anywhere from 30 to 60 minutes). Cool slightly. Cream butter with sugar; beat in egg yolks until lemon colored and thick. Stir in rice; add orange rind and raisins. Blend well. Beat egg whites until stiff peaks form and gently fold into rice mixture. Pour into a 10-inch fluted tube pan which has been dusted with cracker crumbs. Bake at 350 degrees for 50 minutes or until cake tests done. Remove from oven and cool in pan for 20 minutes. Remove from pan and dust with powdered sugar before serving.
Pat Sebek

BEAUTY PARLOR FROSTING

1/2 cup butter or margarine
1/2 cup vegetable shortening
1 cup sugar
3 tablespoons all-purpose flour
2/3 cup milk
1 teaspoon vanilla extract

Cream sugar and shortening until light and fluffy. Stir sugar and flour together, then gradually beat into creamed mixture. Beat at high speed until light and fluffy. Gradually add milk and vanilla, blending at low speed, then beat 5 minutes at high speed. At one point mixture may appear curdly, but will clear with additional beating. Yield: sufficient frosting for 1 (9-inch) layer cake.
Gloria Melaragno

CHOCOLATE PUDDING CAKE

1 (10 to 12 ounce) prepared angel food cake
1 (6-ounce) package chocolate pudding mix
1 (3-ounce) package chocolate pudding mix
5 cups milk
2 cups heavy whipping cream, whipped with 1/4 cup sugar
Finely ground nuts
Cherry halves

Break angel food cake into bite-sized pieces and arrange in bottom of 13x9x2-inch baking pan. Combine milk and pudding mixes in large saucepan and bring to a boil over medium-high heat, stirring constantly. Cook for 3 minutes. Remove from heat and pour over angel food cake in pan. Cool to room temperature. Spread cake with whipped cream, sprinkle with nuts and garnish with cherries. Cover with plastic wrap and chill for several hours before serving. Yield: 12 servings.
Phyllis Mazzella

FRUIT SURPRISE

1 (21-ounce) package yellow cake mix
1/2 cup melted butter
2 eggs, slightly beaten
1 (21-ounce) can cherry or blueberry pie filling
1/2 cup chopped nuts, optional

Mix cake mix, butter and eggs together in large bowl with wooden spoon until smooth. Spread into ungreased 13x9x2-inch baking pan. Pour pie filling over batter and spread to edges; sprinkle with nuts, if desired. Bake at 350 degrees for 40 to 45 minutes. Remove from oven and cool in pan. Top with whipped topping or a glaze made from 1 cup confectioners' sugar and 1 tablespoon water (glaze should be thin enough to drizzle over cake). Yield: 12 servings.
Lee Creadon

AMARETTO ICEBOX CAKE

2 cups heavy cream
6 tablespoons unsweetened cocoa powder
6 tablespoons sugar
2 tablespoons Amaretto liqueur
Pinch of salt
32 chocolate wafers

Combine cream, cocoa, sugar, Amaretto and salt in a bowl. Refrigerate 2 hours, then beat chilled mixture until stiff peaks form. Sandwich chocolate wafers with 1 tablespoon cream mixture. Make stacks of 6 wafers each. Arrange 1 stack of wafers on its side on serving plate. Spread end wafer with cream mixture and press another stack of wafers to it. When all wafers have been used, frost entire roll with cream mixture. Refrigerate 4 hours to overnight. To serve, cut diagonally. Yield: 10 servings.
Nicki Cowan

NO EGG CHOCOLATE CUPCAKES

4 tablespoons butter or margarine
1 cup sugar
1¾ cups all-purpose flour
½ cup cocoa
1¼ teaspoons salt
1 teaspoon baking soda
1 teaspoon baking powder
1¼ cups sour milk

Cream butter or margarine with sugar in large bowl of electric mixer until light and fluffy. Sift dry ingredients together. Add to creamed mixture alternately with sour milk, beginning and ending with flour. Spoon batter into muffin tins which have been greased well or lined with paper cups. Bake at 375 degrees for 20 minutes or until light brown. Frost with whipped cream frosting. Yield: 8 to 10 cupcakes.
Sister Joan

GERMAN POUND CAKE

6 eggs
1 (16-ounce) package confectioners' sugar
1 pound (2 cups) butter or margarine
3 cups all-purpose flour, sifted
2 teaspoons vanilla extract

Beat eggs and confectioners' sugar together in large mixing bowl; add margarine or butter and continue beating. Add flour and vanilla and continue beating for 5 minutes more. Pour batter into a greased and floured 10-inch tube pan or 2 (9x5x3-inch) loaf pans. Bake at 350 degrees for 1 hour and 15 minutes. Remove from oven and turn out onto wire rack to cool. Sprinkle with confectioners' sugar before serving, if desired. *This is an old German recipe.*
Kathy Fagan

ROCKY ROAD CAKE

1 (12-ounce) package semi-sweet chocolate morsels
1/4 cup sugar
4 eggs, separated
1 teaspoon vanilla extract
2 cups whipping cream, whipped to soft peaks
1 cup chopped nuts
1 (10-inch) baked angel food cake, torn into bite-sized pieces

Melt chocolate morsels in top of double boiler over hot, not boiling, water. Stir in sugar. Beat egg yolks and stir in a little egg yolk at a time, stirring constantly and being sure water in bottom pan is not boiling. Cook and stir until smooth. Remove from heat and stir in vanilla. Cool slightly. Beat egg whites until stiff, not dry. Add chocolate mixture to egg whites, a little at a time, mixing until smooth (whites will fall). Fold in whipped cream. Coat bottom of a 13x9x2-inch baking pan with non-stick cooking spray. Layer 1/3 of cake in bottom of pan. Spread 1/3 chocolate mixture over cake and sprinkle with 1/3 nuts. Repeat layers, ending with nuts. Wrap with plastic wrap and refrigerate overnight. This dessert may be frozen if desired. Yield: 10 to 12 servings.
Peggy Rollins
Nicki Cowan

ANGEL FOOD CAKE DESSERT

1 (6-ounce) package chocolate morsels
2 tablespoons water
1 teaspoon sugar
4 eggs, separated
1 cup whipped cream
1 baked angel food cake

Combine chocolate morsels, water and sugar in top of double boiler; place over hot, not boiling, water and stir until melted and smooth. Cool. Beat yolks slightly and stir into cooled chocolate mixture until thoroughly mixed. Beat whites in separate bowl; fold in whipped cream. Combine the 2 mixtures by gently folding chocolate mixture into whipped mixture. Break angel food cake into bite-sized pieces. Layer in serving bowl and pour chocolate sauce over all. Cover tightly with plastic wrap and refrigerate overnight before serving. Yield: 10 to 12 servings.
Nicki Cowan

LEE'S WHIPPED CREAM FROSTING

1 cup sugar
4 tablespoons all-purpose flour
2 eggs
2 cups milk
½ cup butter or margarine
½ cup vegetable shortening
2 teaspoons vanilla extract

In a 4-cup saucepan, mix sugar and flour thoroughly. Beat together milk and eggs. Mix with flour and sugar. Cook over medium heat, stirring constantly, until mixture is a thick paste. Cover with wax paper to prevent coating and cool in refrigerator. While custard is cooling, cream margarine, shortening and vanilla. Add cooled custard a couple of tablespoons at a time. Whip well between each addition. Whip until very light and creamy.
Lee Creadon
Frances Willson

QUICK AND EASY CHOCOLATE FROSTING

½ cup butter or margarine
4 tablespoons cocoa
1 tablespoon vanilla extract
2 cups confectioners' sugar
1 egg

Melt margarine or butter in saucepan over low heat. Remove from heat and stir in cocoa and vanilla. Pour into small bowl of electric mixer; add confectioners' sugar. Add egg and beat until light and fluffy. Spread on cake as desired. Yield: enough for 13x9x2-inch cake.
Michele Leahy

LINZER TORTE

3 cups all-purpose flour
1 cup sugar
1 teaspoon baking powder
Pinch of baking soda
1 cup butter or margarine
5 eggs, separated
2 teaspoons vanilla extract
2 tablespoons powdered sugar
*Jam**
1½ cups chopped walnuts

Sift flour, sugar, baking powder and soda together in large mixing bowl. Blend in butter or margarine, egg yolks and vanilla with pastry blender. Mixture should look like pie dough. Do not handle too much. Pat into bottom of on 15x10x2-inch baking sheet and one 8-inch square pan. Spread your choice of jam over dough. Sprinkle on ½ cup chopped nuts. Beat egg whites until soft peaks form; spread over nuts. Sprinkle with confectioners' sugar. Sprinkle on remaining nuts. Bake at 350 degrees for about 30 minutes. Cut into squares when cooled. *Use your choice of jam - strawberry, pineapple, apricot or raspberry. Yield: 16 to 20 servings.
Janet Barkawsh

FRESH BLUEBERRY PIE

Pastry for 2-crust pie:

2 cups sifted all-purpose flour
1 teaspoon salt
¾ cup vegetable shortening
4 tablespoons water

Stir together flour and salt in a large bowl. Add shortening and cut in with pastry blender until mixture is uniform. Sprinkle water over mixture and stir with fork until blended. Work dough into a firm ball with hands. Divide in ½ and roll out on floured surface to ⅛-inch thickness.

Blueberry filling:

⅞ cup sugar
5 tablespoons all-purpose flour
½ teaspoon ground cinnamon
4 cups fresh blueberries
1½ tablespoons lemon juice

Combine sugar, flour and cinnamon; add blueberries and toss lightly to coat. Stir in lemon juice and turn into pastry-lined 9-inch pie plate. Cover with top crust, seal and crimp edges and cut several slits in top to allow steam to escape. Bake at 425 degrees 30 to 40 minutes, or until crust is golden brown and juices bubble up through slits in crust. Yield: 6 to 8 servings.
Rosemary Balchak

BEST APPLE PIE

Pie crust for 2 crust pie
5 large cooking apples (Rome) or 6 or 7 medium size apples (McIntosh) sliced thinly
⅓ cup firmly packed light brown sugar
⅓ cup sugar
1 tablespoon cornstarch or 2 tablespoons all-purpose flour
1½ teaspoons ground cinnamon
⅓ teaspoon salt
3 tablespoons lemon juice
6 teaspoons butter

Mix dry ingredients and then add to sliced apples while tossing. Add lemon juice and toss gently. Let stand 10 minutes; fill the unbaked pie crust and add 6 teaspoons butter on top. Place second crust over apples and seal edges. For crispy and sugary top, brush top of pie shell lightly with a heavy mixture of sugar dissolved in milk. Bake at 400 degrees for 45 minutes. Yield: 6 to 8 servings.
Joe Kovach

READY-TO-GO PIE CRUST MIX

6 cups sifted all-purpose flour
1 tablespoon salt
2⅓ cups vegetable shortening

Mix flour and salt in a large bowl. Cut in shortening with pastry blender until mixture resembles fine crumbs. Store in covered container (does not need to be refrigerated). Yield: 7 to 8 cups.

Single 8- or 9-inch pastry crust:

1½ cups Ready-To-Go Pie Crust Mix
3 tablespoons water

Combine water with pie crust mix, a tablespoon at a time, tossing lightly with a fork. When all water has been added and mixed, work dough with hands into a firm ball. Roll out on floured surface.

Double 8- or 9-inch pastry crust:

2¼ cups Ready-To-Go Pie Crust Mix
4 tablespoons water

Mix as for single crust, rolling only ½ at a time.

Double 10-inch crust:

3 cups Ready-To-Go Pie Crust Mix
6 tablespoons water

Mix as for single crust, rolling only ½ at a time.
Rosemary Balchak

MOCHA MUD PIE

½ (9-ounce) package chocolate wafers
4 tablespoons butter, melted
1 quart coffee ice cream, softened
1½ cups fudge sauce

Crush wafers and stir in butter. Mix well and press onto bottom and sides of a 9-inch pie plate. Cover crust with ice cream and freeze until firm. When pie is firm, top with cold fudge sauce. Leave pie in freezer about 10 hours before serving. To serve, cut into wedges and serve on chilled plates with chilled forks. Top with whipped cream and slivered almonds. Yield: 8 servings.
Rosemary Balchak

SOUR CREAM APPLE OR PEACH PIE

¾ cup sugar
2 tablespoons all-purpose flour
⅛ teaspoon salt
1 cup dairy sour cream
1 egg, well-beaten
½ teaspoon vanilla extract
4 cups finely chopped tart apples or 4 cups thinly sliced fresh peaches

Topping:

⅓ cup sugar
⅓ cup all-purpose flour
¼ cup butter or margarine
1 (9-inch) unbaked pie shell

Sift ¾ cup sugar, 2 tablespoons flour and salt together in large bowl. Add cream, eggs and vanilla and mix well. Fold in apples or peaches. Spoon into prepared pie shell and bake at 425 degrees for 15 minutes. Reduce heat to 350 degrees and continue baking for 30 minutes more. Blend ⅓ cup sugar, ⅓ cup flour and butter or margarine to make crumb topping. Remove pie from oven and sprinkle on topping; return to oven and bake for 15 minutes more. Remove from oven and refrigerate immediately until cool. Yield: 8 servings.
Sue Mahon

CHOCOLATE ANGEL PIE

Crust:

4 or 5 egg whites, room temperature
¼ teaspoon cream of tartar
Pinch of salt
½ cup sugar
1 cup chopped nuts

Beat egg whites in small mixing bowl until soft peaks form; add cream of tartar and salt and beat until stiff. Gradually add sugar, about 1 tablespoon at a time, beating constantly. Fold in nuts. Spread in 9-inch pie plate and bake at 300 degrees for 40 minutes.

Filling:

1 bar German sweet chocolate, melted and cooled
2 tablespoons water
1 cup heavy cream, whipped

Stir water into cooled chocolate; fold in whipped cream. Spoon into cooled pie shell and refrigerate. Garnish with more whipped cream before serving. Yield: 6 or 8 servings.
Sue Mahon

MALTED MILK PIE

Crust:

1½ cups flaked coconut
2 tablespoons melted margarine
2 tablespoons sugar
Pinch of ground cinnamon
¼ cup finely crushed graham crackers, vanilla wafers or chocolate wafers

Combine all ingredients and press onto bottom and sides of a 9-inch pie plate. Bake a 375 degrees for 10 to 12 minutes; cool.

Filling:

6 (2.5-ounce) malted milk candy bars
¼ cup milk
1 tablespoon brewed coffee
1 quart vanilla ice cream, softened

Chop candy into chunks, reserving 2 bars for garnish. Combine chopped candy, milk and coffee in a saucepan; cook over low heat until melted and smooth. Remove and cool to room temperature. Place softened ice cream in a large bowl; stir in chocolate mixture until well-blended. Spoon into cooled pie shell. Place in freezer for 3 to 4 hours. Remove to refrigerator for 20 minutes before serving. Garnish with sliced reserved candy bars. Yield: 6 to 8 servings.
Edna Stein

JUST RIGHT PUMPKIN PIE

Pastry for 9-inch pie shell
2 tablespoons butter or margarine
1½ cups canned pumpkin
1 teaspoon ground ginger
1 teaspoon ground cinnamon
¼ teaspoon ground mace
¼ teaspoon ground cloves
2 eggs
2 tablespoons all-purpose flour
½ cup firmly packed light brown sugar
½ cup sugar
½ teaspoon salt
1 cup milk

Line a 9-inch pie plate with pastry and refrigerate while making filling. Preheat oven to 450 degrees. Melt butter or margarine and stir into pumpkin along with ginger, cinnamon, mace and cloves. Using separate bowl, beat eggs until frothy and stir in flour, sugars, salt and milk. Combine egg and pumpkin mixtures gently. Pour filling into reserved pie shell and place in oven. Bake for 15 minutes; reduce heat to 375 degrees, and continue baking for 45 minutes more or until tip of knife inserted in center of pie comes out clean. Serve warm or cold with whipped cream. Yield: 6 to 8 servings.
Rosemary Corcoran

GEORGIA'S PEANUT BUTTER PIE

⅔ cup dry roasted peanuts, chopped fine
1 cup all-purpose flour
½ cup butter or margarine, softened
⅓ cup smooth peanut butter
1 cup powdered sugar
1 (8-ounce) package cream cheese, softened
1 cup non-dairy whipped topping
1 (3-ounce) package instant chocolate pudding mix
1 (3-ounce) package instant vanilla pudding mix
2¾ cups milk

Blend peanuts, flour and margarine in large bowl until crumbly; press into greased 10-inch pie plate or 13x9x2-inch baking pan. Bake at 350 degrees for 15 to 20 minutes. Cool. Blend peanut butter, powdered sugar and cream cheese until smooth; fold in 1 cup whipped topping. Spread over cooled crust. Mix puddings together in large bowl of electric mixer; add milk and beat well. Spread over cream cheese layer. Top with more whipped topping and garnish with shaved chocolate or chopped peanuts. Refrigerate until thoroughly chilled (overnight is best). Yield: 12 to 16 servings.
Kay Holman

VANILLA WAFER STRAWBERRY PIE

1⅓ cup crushed vanilla wafers
¼ cup melted butter or margarine
2 tablespoons sugar
1 envelope unflavored gelatin
¼ cup water
1 pint strawberries, washed and hulled and puréed
2 egg whites
¼ cup sugar
½ cup heavy cream, whipped
14 whole vanilla wafers

Preheat oven to 350 degrees. Mix vanilla wafer crumbs with butter and sugar until thoroughly blended. Press firmly over bottom and up side of 9-inch pie plate to form crust. Bake for 8 minutes. Remove from oven; let cool completely on wire rack. Sprinkle gelatin over water in a small saucepan; let stand 5 minutes to soften. Heat over low heat, stirring constantly, until gelatin dissolves. Stir into puréed berries; chill until mixture is almost set. Beat egg whites in a small bowl with electric mixer at high speed until soft peaks form. Gradually add sugar, beating constantly, until whites are stiff and glossy. Fold whites and whipped cream into puréed strawberry mixture. Pour filling into cooled crust. Insert whole vanilla wafers around edge of filling to garnish. Chill 4 hours or until set.
Jean Croyle

HEAVENLY LEMONY PIE

Crust:

1 cup sugar
1/4 teaspoon cream of tartar
4 egg whites

Sift together sugar and cream of tartar. Beat egg whites until stiff but not dry. Gradually add sugar mixture, about 2 tablespoons at a time, beating after each addition until sugar is dissolved. Take care not to underbeat. Lightly grease a 10-inch pie plate and spread meringue in plate. Do not bring meringue too close to rim of plate, as it will puff up as it bakes. Bake at 275 degrees for 1 hour.

Filling:

4 egg yolks
1/2 cup sugar
3 tablespoons lemon juice
2 teaspoons grated lemon rind
1 1/2 cups heavy cream
1/8 teaspoon salt
1 teaspoon vanilla extract
1 1/2 teaspoons sugar

Beat egg yolks lightly, stir in sugar and lemon juice, and cook in top of double boiler over hot water, stirring constantly, until thickened. Remove from heat, stir in rind and cool slightly. Whip cream; add salt, vanilla and 1 1/2 teaspoons sugar. Fold 1/2 the whipped cream mixture into cooled lemon mixture. Fill meringue shell with lemon mixture (this may be done as soon as the meringue comes from the oven). Cover lemon filling with remaining whipped cream mixture. Refrigerate 24 hours. May be garnished with mint sprigs, thin lemon slices, or grated chocolate. Yield: 6 servings.
A Friend

FROSTY STRAWBERRY PIE

1 (10-ounce) package frozen strawberries, thawed
1 unbeaten egg white, room temperature
1/2 cup sugar
2 teaspoons lemon juice
1 cup heavy whipping cream

Combine strawberries, egg white, sugar and lemon juice in a large mixing bowl. Beat mixture with an electric mixer at high speed until thick and creamy, 5 to 8 minutes. In a separate bowl, beat whipping cream until thick. Fold gently but thoroughly into strawberry mixture. Spoon lightly into baked pie shell. Freeze 4 to 6 hours, or overnight.
Eileen Barlock

EASY FRENCH SILK CHOCOLATE PIE

¾ cup sugar
½ cup butter or margarine, softened
2 squares unsweetened chocolate, melted and cooled
1 teaspoon vanilla extract
2 eggs
1 (9-inch) graham cracker or regular pie shell, baked and cooled
Whipped cream

Cream sugar and butter in large bowl of electric mixer until light and fluffy. Add melted chocolate and vanilla, beating well. Add eggs, 1 at a time, beating 5 minutes after each. Pour mixture into crust and chill several hours or overnight. Garnish with whipping cream and shaved chocolate before serving. Yield: 6 or 8 servings.
Sue Mahon

EGGNOG CHIFFON PIE

2 envelopes unflavored gelatin
4 cups dairy eggnog
¼ cup sugar
¼ teaspoon ground nutmeg
4 teaspoons rum
1 cup heavy cream, whipped
1 (10-inch) graham cracker pie shell

Sprinkle gelatin over 1 cup cold eggnog in top of double boiler to soften. Place over boiling water, add sugar and stir until gelatin and sugar are dissolved. Add remaining eggnog, nutmeg and rum. Chill until mixture is the consistency of unbeaten egg white. Whip until light and fluffy; fold in whipped cream. Turn into pie shell and refrigerate until firm. Top with additional whipped cream and garnish, if desired with shaved chocolate and chopped maraschino cherries. Yield: 6 servings.
Betty Karaffa

PEANUT BUTTER PIE

8 ounces cream cheese, softened
¾ cup powdered sugar
½ cup peanut butter
1 (9-ounce) carton frozen whipped topping, thawed
1 (9-inch) graham cracker pie crust

Combine cream cheese, sugar and peanut butter; beat until fluffy. Fold in ½ of whipped topping. Spread in prepared crust; top with remaining whipped topping. Chill at least 2 hours before serving. Yield: 6 servings.
Sister Claudia Liclachowski, C.S.F.N.

BANANA SPLIT PIE

2 (8-inch) prepared graham cracker pie shells or 1 graham cracker crust in a (13x9x2-inch) pan
½ cup butter or margarine
2 cups confectioner's sugar
2 eggs
1 teaspoon vanilla extract
3 bananas
2 cups drained crushed pineapple
1 (12-ounce) container non-dairy frozen whipped topping, thawed
1 (4-ounce) jar maraschino cherries
1 cup chopped walnuts

Combine butter or margarine, sugar, eggs and vanilla in small bowl and beat until fluffy. Spoon into baked pie shell. Slice bananas over cream mixture. Spread drained pineapple over bananas. Cover to edges with whipped topping, cherries, then nuts. Refrigerate until firm. Yield: two (8-inch) pies or one 13x9x2-inch pie.
Sister Patricia Ann, O.S.U.

TWO-MINUTE LEMONADE PIE

1 (9-inch) graham cracker crust or regular crust
1 (8-ounce) container non-dairy frozen whipped topping
1 (14-ounce) can sweetened condensed milk
1 (6-ounce) can frozen lemonade concentrate, thawed
Lemon slices for garnish

Mix whipped topping, milk and lemonade in large bowl with electric mixer for two minutes. Pour into pie shell. Chill several hours or overnight. Garnish with lemon slices before serving, if desired. *This is a great refreshing summer dessert. You won't believe how easy!*
Colleen Fitzgerald

POOR MAN'S PECAN PIE

1 cup sugar
1 cup margarine
1 cup dark corn syrup
3 eggs
1 cup uncooked oatmeal
1 teaspoon vanilla extract
1 (9-inch) unbaked pastry shell

Combine sugar, margarine and syrup in saucepan; heat until melted. Add remaining ingredients and mix well. Pour into pastry shell and bake at 350 degrees for 1 hour. Yield: 6 servings.
Sister Joan

WALNUT FUDGE PIE

1/4 cup butter
3/4 cup firmly packed brown sugar
3 eggs
1 (12-ounce) package semi-sweet chocolate morsels, melted
2 teaspoons instant coffee powder
1 teaspoon rum extract
1/4 cup all-purpose flour
1 cup coarsely broken walnuts
1 (9-inch) unbaked pie shell
1/2 cup walnut halves for decoration

Cream butter with sugar in small mixing bowl; beat in eggs, one at a time. Fold in melted chocolate, instant coffee, and rum extract. Combine flour and 1 cup walnuts, then stir into batter. Pour into prepared pie shell and garnish with remaining 1/2 cup walnuts. Bake at 375 degrees for 25 minutes. Cool completely before cutting. Garnish with whipped cream to serve, if desired. Yield: 8 servings.
Lynne Della Donna

CARAMEL CRUNCH APPLE PIE

1 unbaked 9-inch pastry shell
28 caramels
2 tablespoons water
6 cups tart, peeled, cored and sliced apples
3/4 cup all-purpose flour
1/3 cup sugar
1/2 teaspoon cinnamon
1/3 cup butter or margarine
1/2 cup chopped walnuts

Preheat oven to 375 degrees. Melt caramels with water in saucepan over low heat, stirring occasionally, until melted and smooth. Layer apples and caramels, alternately, in pastry shell. In a small bowl, combine flour, sugar and cinnamon. Cut in butter until consistency of coarse crumbs. Stir in nuts. Sprinkle mixture over apples. Bake for 40 to 45 minutes.
Sue Robinson

WALNUT PIE CRUST

1 1/4 cup finely chopped walnuts
2 tablespoons butter, softened
3 tablespoons sugar
1/4 cup all-purpose flour

Combine all ingredients in a bowl, mixing well. Press onto bottom and sides of a 9-inch pie pan. Bake at 400 degrees for 10 minutes. Cool and fill with desired filling. *This crust is great with any cream pie. You can also add mini chocolate morsels to mixture.*
Patti Lovejoy

CINDERELLA CHEESE PIE

1 (9 or 10-inch) pastry shell, baked
1 tablespoon (1 envelope) unflavored gelatin
1½ cups milk
1 (3-ounce) package cream cheese
1 (16-ounce) can pumpkin pie filling
2 eggs, separated
1 (3-ounce) package butterscotch pudding mix

Soften gelatin in ½ cup milk. Combine cream cheese, pumpkin pie filling and egg yolks in a small bowl. Beat until smooth. Combine 1 cup milk and pudding mix in saucepan; add pumpkin mixture and gelatin. Cook over medium heat until mixture thickens and is bubbly. Chill in refrigerator until slightly thickened but not set. Beat egg whites until stiff but not dry. Fold into chilled filling. Spoon filling into baked pie shell. Chill for several hours, or overnight. Serve with whipped cream garnish.
Rita Grennan

CHOCOLATE CANDY BAR PIE

1 (9-inch) baked graham cracker pie shell
3 (1.7-ounce) chocolate with almond candy bars
16 large marshamallows
½ cup chocolate morsels
⅓ cup milk
1 cup heavy whipping cream, whipped with sugar to taste

Melt chocolate bars, marshmallows, chocolate morsels and milk in saucepan over low heat. Stir until smooth. Remove from heat and cool. Fold whipped cream into cooled mixture and spoon into prepared pie shell. Refrigerate until serving time. *May add ½ cup crushed peanuts to pie shell if desired.* Yield: 8 servings.
Kay Kelly

SHIRLEY'S MACAROONS

2 egg whites
½ teaspoon vanilla extract
1 cup sugar
2 cups corn cereal flakes
½ cup chopped nuts
1 cup shredded coconut

Beat egg whites with vanilla in small mixing bowl until stiff. Carefully fold in sugar until blended. Fold in cereal, nuts and coconut. Drop by rounded teaspoonsful onto a well-greased 15x10x1-inch cookie sheet. Bake at 350 degrees for 10 minutes. Cookie dough will be very loose when spooned onto baking sheet but spreads and holds together when baked. Yield: 5 dozen cookies.
Shirley Zirm

CHOCOLATE-FILLED THIMBLE COOKIES

Dough:

3/4 cup butter or margarine
1/2 cup firmly packed brown sugar
1 egg, separated
1/2 teaspoon vanilla extract
1 1/2 cups sifted all-purpose flour
1/4 teaspoon salt
1 cup finely chopped nuts

Cream butter or margarine and brown sugar in large bowl of electric mixer until light and fluffy. Blend in egg yolk and vanilla. Sift flour and salt; add to batter and mix thoroughly. Chill dough, covered, for easier handling (at least 1 hour). Shape dough into into balls about 1-inch in diameter. Dip each ball into slightly beaten egg white, then into chopped nuts. Place on ungreased baking sheets. Make an indentation in center of each cookie with floured finger or thimble. Bake at 350 degrees for 10 to 15 minutes, or until nicely browned. Remove from oven and cool while preparing filling. Yield: about 3 dozen cookies.

Chocolate filling:

3/4 cup semi-sweet chocolate morsels
1 tablespoon vegetable shortening
2 tablespoons light corn syrup
1 tablespoon water
1 teaspoon vanilla extract

Combine chocolate morsels with shortening in top of double boiler. Place over hot, not boiling, water and stir until smooth. Remove from heat and stir in corn syrup, water and vanilla. Stir until smooth. Spoon about 1 teaspoonful chocolate filling into hollow of each cookie. Use all filling. Let cookies stand until chocolate hardens. Store in flat container. Do not stack cookies.
Kaye Sarby

MOLASSES COOKIES

3/4 cup vegetable shortening or butter
1 cup firmly packed brown sugar
1 egg
1/4 cup dark molasses
2 1/4 cups all-purpose flour
2 teaspoons baking soda
1/4 teaspoon salt
1/2 teaspoon ground cloves
1 teaspoon ground cinnamon
1 teaspoon ground ginger
Sugar

Cream shortening or butter and sugar in large bowl of electric mixer until light and fluffy. Beat in egg and molasses. Sift flour, soda, salt and spices together; add to creamed mixture and blend well. Roll pieces of dough into 1-inch balls. Roll in sugar to coat; place on 15x10x1-inch cookie sheets. Sprinkle each cookie with a few drops water. Bake at 375 degrees for 10 to 15 minutes. Yield: 2 or 3 dozen cookies.
Thomas More Program

FOREIGN COOKIES

2 cups butter
2 cups lard (vegetable shortening may be substituted)
3 cups sugar
1 teaspoon salt
8 eggs
12 to 16 cups sifted all-purpose flour

Work butter, lard, sugar, salt, 2 whole eggs and 6 egg yolks together by hand in large bowl until creamed. Using hands, gradually mix in enough flour to keep dough from adhering to bowl or hands. (Entire 16 cups flour may not be necessary; work in small amount at a time.) Shape blended dough into a loaf, cover with waxed paper or plastic wrap and chill for several hours or overnight (for easier handling). Remove from refrigerator and slice pieces from whole loaf about ½-inch thick. Working with 1 piece at a time, flatten with palm of hand (not rolling pin) on floured board to desired thickness. Cut with cookie cutters of desired shape. Place cookies on greased 15x10x1-inch cookie sheets. Brush with topping. Bake at 350 degrees for 20 minutes or until golden.

Topping:

2 egg whites
¾ cup ground walnuts
¼ cup sugar (or more, to taste)

Brush cookie tops with slightly beaten egg whites; sprinkle with mixture of ground nuts and sugar.
Eileen Barlock

BOW TIES

3 egg yolks
1 egg
½ teaspoon salt
¼ cup powdered sugar
1 tablespoon rum extract
1 teaspoon vanilla extract
1 cup sifted all-purpose flour

Beat egg yolks, egg and salt together in small bowl of electric mixer for about 10 minutes, or until very stiff. Add powdered sugar and extracts and mix well. Add flour all at once; stir to blend. Turn out onto floured board and knead for about 7 minutes. Divide dough into halves. Roll 1 ball of dough very thin and cut into squares. Cut a slit in center of each square and bring one corner through slit. Fry immediately in deep (at least 2 inches) hot (375 degrees) fat, turning to brown lightly on each side. Remove from fat with slotted spoon or tongs; drain on paper toweling and sprinkle with powdered sugar. Repeat with remaining ½ of dough. Yield: 3 dozen bow ties.
Janet Borkowski

BUTTER HORN COOKIES

2 cups sifted all-purpose flour
1 teaspoon baking powder
1/4 teaspoon salt
1/2 cup butter
1/2 package (1 1/2 teaspoons) active dry yeast
2 tablespoons warm water
2 eggs, separated
1/4 cup dairy sour cream
1/2 teaspoon vanilla extract
1/2 cup sugar
1/2 cup finely ground walnuts
1/2 teaspoon almond extract
Powdered sugar for sprinkling

Measure sifted flour. Stir flour, baking powder and salt together in mixing bowl. Cut in butter. Dissolve yeast in water. Stir in egg yolks, sour cream and vanilla. Blend into flour mixture. Refrigerate for 1 hour. Heat oven to 400 degrees. Beat egg whites until foamy, gradually adding sugar; beat until stiff. Fold in nuts and almond extract. Divide dough into 4 parts. Roll each part into a 9-inch circle on lightly floured board, and sprinkle with powdered sugar. Cut each circle into 12 wedges. Spread 1 heaping teaspoon of meringue on each wedge; roll, beginning at wide end. Bake on lightly greased baking sheet for 10 to 12 minutes, or until golden brown. Sprinkle with powdered sugar. Yield: 4 dozen.
Janet Borkowski

SOUR CREAM COOKIES

1/2 cup vegetable shortening
1 1/2 cups sugar
2 eggs
1 cup dairy sour cream
1 teaspoon vanilla extract
2 3/4 cups all-purpose flour
1/2 teaspoon baking soda
1/2 teaspoon baking powder
1/2 teaspoon salt

Cream shortening and sugar together in large bowl of electric mixer until light and fluffy; stir in sour cream and vanilla. Sift flour, soda, baking powder and salt together and add to creamed mixture. Beat well. Cover and chill in refrigerator for 1 hour. Remove from refrigerator and drop onto an ungreased 15x10x1-inch cookie sheet. Bake at 400 degrees for 8 to 10 minutes. Remove to wire rack to cool. Frost. Yield: about 3 dozen.

Icing:

4 tablespoons butter or margarine
1 cup powdered sugar
1 teaspoon vanilla extract
1 or 2 tablespoons hot water

Brown butter in saucepan until golden. Add sugar, vanilla and hot water as needed; stir until smooth. Use to frost cookies.
Sue Robinson

SAINT NICHOLAS COOKIES

½ cup sugar
½ cup butter or margarine
½ cup firmly packed brown sugar
1 large egg, beaten
2 cups all-purpose flour
½ teaspoon salt
½ teaspoon baking soda
½ teaspoon baking powder
1½ teaspoons ground cinnamon
¼ teaspoon ground nutmeg
¼ teaspoon ground cloves
1-ounce chopped, blanched almonds (optional)

Cream sugar and butter or margarine in large bowl of electric mixer; beat in egg. Sift dry ingredients together and add to dough; blend well. Stir in almonds. Cover bowl and refrigerate until thoroughly chilled (at least 1 hour). Remove from refrigerator and roll out on lightly floured board to about ⅛-inch thickness. Cut into desired shapes, place on ungreased baking sheet and bake at 400 degrees for 5 minutes or until lightly-browned. Frost when cooled. Yield: 2½ to 3 dozen cookies.

Frosting:

2 cups powdered sugar
1 teaspoon almond extract
Water

Sift sugar into mixing bowl; beat in extract and about 2 tablespoons water until spreading consistency. Use to frost cookies.
Helen Wanyerka

OLD-FASHIONED PEANUT BUTTER COOKIES

3 cups sifted all-purpose flour
2 teaspoons baking soda
½ teaspoon salt
1 cup vegetable shortening
1 cup sugar
1 cup firmly packed brown sugar
2 eggs
1 cup peanut butter (smooth or crunchy)
1 teaspoon vanilla extract

Sift flour, soda and salt together. Set aside. Cream shortening and sugars well in large bowl of electric mixer. Add eggs, 1 at a time, beating after each addition. (Batter should be light and fluffy.) Beat in peanut butter and vanilla until very light. Gradually stir in flour mixture; blend. Shape into walnut-size balls. Place on lightly-greased 15x10x1-inch cookie sheets and press each cookie with a fork that has been dipped into sugar. (Press both ways, dipping fork into sugar each time, to form criss-cross design.) Bake at 375 degrees for 12 to 15 minutes or until lightly-browned. Remove to wire rack to cool. Yield: about 50 cookies.
Rosemary Corcoran

PUMPKIN TREAT

1 cup butter or margarine
1 cup sugar
1 cup prepared pumpkin
1 egg
1 teaspoon vanilla extract
2 cups all-purpose flour
1 teaspoon baking powder
1 teaspoon baking soda
1 teaspoon ground cinnamon
½ teaspoon salt

Cream butter and sugar in large bowl of electric mixer until light and fluffy. Add pumpkin, egg and vanilla and beat well. Sift flour, baking powder, soda, cinnamon and salt together and gradually add to mixture. Blend well. Drop batter by teaspoonsful onto greased 15x10x1-inch cookie sheet. Bake at 375 degrees for 10 to 15 minutes. Remove to wire rack to cool. Frost. *For variety, stir ½ cup chopped dates, raisins or nuts into batter before baking.* Yield: 2 or 3 dozen.

Frosting:

½ cup firmly packed brown sugar
¼ cup milk
3 tablespoons butter or margarine
¾ teaspoon vanilla extract
1 cup powdered sugar

Combine brown sugar, milk and butter in saucepan; cook over medium-high heat for 2 minutes, stirring. Remove from heat and cool. Stir in vanilla and powdered sugar until smooth. Use to frost cookies.
Shirley Zirm

CHINESE FORTUNE COOKIES

1⅔ cup sugar
¾ cup egg whites, unbeaten
Salt to taste
1 cup butter, melted
1 cup all-purpose flour
½ teaspoon vanilla extract

Stir sugar into egg whites until dissolved. Add butter, flour and vanilla. Beat until well-blended. Drop by teaspoonfuls, 2 inches apart, on a greased baking sheet. Bake at 375 degrees for 5 minutes or until edges curl. Remove from oven and place fortunes on cookies. Fold cookies in ½ once, then mold over a wooden spoon handle or stand cookies in muffin pan cups to cool. You MUST work fast. If the cookies harden before you can fold them return them to the oven briefly. *Since speed is important, prepare witty, wise or romantic fortunes ahead of time and have them folded and ready to insert in the warm cookies.* Yield: 5 dozen cookies.
Ralph Kroggel

KATHY'S CUT-OUT COOKIES

3 cups all-purpose flour
1 teaspoon salt
1 teaspoon baking soda
1¼ cups sugar
⅔ cup vegetable shortening
2 eggs, beaten
2 tablespoons milk with 4 drops lemon juice or vinegar
1 teaspoon vanilla extract

Sift together flour, salt, soda and sugar into a bowl. Add remaining ingredients and mix well. Roll out on a floured surface. Cut with floured cookie cutters and bake 5 to 8 minutes at 350 degrees. Cookies should not brown. Cool and frost. Yield: about 3 dozen.

Frosting:

¼ cup vegetable shortening
¼ cup butter
1 teaspoon vanilla extract
2 egg whites
1 (16-ounce) package powdered sugar
Dash of salt
Food coloring, optional

Combine all ingredients until smooth, adding a small amount of milk if necessary for desired consistency. *Children love to help bake and frost these cookies.*
Kathy Story

MOM WOLL'S CUT-OUT SUGAR COOKIES

1¼ cups butter or margarine
1½ cups sugar
1½ cups vegetable shortening
2 eggs
2 egg yolks
2 teaspoons vanilla extract
1 teaspoon baking powder
1 teaspoon salt
7½ cups all-purpose flour

Cream butter or margarine with sugar in large bowl of electric mixer until light and fluffy; beat in eggs and egg yolks. Add remaining ingredients and mix by hand with wooden spoon. Roll out onto covered board which has been sprinkled with equal parts of sugar and flour. Cut cookies into desired shapes and gently place on ungreased 15x10x1-inch baking sheets. Bake at 400 degrees for 5 or 6 minutes. *Dough rolls out much easier if it is first chilled in the refrigerator for 2 or 3 hours.* Yield: 8 dozen or more.
Mindy Woll

MARZIPAN TASSIES

1/3 cup butter (no substitute)
1/4 cup confectioners' sugar
1 egg yolk
1/4 teaspoon almond extract
1 cup all-purpose flour

Cream butter and sugar thoroughly with electric mixer; add egg yolk and extract; mix well. Blend in flour, then chill dough about 1 hour. Pinch off marble-size pieces and press into bottoms and sides of ungreased tiny muffin tins. Bake at 375 degrees 3 to 4 minutes.

Filling:

1/3 cup butter (no substitute)
1 (4-ounce) can almond paste
1/2 cup sugar
2 eggs
2 teaspoons almond extract
1/2 cup powdered sugar
Orange or lemon juice
1/4 teaspoon almond extract

Cream butter and almond paste until smooth; beat in sugar. Blend in eggs and 2 teaspoons extract. Spoon mixture into baked shells, then bake at 350 degrees 15 minutes. While tassies bake, prepare a thin frosting of 1/2 cup powdered sugar and small amount of juice, adding almond extract. Frost centers of warm tassies. These may be made in advance and frozen. *Follow instructions accurately. This is a challenge, but your compliments will be well worth the effort.* Yield: 36 (1 3/4-inch cupcakes).
Holly Hura, Registered Dietitian, Parmadale

ALMOND MOONS

2 cups sweet butter, softened
1 pound almonds, blanched and ground
5 cups all-purpose flour
6 tablespoons powdered sugar
1 egg

Mix butter and flour with wooden spoon. Add nuts, sugar and egg. Knead together until well-blended. Roll small amount between palms into crescent shape and arrange on cookie sheet. Repeat with remaining dough. Bake at 350 degrees about 15 minutes, until light brown. Roll warm cookies in powdered sugar. Lay out sugared cookies and when all are finished, roll in powdered sugar again. Cool and store in covered containers between layers of waxed paper. Yield: 6 dozen.
Betty Karaffa

FRANCES' COOKIES

1 cup all-purpose flour
1/2 teaspoon baking soda
1/2 teaspoon baking powder
1/4 teaspoon salt
1/2 cup vegetable shortening
1/2 cup firmly packed brown sugar
1/2 cup sugar
2 eggs, beaten
1 cup corn or wheat cereal flakes
1/2 cup shredded coconut (or additional 1/2 cup cereal)

Sift flour, baking soda, baking powder and salt together; set aside. Cream shortening and sugars together in large bowl of electric mixer until light and fluffy. Add eggs and mix well. Stir in cereal flakes and coconut. Gently stir in dry ingredients. Drop by teaspoonsful onto greased 15x10x1-inch cookie sheets; bake at 350 degrees for about 12 to 15 minutes or until lightly browned. Yield: about 3 dozen cookies.
Frances Willson

LACE WAFER COOKIES

2/3 cup quick oats
1/2 cup all-purpose flour
1/3 cup firmly packed light brown sugar
1/4 cup dark corn syrup
3 tablespoons corn oil margarine, softened

Place oats in blender. Cover and blend on medium speed for 30 seconds, or until finely chopped. In a medium bowl, stir together oats, flour, sugar, corn syrup and margarine until mixture is well blended. Using 1 level teaspoon of dough per cookie, form dough into balls and place 2 inches apart on well-greased 15x10x1-inch cookie sheet. Flatten each ball into a 3-inch circle by placing a 3-inch square of waxed paper on top of ball and using the bottom of a glass. Remove waxed paper. Bake in 375 degree oven for 3 to 5 minutes until cookies are flat and bubbly. Remove from oven and bang cookie sheet briskly on countertop to stop bubbling on surface. Cool 1 to 2 minutes. With a metal spatula, remove wafers from cookie sheet, one at a time, and roll around handle of a wooden spoon. Place rolled cookies on wire rack. If cookies cool before rolling, return to oven until they are heated. Cookies may also be left flat. Yield: 3 dozen.
Sister Patricia Ann

DONNA'S BUTTER COOKIES

1/2 pound butter (1 cup)
1 1/2 cups powdered sugar
1 egg
1 teaspoon vanilla extract
1 teaspoon cream of tartar
1 teaspoon baking soda
2 1/2 cups all-purpose flour

In a bowl, cream together butter and sugar. Add remaining ingredients, one at a time. Mix well. Roll out on a floured board and cut with a cookie cutter. Bake in a 350 degree oven for 8 to 10 minutes. Yield: about 4 dozen.
Donna Barnett

MADELEINES

3/4 cup melted butter
2 eggs
1 cup sugar
1 cup sifted all-purpose flour
1 teaspoon vanilla extract
1 tablespoon rum

Preheat oven to 450 degrees. Heat eggs and sugar in top of double boiler until lukewarm; stir and remove from heat. Beat with electric mixer until very creamy and light. Add flour gradually to cooled butter mixture. Stir in vanilla and rum. Brush madeleine tins with melted butter. Pour batter into tins, filling 1/2 full. Bake about 15 minutes on second shelf of oven. Turn out onto cookie sheets to cool. Yield: 2 dozen.
Karen West

MAPLE SYRUP OATMEAL COOKIES

1 cup all-purpose flour
1/4 teaspoon salt
1 teaspoon baking powder
1 cup quick oats
1/2 cup chopped walnuts
1 egg
1/2 cup vegetable shortening
3/4 cup maple syrup
1/2 teaspoon vanilla extract

Sift flour, salt and baking powder together into large bowl. Add oats and walnuts; mix well. In separate bowl, cream egg and shortening until fluffy. Add maple syrup and vanilla and mix well. Stir mixture into dry ingredients until blended. Drop by heaping teaspoonsful onto greased 15x10x1-inch cookie sheets, about 2 inches apart. Bake at 400 degrees for 8 to 12 minutes or until golden brown. Yield: about 3 dozen.
Dolores Sygula

CHOCOLATE SURPRISE COOKIES

3 cups all-purpose flour
1 teaspoon baking soda
½ teaspoon salt
1 cup butter or margarine
1 cup sugar
½ cup firmly packed brown sugar
2 eggs
2 tablespoons water
1 teaspoon vanilla extract
3 pounds chocolate top nonpareils

Sift flour, soda and salt together and set aside. Cream butter or margarine with sugars in large bowl of electric mixer. In small bowl, beat eggs, water and vanilla together; add to creamed mixture and beat well. Add flour mixture slowly, beating until blended. Cover and refrigerate overnight. Remove from refrigerator and pinch off dough in marble-size pieces and press around a chocolate nonpareil so that dough surrounds edges of candy. (Be careful not to use too much dough or cookies will be too large.) Place on greased 15x10x1-inch cookie sheet. Bake at 350 degrees for 10 to 12 minutes or until cookies are golden brown. Remove to wire rack to cool. Yield: about 35 to 40 cookies.
Nicki Cowan
Betty Karaffa

COCONUT COOKIES ROYAL

1 cup butter or margarine
1 cup firmly packed brown sugar
1 cup granulated sugar
2 eggs
2 teaspoons vanilla extract
2 cups all-purpose flour
1 teaspoon salt
1 teaspoon baking powder
1 teaspoon baking soda
2 cups quick oats
1½ cups flaked coconut
1 cup chopped nuts

Cream butter or margarine with sugars in large bowl of electric mixer until light and fluffy. Beat in eggs and vanilla. Sift dry ingredients together and add to creamed mixture until blended. Stir in coconut, oats and nuts. Mix well. Drop by heaping teaspoonsful about 2 inches apart onto greased 15x10x1-inch baking sheets. Bake at 350 degrees for about 8 minutes or until lightly browned. Remove from pan at once to cool. Yield: 8 dozen.
Debbie Rush
Nicki Cowan

CHOCOLATE GLOBS

1/2 cup vegetable shortening
2 cups sugar
2 eggs, beaten well
4 cups all-purpose flour
2 teaspoons baking soda
1/2 teaspoon baking powder
1/2 cup cocoa
1 cup sour milk
1 cup boiling water
1 teaspoon vanilla extract

Cream shortening and sugar in large bowl of electric mixer; beat in eggs. Sift dry ingredients together and add to batter along with milk, water, and vanilla. Mix well. Drop batter by teaspoonfuls onto ungreased baking sheets. Bake at 450 degrees for 5 minutes. Remove from oven and cool on wire rack. Prepare filling as directed below. Yield: 2 or 3 dozen.

Filling:

5 tablespoons all-purpose flour
1 cup milk
1 cup sifted powdered sugar
1/4 cup butter or margarine
1/2 cup vegetable shortening
1/2 teaspoon salt
1 teaspoon vanilla extract

Combine flour and milk in saucepan with wire whisk; place over medium heat and cook, stirring constantly, until thickened. Cool. In large bowl, cream together cooled flour/milk mixture, sugar, margarine, shortening, salt and vanilla; beat well. Use filling between two cookies to make a "sandwich".
Betz Spacek

GINGERBREAD COOKIES

2/3 cup firmly packed dark brown sugar
2/3 cup molasses
2 teaspoons ground ginger
1/2 teaspoon ground cinnamon
1/4 teaspoon ground cloves
2 teaspoons baking soda
2/3 cup butter or margarine
1 egg
5 cups all-purpose flour

Heat brown sugar, molasses, ginger, cloves and cinnamon to boiling in saucepan over medium heat. Remove from heat and add soda. Pour mixture over butter in large mixing bowl. Stir until butter is melted. Add egg and beat well. Stir in flour until thoroughly mixed. Turn out onto board and knead dough well; shape into ball. Place in bowl, cover with plastic wrap, and refrigerate until firm (several hours or overnight). Remove from refrigerator, roll out onto lightly floured board and cut in desired shape with cookie cutters (naturally, gingerbread men are best!). Gently place cookies on greased 15x10x1-inch cookie sheet and bake at 325 degrees for 10 minutes. Remove to wire rack to cool. Yield: 6 to 8 dozen.
Eileen Barlock

MELTING DREAM COOKIES

1¼ cups sifted all-purpose flour
¼ cup cornstarch
½ cup powdered sugar
¾ cup butter (no substitute)

Sift dry ingredients together; add butter and mix with fingers. Chill at least 1 hour. Roll into walnut-size balls. Place on ungreased cookie sheets and flatten with fork. Sprinkle with sugar (may use tinted sugar for holiday cookies) and bake at 300 degrees until very lightly browned, about 25 minutes. Cool on wire racks. Yield: 2 to 3 dozen.
Shirley Herbst

ORANGE DROP COOKIES

1 cup vegetable shortening
2 cups sugar
1 cup sour milk (or 1 cup milk plus 1 tablespoon vinegar)
¾ cup orange juice
2 eggs
5 cups all-purpose flour
2 teaspoons baking powder
2 teaspoons baking soda
1 teaspoon salt

Cream shortening in large bowl of electric mixer; gradually add sugar, beating until light and fluffy. Add eggs and beat well. Sift dry ingredients together and add to creamed mixture alternately with sour milk and orange juice. Drop by teaspoonful onto greased 15x10x1-inch cookie sheets. Bake at 350 degrees for 10 to 12 minutes. Remove to wire rack to cool. Frost with mixture of powdered sugar and orange juice. Yield: about 7 or 8 dozen.
Carol Brady

GINGER COOKIES

3 tablespoons vegetable shortening
¼ cup dark brown sugar, packed
1 egg, beaten
1½ cups all-purpose flour
¼ cup cornstarch
½ teaspoon baking powder
½ teaspoon ground cinnamon
¼ teaspoon ground allspice
¼ teaspoon ground cloves
¾ teaspoon baking soda
½ teaspoon salt
1 tablespoon ground ginger
½ cup dark molasses
½ cup dairy sour cream

Cream shortening and sugar until fluffy. Add egg and blend well. Combine dry ingredients. Add alternately with molasses and sour cream, mixing well after each addition. Drop by spoonsful onto a greased baking sheet. Bake at 375 degrees for 15 to 20 minutes. Yield: 3 dozen cookies.
Mike Pitroski

CHILDREN'S OATMEAL COOKIES

2 cups all-purpose flour
1 teaspoon salt
¼ teaspoon baking soda
2 eggs
¾ cup firmly packed brown sugar
1 teaspoon vanilla extract
¾ cup vegetable shortening
2 cups quick-cooking oatmeal
½ cup powdered sugar

Sift flour, salt and soda into large bowl. Add eggs, brown sugar and vanilla; mix well. Cut in shortening until blended. Add oatmeal and work together. Sprinkle countertop or board with powdered sugar; roll out dough into a ¼-inch thickness. Cut dough with cookie cutters into desired shapes and transfer to greased 15x10x1-inch cookie sheets. Bake at 350 degrees for 10 to 12 minutes. Tops may be decorated with candy or sugar sprinkles before baking, if desired. If sugar sprinkles are not used, cookies may be frosted. *This recipe is fun for children to make at holiday time. I remember making them with my Mother every Christmas when I was a little girl and continued the tradition with my own daughter.* Yield: about 6 dozen cookies.
Eileen Barlock

FORGOTTEN CHRISTMAS COOKIES

2 egg whites
¼ teaspoon cream of tartar
Pinch of salt
1 cup sugar
2 or 3 drops green food coloring, optional
1 (8-ounce) package mint chocolate morsels, or semi-sweet chocolate morsels.

Preheat oven to 350 degrees before making cookies *(important)*. Beat egg whites and cream of tartar in small bowl of electric mixer until soft peaks form; add salt. Beat in sugar gradually, about 1 tablespoon at a time, until all has been added and whites are stiff. Add food coloring until desired color is achieved. Fold in chocolate morsels. *Turn oven off.* Drop dough onto a waxed paper-lined 15x10x1-inch cookie sheet. Place in hot oven and leave overnight (10 hours). *Do not open oven door during this time.* Yield: about 2 dozen cookies.
Sue Polacek
Carolyn Hayek

ORIENTAL ALMOND COOKIES

1 cup vegetable shortening (may use lard for crisper cookies)
1 cup sugar
2 eggs
2 teaspoons almond extract
3 cups all-purpose flour, sifted with ¼ teaspoon baking soda
1 egg, beaten
24 canned almonds

Beat shortening or lard with sugar until light. Add eggs and almond flavoring, then gradually beat in flour, beating until smooth. Roll into walnut-size balls, place on cookie sheets and press to flatten. Press an almond into the center of each cookie and brush with beaten egg. Bake at 325 degrees 25 minutes, or until golden brown. Yield: 2 dozen.
Michele Cotner

OATMEAL COOKIES

½ cup vegetable shortening
¾ cup firmly packed brown sugar
1 egg
¼ cup buttermilk or sour milk
1 cup all-purpose flour
½ teaspoon baking soda
½ teaspoon baking powder
½ teaspoon salt
½ teaspoon ground cinnamon
½ teaspoon ground nutmeg
1½ cups rolled oats
½ cup raisins
¼ cup chopped walnuts

In a bowl cream shortening, brown sugar and eggs until light and fluffy. Stir in milk. Sift all dry ingredients and stir into creamed mixture. Stir in oats, raisins and nuts. Drop from tablespoon 2 inches apart on a greased 15x10x1-inch cookie sheet. Bake at 400 degrees for 8 minutes.
Lisa Dakdduk

SNOWBALLS

1 cup butter or margarine
¼ cup sugar
2 cups ground pecans or walnuts
2 cups sifted all-purpose flour

Cream butter or margarine in bowl of electric mixer until softened; stir in sugar, nuts and flour. Mix well. Shape into balls, using about 1 tablespoon dough for each cookie. Place on ungreased baking sheet and bake at 300 degrees for 30 to 40 minutes, checking about every 15 minutes. Cookies should be firm to touch and light brown when done. Roll in powdered sugar after they have cooled for about 5 minutes, if desired. Yield: 4 to 6 dozen.
Diane Cassell

PUMPKIN SQUARES

Crust:

1 cup all-purpose flour
½ cup quick oats
½ cup firmly packed light brown sugar
½ cup butter or margarine

Preheat oven to 375 degrees. Generously flour a 13x9x2-inch baking pan. Set aside. In a small bowl, combine first 3 ingredients for the crust. Cut butter or margarine in with a pastry blender, or 2 knives used scissor fashion until mixture resembles coarse crumbs. Press into bottom of prepared pan and bake for 12 to 15 minutes until crust is a light, golden brown. Remove from oven. Reduce oven temperature to 350 degrees.

Filling:

1 (16-ounce) can pumpkin
1 (13-ounce) can evaporated milk
2 eggs
¾ cup sugar
1 teaspoon ground cinnamon
½ teaspoon ground ginger
½ teaspoon salt
¼ teaspoon ground cloves

Prepare filling while crust bakes. In a medium-sized mixing bowl, place ingredients for filling. Beat at low speed until mixed. Increase speed to medium and beat for 3 minutes. Pour into baked crust. Bake for 15 to 20 minutes, or until set.

Topping:

1 cup firmly packed light brown sugar
1 cup chopped walnuts
¼ cup butter or margarine
2 tablespoons all-purpose flour

Combine with fork until crumbly. Sprinkle on baked mixture; return to oven for 10 to 15 minutes until deep golden color. Yield: 15 bars.
Kay Holman

QUICKEST COOKIES EVER

1 refrigerated slice-and-bake sugar cookie roll
1 (6-ounce) package semi-sweet chocolate morsels

Prepare cookies according to package directions. Melt chocolate morsels in top of double boiler over hot (not boiling) water and dip half the cookie in chocolate. Set on waxed paper to cool. *These are so easy, but look like you have "slaved over a hot oven" to prepare them!*
Lynn Malo

CRUNCHY PEANUT BUTTER BARS

1 cup sugar
1 cup light corn syrup
2 cups peanut butter (smooth or crunchy)
4 cups crisp rice cereal puffs
1 (6-ounce) package chocolate morsels
1 (6-ounce) package butterscotch morsels

Combine sugar and corn syrup in saucepan and cook over medium heat until sugar is dissolved. Remove from heat. Blend in peanut butter. Stir in cereal until well-mixed. Spread in buttered 13x9x2-inch baking pan and set aside. Melt chocolate and butterscotch morsels together in top of double boiler over hot, not boiling, water. Stir until smooth. Spread over cookies in pan. Cut into squares immediately. *This cookie freezes well.* Yield: about 16 bars.
Shirley Zirm

APRICOT NUT BARS

2 cups butter or margarine
2 cups sugar
4 egg yolks
4 cups all-purpose flour
2 cups chopped walnuts
1 (18-ounce) jar apricot preserves

Cream butter or margarine and sugar with egg yolks in large bowl of electric mixer until light and fluffy. Slowly blend in flour. Stir in chopped walnuts (batter will be stiff). Pat ½ of dough into a greased and floured 13x9x2-inch baking pan. Spread with apricot preserves. Roll out remaining dough on floured board and cut into strips. Criss-cross strips over top of preserves. Bake at 325 degrees for 55 to 60 minutes. Cool completely before cutting into bars. Yield: 16 to 20 bars.
Anna Mae Zastawny
Sister Madeline

CHOCOLATE DELIGHT BARS

½ cup butter or margarine
1 egg yolk
2 tablespoons water
1¼ cups all-purpose flour
1 teaspoon sugar
1 teaspoon baking powder
1 (12-ounce) package semi-sweet chocolate morsels

Beat butter, egg yolk and water until light. Stir in flour, sugar and baking powder and mix well. Press into a 13x9x2-inch baking pan and bake at 350 degrees for 10 minutes. Remove from oven and immediately sprinkle with chocolate morsels. Return to oven for 1 minute. Remove and spread chocolate evenly over surface.

Topping:

2 eggs
¾ cup sugar
6 tablespoons butter, melted
2 teaspoons vanilla extract
2 cups ground nuts

Beat eggs until thick, then add sugar and beat well. Stir in butter and vanilla. Add chopped nuts and spread over chocolate layer. Return to oven and bake 30 to 35 minutes. Yield: about 18.
Kay Kelly

BUTTERSCOTCH CHEESECAKE BARS

1 (12-ounce) package butterscotch morsels
⅓ cup margarine or butter
2 cups graham cracker crumbs
1 cup chopped nuts
1 (8-ounce) package cream cheese, softened
1 (14-ounce) can sweetened condensed milk
1 teaspoon vanilla extract
1 egg

Preheat oven to 350 degrees. In medium saucepan melt butterscotch morsels and margarine. Stir in graham cracker crumbs and nuts. Press ½ of mixture firmly into bottom of greased 13x9x2-inch baking pan. In large mixing bowl, beat cream cheese until fluffy. Continue beating and add condensed milk, vanilla and egg. Mix well. Pour into prepared pan and top with remaining crumb mixture. Bake for 25 to 30 minutes, or until toothpick inserted into center comes out clean. Cool to room temperature. Chill before cutting into bars. Refrigerate leftovers. Yield: 18 to 24 bars.
Anna Mae Zastawny

READY-TO-GO BROWNIE MIX

4 cups all-purpose flour
1 tablespoon plus 1 teaspoon baking powder
1 tablespoon salt
8 cups sugar
2½ cups unsweetened cocoa powder
2 cups vegetable shortening

Combine flour, baking powder, salt, sugar and cocoa; stir together well. Cut in shortening until mixture resembles coarse meal. Store in air tight container in a cool, dry place, or in refrigerator for up to 6 weeks. *This mix is great if you want the convenience of a mix, but enjoy homemade brownies.* This amount will make 5 batches of soft, fudgy brownies. Yield: 16 cups.

Quick and Easy Brownies:

3 cups Ready-to-Go Brownie Mix
3 eggs, beaten
1½ teaspoons vanilla extract
½ cup chopped pecans

Combine all ingredients, stirring until well-mixed. Spoon into greased and floured 8-inch square pan; bake at 350 degrees for 35 to 40 minutes. Yield: 16 brownies.
Betz Spacek

HONEY BACKPACK BARS

½ cup vegetable shortening
½ cup honey
½ cup firmly packed brown sugar
1 egg
1 teaspoon vanilla extract
¾ cup all-purpose flour
½ teaspoon baking soda
½ teaspoon baking powder
¼ teaspoon salt
1 cup shredded coconut
1 cup rolled oats
½ cup sesame seed

Cream shortening, honey and sugar well in large bowl of electric mixer; beat in egg and vanilla. Sift flour, soda, baking powder and salt together and beat into creamed mixture. Stir in coconut, oats and sesame seed. Spread mixture into a greased 15x10x1-inch jellyroll pan. Bake in preheated 350 degree oven for 25 to 30 minutes. Cool in pan and cut into bars. Remove each bar from pan, roll in powdered sugar and wrap individually for backpacking. Yield: 36 bars.
Sister Joan

CHEWY TURTLE BARS

1 (18.5-ounce) box Swiss chocolate cake mix
½ cup butter or margarine, melted
⅔ cup evaporated milk (5.3-ounce can)
1 (14-ounce) package light caramels
1 (12-ounce) package chocolate morsels
1 cup coarsely chopped pecans

Preheat oven to 350 degrees. In a bowl, mix together cake mix, margarine and ⅓ cup of evaporated milk. Beat at high speed. Place ½ of mixture in a greased 13x9x2-inch baking pan. Press mixture well into bottom of pan. Bake for 6 minutes. Remove from oven and cool to room temperature. Unwrap caramels and place in a pan with remaining evaporated milk; stir over medium heat until smooth. Pour mixture evenly over baked chocolate crust and spread with a spatula. Sprinkle chocolate chips and nuts on top. Cut small pieces of remaining dough and flatten with hands. Cover the caramel, chip and nut layer as much as possible. Bake for 15 to 18 minutes. Cool and then cut into bars. Freeze if desired. *Wonderful!*
Edna Stein
Dana Barlock

WALNUT CHEESECAKE BARS

⅓ cup butter or margarine
⅓ firmly packed brown sugar
1 cup all-purpose flour
½ cup chopped walnuts
¼ cup sugar
1 (8-ounce) package cream cheese, softened
1 egg, slightly beaten
2 tablespoons milk
1 tablespoon lemon juice
½ teaspoon vanilla extract

Cream butter and brown sugar until light; add flour and nuts. Stir with a wooden spoon until crumbly. Set aside 1 cup for topping. Press remaining crumbs into ungreased 8-inch square pan. Bake at 350 degrees for 12 to 15 minutes. Cool completely. Combine sugar and cream cheese in small bowl; beat until smooth. Add remaining ingredients and beat well. Spread evenly over cooled prepared crust. Sprinkle reserved crumbs over top. Bake at 350 degrees for 25 to 30 minutes. Cool before cutting into bars. Refrigerate cookies. Yield: 16 bars.
Gloria Rosenbush
Jan Gabbert

TOFFEE-NUT BARS

Pastry Layer:

1/4 cup vegetable shortening
1/4 cup butter or margarine
1/2 cup firmly packed brown sugar
1 cup sifted all-purpose flour

Preheat oven to 350 degrees. In a bowl, mix together shortening, butter and brown sugar. Stir in flour. Cover bottom of ungreased 13x9x2-inch baking pan with dough. Press dough and flatten with hand. Bake for 10 minutes.

Topping:

2 eggs, beaten
1 cup firmly packed brown sugar
1 teaspoon vanilla extract
2 tablespoons all-purpose flour
1 teaspoon baking powder
1/2 teaspoon salt
1 cup shredded coconut
1 cup chopped nuts (almonds, walnuts or pecans)

Add brown sugar and vanilla to beaten eggs. Mix together flour, baking powder and salt; stir into egg mixture. Stir in coconut and nuts. Spread mixture over baked pastry layer. Return to oven and bake for 25 minutes, or until golden brown. Cool slightly and cut into bars. Yield: 24 to 36 bars.
Betzy Spacek

WALNUT RAISIN BARS

1 cup sugar
2/3 cup butter or margarine
1 teaspoon vanilla extract
1 egg
2 cups all-purpose flour

Cream butter or margarine, sugar, vanilla and egg in large bowl of electric mixer. Stir in flour. Press dough into ungreased 13x9x2-inch baking pan. Bake at 350 degrees for 15 minutes or until edges are lightly browned.

Topping:

3 eggs
2/3 cup sugar
1/2 cup light or dark corn syrup
1/4 cup unsulfured molasses
1 teaspoon vanilla extract
1 cup walnuts, broken or coarsely chopped
1 cup seedless raisins

Beat eggs; add sugar, corn syrup, molasses and vanilla and blend. Stir in walnuts and raisins. Pour over prepared crust. Bake at 350 degrees for 25 to 30 minutes or until set. Cool. Cut into bars measuring about 2x1 1/2-inches. Yield: 36 bars.
Eileen Barlock

PUMPKIN BARS

4 eggs
1⅔ cups sugar
1 cup vegetable oil
1 (16-ounce) can pumpkin
1 teaspoon salt
1 teaspoon baking soda
2 teaspoons baking powder
2 teaspoons ground cinnamon
2 cups all-purpose flour

Beat eggs with sugar until light and fluffy in large bowl of electric mixer; beat in pumpkin and oil. Sift dry ingredients together and add to creamed mixture, beating well. Spoon into a greased 13x9x2-inch baking pan. Bake at 350 degrees for 25 to 30 minutes. Remove from oven and cool in pan. Frost. Yield: 36 bars.

Icing:

1 (3-ounce) package cream cheese, softened
½ cup butter or margarine, softened
2 cups powdered sugar
1 teaspoon vanilla extract

Beat cream cheese, butter and sugar until light and fluffy; add vanilla and beat until smooth. Spread over cooled pumpkin bars.
Nicki Cowan

RAISIN BARS

2 cups seedless raisins
2 cups hot water
1 cup vegetable oil
2 cups sugar
2 eggs, beaten
3½ cups all-purpose flour
½ teaspoon salt
2 teaspoons baking soda
2 teaspoons ground cinnamon
2 teaspoons ground nutmeg
2 teaspoons ground allspice
2 teaspoons ground cloves

Combine raisins and hot water in a large bowl. Let stand for 5 minutes. Add remaining ingredients and blend until smooth. Bake in a 15x10x2-inch pan at 375 degrees for 35 minutes. Cool and cut into squares. Yield: 24 to 36 bars.
Helen Wanyerka

BANANA NUT SQUARES

2/3 cup margarine
1 1/2 cups sugar
2 egg yolks
3 ripe bananas
1 1/2 cups cake flour
1 teaspoon baking soda
1/4 teaspoon salt
4 tablespoons dairy sour cream
1/2 teaspoon vanilla extract
2 egg whites
1/2 cup chopped nuts

In a bowl cream together margarine, sugar and egg yolks until smooth and fluffy. Add mashed, ripe bananas. In another bowl, sift and measure cake flour, baking soda, salt and sour cream. Add to first mixture. Mix well and add vanilla. Beat egg whites until fluffy and fold into mixture. Add chopped nuts. Pour into a greased 13x9x2-inch baking pan. Bake at 350 degrees for 45 minutes.

Frosting:

2 tablespoons all-purpose flour
2 tablespoons margarine
1/2 teaspoon salt
3/4 cup milk
4 tablespoons sugar
1 cup vegetable shortening
6 tablespoons powdered sugar
2 teaspoons vanilla extract

In a saucepan, cook flour, margarine, salt, milk and sugar until thick. Remove from heat and cool. When cool, add shortening, powdered sugar and vanilla to thickened mixture and beat with an electric mixer at high speed until fluffy. Frost and cut into squares. Yield: 12 to 24 bars.
Anna Mae Zastawny

RASPBERRY BARS

3/4 cup butter or margarine
1 cup firmly packed brown sugar
1 1/2 cups all-purpose flour
1 teaspoon salt
1/2 teaspoon baking soda
1 1/2 cups quick oats
1 (10-ounce) jar raspberry preserves
Chopped nuts, optional

Cream butter or margarine and sugar in large bowl of electric mixer until light and fluffy. Add flour, soda and salt and mix well. Stir in oats (mixture will be crumbly). Press 1/2 of mixture into a greased 13x9x2-inch baking pan and spread preserves over top. Sprinkle remaining 1/2 dough over preserves, sealing outside edges. Sprinkle with nuts, if desired. Bake at 400 degrees for 20 to 25 minutes. Remove from oven and cool before cutting into bars. Yield: 18 to 36 bars.
Eileen Barlock

DATE-WALNUT DOUBLE DECKERS

Pastry Layer:

1¼ cups sifted all-purpose flour
⅓ cup sugar
½ cup butter or margarine

Preheat oven to 350 degrees. Combine flour, sugar and butter in a bowl and blend to fine crumbs. Press into bottom of greased 9-inch square baking pan. Bake for 20 minutes, or until edges are slightly browned.

Top Layer:

⅓ cup firmly packed light brown sugar
⅓ cup granulated sugar
2 eggs
1 teaspoon vanilla extract
2 tablespoons all-purpose flour
1 teaspoon baking powder
½ teaspoon salt
¼ teaspoon ground nutmeg
1 cup chopped walnuts
1 (8-ounce) package chopped, pitted dates

Combine brown sugar, sugar, eggs and vanilla in a bowl and beat well. Sift together flour, baking powder, salt and nutmeg; add to sugar mixture. Stir in dates and walnuts. Spoon batter into baking pan over hot pastry. Bake 20 minutes. Cool. Sprinkle with powdered sugar, if desired, and cut into bars. Yield: 9 bars.
Nicki Cowan

BUTTERSCOTCH BROWNIES

1 (6-ounce) package butterscotch morsels
¼ cup butter or margarine
1 cup firmly packed brown sugar
2 eggs, slightly beaten
½ teaspoon vanilla extract
1 cup all-purpose flour
1 teaspoon baking powder
¾ teaspoon salt
⅓ cup chopped walnuts

Melt butterscotch morsels with butter or margarine in top of double boiler over hot, not boiling, water. Remove from heat and stir in brown sugar. Cool for 5 minutes. Stir eggs and vanilla into cooled mixture. Add flour, baking powder and salt and mix well. Stir in chopped walnuts. Pour batter into greased and floured 13x9x2-inch baking pan and bake at 350 degrees for 25 minutes. Yield: 24 brownies.
Thomas More Program

SWEET DREAMS AND PICKLED DELIGHTS

Candies, Jams, Jellies, Pickles and Preserves

PEANUT BRITTLE

2 cups sugar
1 cup light corn syrup
4 tablespoons butter
1 teaspoon salt
1 cup raw peanuts
1 teaspoon vanilla extract
1 teaspoon baking soda

Put all ingredients, except soda and vanilla, in a large skillet. Cook over medium heat, stirring constantly. Observe color of mixture closely. When it turns golden brown in color (about 15 minutes), rapidly add vanilla and baking soda, mixing well. Remove foamy mixture from heat and spread on buttered 15x10x1-inch jelly roll pan the thinner the better. Break into bite-size pieces when cool.
Julee Brice

CARAMEL CANDY CHEWS

28 caramels
3 tablespoons margarine
2 tablespoons water
1 (3-ounce) can chow mein noodles
1 cup peanuts
1 (6-ounce) package semi-sweet chocolate morsels
2 tablespoons water

Melt caramels with margarine and water in a saucepan over low heat. Stir occasionally until sauce is smooth. Remove from heat. Add noodles and peanuts; toss until well coated. Drop by rounded teaspoonfuls onto greased cookie sheet. Melt chocolate pieces with water in saucepan over low heat. Top chews with melted chocolate mixture. Chill until firm. Yield: 2½ dozen.
Lynne Della Donna

CARAMEL

2 cups sugar
Few grains salt
2 cups light corn syrup
½ cup butter or margarine
2 cups evaporated milk
1 teaspoon vanilla extract

Put sugar, salt and corn syrup in a saucepan and cook over low heat until bubbly. Continue cooking and add butter; let melt. Gradually add canned milk so mixture does not stop boiling. Stir constantly. Add vanilla; stir. Pour into a buttered 13x9x2-inch pan. Cool. When cool, cut into pieces.
Julee Brice

MILLION DOLLAR FUDGE

4½ cups sugar
⅛ teaspoon salt
2 tablespoons butter or margarine
1 (13-ounce) can evaporated milk
1 (12-ounce) package semi-sweet chocolate morsels
1 (12-ounce) package German sweet chocolate
1 pint marshmallow cream
2 cups chopped nuts

Bring sugar, salt, butter or margarine and milk to a boil in large saucepan; stirring constantly; boil for 6 minutes. Remove from heat immediately and pour over semisweet chocolate, German sweet chocolate, marshmallow cream and nuts in large mixing bowl. Beat until chocolate is completely melted. Pour into buttered 13x9x2-inch pan and let stand to cool. Cut into pieces before serving. Keep stored in tightly covered container. Keeps well.
Jo Jennings

CRISPY CEREAL BALLS

½ cup butter or margarine
1 cup sugar
1½ cups chopped dates
1 egg, beaten
1 teaspoon vanilla extract
3 cups crispy rice cereal
Coconut, optional

Melt butter in saucepan. Add sugar, dates, beaten egg and salt; cook until thick. Add crispy cereal and mix well. Form into 1½ to 2-inch balls and roll in coconut, if desired. Store in a covered container.
Eileen Barlock

CHINESE SNACKS

1 (12-ounce) package butterscotch morsels (or peanut butter morsels)
1 (5-ounce) can chow mein noodles
½ cup Spanish or salted peanuts
½ cup raisins, optional

Melt morsels over low heat in saucepan. Stir in remaining ingredients. Drop by tablespoons on waxed paper. Refrigerate for 30 minutes. Ready to eat. May be removed from refrigerator if stored in a cool place.
Rosemary Corcoran

FABULOUSLY EASY FUDGE

4 cups sugar
1 cup milk
1 cup butter or margarine
1 teaspoon vanilla extract
¼ pound marshmallows (about 20)
2 (1-ounce) squares unsweetened chocolate
1 (12-ounce) package semi-sweet chocolate morsels
1 (12-ounce) package chocolate stars
1 cup broken walnuts or pecans

In a heavy 4-quart saucepan, stir sugar, milk and butter over medium heat until sugar dissolves and mixture comes to a boil. Boil hard, uncovered, for 2 minutes. Remove from heat and add vanilla. Stir in marshmallows, unsweetened chocolate, chocolate pieces and chocolate stars; stir until melted. (If mixture cools too much for chocolate to melt, place over hot water or very low heat and stir until melted). Add nuts and pour into a greased 13x9x2-inch buttered pan; let set. Cut into squares. Yield: 5 pounds.
Sister Joan

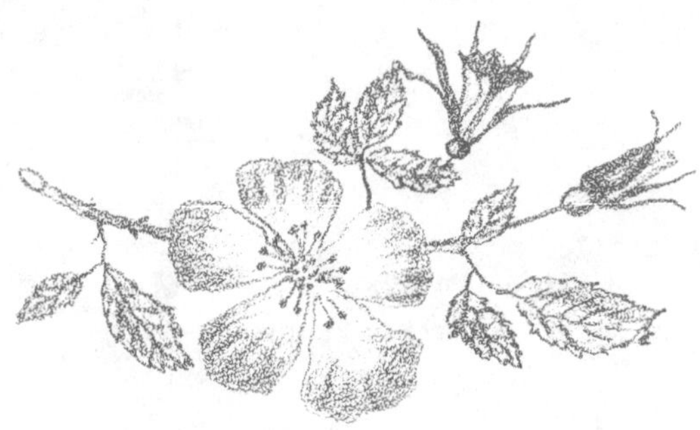

EASY CHOCOLATE TRUFFLES

8 ounces milk chocolate
1 (8-ounce) package semi-sweet chocolate
1 egg
2 egg yolks
2 tablespoons margarine, softened
Chopped nuts or coconut

Melt chocolate. Add egg and egg yolks 1 at a time, beating until smooth after each addition. Add margarine and beat until smooth. Chill until firm enough to hold shape, about 45 minutes. Shape into 1-inch balls and roll in nuts or coconut. Store in refrigerator. Yield: 3 dozen.
Sherry Stenger

CHOCOLATE PEANUT BUTTER FUDGE

2 (1-ounce) squares unsweetened chocolate
4 tablespoons butter or margarine
½ cup light corn syrup
1 teaspoon vanilla extract
1 tablespoon water
1 (16-ounce) package powdered sugar
⅓ cup instant non-fat dry milk
½ cup peanut butter

Melt chocolate and butter or margarine in top of 2-quart double boiler over hot, not boiling, water. Combine milk and sugar and set aside. Stir syrup, vanilla and water into chocolate mixture. Add ½ the sugar/milk mixture and blend. Add remaining milk mixture and continue stirring until mixture is blended and smooth. (Should still be shiny but thick enough to pile.) Beat in peanut butter. Remove from heat and add nuts. Pour into buttered pan. Cool and cut into squares to serve. Yield: 1¾ pounds.
Frances Willson

BUCKEYES

1 (12-ounce) jar peanut butter
⅔ cup butter or soft margarine
1 teaspoon vanilla extract
1 (16-ounce) box powdered sugar
1 (12-ounce) package semisweet chocolate morsels
1 (12-ounce) package milk chocolate morsels
½ cup grated paraffin wax

Combine peanut butter, margarine, vanilla and powdered sugar in large mixing bowl; mix well. Roll into balls and place on ungreased cookie sheet. Refrigerate for 2 or 3 hours. Combine chocolate morsels with grated paraffin in top of double boiler. Place over hot, not boiling, water and stir until mixture is melted and smooth. Remove peanut butter balls from refrigerator and dip into melted chocolate. Drop on waxed paper to set. Store in airtight container in refrigerator until ready to serve. Yield: about 75 or 80 balls.
Jeanne Baker
Blanche Kwiatkowski
Diane Cassell

ENGLISH TOFFEE

1 cup butter
1 cup sugar
⅓ cup hot water
¾ cup semi-sweet chocolate morsels
¼ cup chopped nuts

Stir butter and sugar together in heavy saucepan over medium-high heat, boiling until golden brown (hard ball stage on candy thermometer). Wash down side of pan with hot water after butter has melted to remove any grains of sugar. Pour onto buttered 15x10x1-inch baking sheet and sprinkle chocolate morsels over top immediately. When chocolate has melted, spread to cover toffee with chocolate. Sprinkle on nuts. Set aside to completely cool. When hard, hit with a knife to crack into bite-sized pieces. Keep stored in airtight container.
Julee Brice

LOLLIPOPS

2 cups sugar
⅔ cup light corn syrup
1 cup water
⅛ teaspoon salt
⅛ teaspoon oil of peppermint
Red food color, as desired

Place lollipop sticks at intervals on a heavily oiled cookie sheet or on a silicone paper. Combine sugar, corn syrup, water and salt in a 2-quart saucepan. Stir well and cover with tight lid. Bring to a rolling boil; remove lid and place candy thermometer in pan. Cook, without stirring, to 310 degrees. Remove from heat. Add peppermint and food color, stirring only enough to mix. Working quickly, drop hot syrup by spoonsful in mounds, covering one end of the sticks. When hardened and cool, wrap individually and store in a airtight container. Yield: 8 to 12 lollipops.
Patti Lovejoy

PECAN DELIGHTS

1 (16-ounce) package soft carmels
4 tablespoons heavy cream
2½ cups pecan halves, or walnut halves
Dipping chocolate, optional

Melt carmels and heavy cream in top of double boiler over hot, not boiling, water. Sprinkle nuts thickly in the bottom of a pan. Cool carmel mixture slightly; then drop by spoonfuls over the nuts. Let stand until firm. Cover and store. *If desired carmels may be dipped in melted chocolate letting tips of nuts show.* Yield: 40 pieces.
Eileen Barlock

PARTY POPCORN

1 cup pecan halves
1 cup slivered almonds
12 cups popped corn
½ teaspoon salt
½ cup butter or margarine
½ cup brown sugar, firmly packed

Preheat oven to 350 degrees. Spread pecan halves and slivered almonds in a single layer in roasting pan. Bake 10 to 15 minutes, stirring often, until nuts are lightly browned. Remove from oven; add popped corn and salt. Melt butter and brown sugar in a small saucepan over medium heat. Stir into popcorn-nut mixture until well coated. Bake 10 minutes longer, stirring only once, until golden brown. Remove from oven and cool in pan. Store in tightly covered containers. Yield: approximately 3½ quarts.
Barb Radthe

MERINGUE NUTS

1 pound pecans or almonds (or ½ walnuts)
1 cup sugar
Dash of salt
2 eggs, beaten slightly
½ cup butter or margarine

Place nuts on baking sheet and toast in oven at 350 degrees until brown. In a bowl, combine sugar, salt and eggs. Beat until stiff. Fold toasted nuts into meringue. Melt butter on a 15x10x1-inch baking sheet and spread nut mixture over butter. Bake at 325 degrees for 30 minutes. Check and turn pan every 10 minutes. When cool break apart.
Mary Lou Misciasci

CREAM CHEESE MINTS

1 (3-ounce) package cream cheese
3 to 3½ cups powdered sugar
Flavoring of your choice
Food coloring
Candy molds

Soften cream cheese, add flavoring and food coloring: peppermint with red, for example. Work in confectioners' sugar until smooth - the more sugar you can work into it the better the candy tastes. Roll in small balls, dip one side in sugar and press into mold. Turn out on wax paper and let air dry overnight. These freeze well. Yield: 3 dozen.
Kay Kelly
Sister Joan

PEACH FREEZER JAM

2 cups ripe peaches (about 2 pounds)
3 tablespoons lemon juice
4 cups sugar
¾ cups water
1 (1¾-ounce) box powdered fruit pectin

Wash peaches and remove stems, skins and pits. Crush peaches and measure 2 cups; place in a medium-size bowl. Add sugar and lemon juice and mix well. Let stand for 10 minutes. Mix water and pectin in small saucepan. Bring mixture to a boil and boil for 1 minute, stirring constantly. Remove from heat and stir pectin into fruit. Continue to stir about 2 minutes. Ladle into sterilized freezer jars or plastic freezer containers. Leave ½-inch headspace. Seal immediately with sterilized tight fitting lids. *Do not seal with paraffin.* Let jars or plastic containers stand at room temperature until jam is set, (this may take 24 hours) and then freeze. Yield: 5 or 6 half-pint jars.
Patti Lovejoy

LOW-CALORIE STRAWBERRY JAM

1 quart fresh strawberries, hulled and crushed
Water
1 (1¾-ounce) package diet powdered fruit pectin
Artificial sweetner to equal ¾ cup sugar
1 teaspoon pineapple extract

Crush berries thoroughly in food processor or blender. Place crushed berries in a quart measure and fill to 1 quart mark with water. In a 4-quart kettle place berry mixture and powdered pectin. Mix well with wire wisk. Cook over high heat, stirring constantly; bring to a boil and boil rapidly for 2 minutes. Remove from heat and add artificial sweetner and pinapple extract. Stir for 5 minutes and pour into hot, sterilized jars leaving ⅛-inch space on top. Apply lids according to package direction and process in boiling water bath for 5 minutes. Cool on a rack or towel, away from drafts. Check seals the next day. Yield: three 8-ounce jars, plus 4-ounces to eat immediately. Whole recipe contains about 450 calorie or 10 calories per ½-ounce serving.
Jo Jennings

BLUEBERRY-CHERRY JAM

1 quart fresh blueberries
1 quart fresh sour cherries
1 tablespoon lemon juice
1 (1¾-ounce) package powdered fruit pectin
7 cups sugar
¼ teaspoon almond extract
10 jelly glasses
Melted paraffin wax

Wash and stem blueberries and cherries. Crush gently; pour into heavy kettle or large heavy saucepan; add lemon juice and pectin. Place over medium-high heat and bring to a boil, stirring constantly. Add sugar all at once. Bring to a full, rolling boil, stirring constantly and boil for 1 minute. Remove from heat, add almond extract and skim off top foam. Pour into hot, sterilized jelly glasses and cover with hot, melted paraffin wax. Yield: 10 medium jelly glasses.
Jo Jennings

ORANGE JELLY

3¼ cups sugar
1 cup water
3 tablespoons lemon juice
½ bottle liquid pectin
1 (6-ounce) can or ¾ cup frozen concentrated orange juice

Stir sugar into water in heavy saucepan. Place over high heat and stirring constantly, bring quickly to full, rolling boil that cannot be stirred down. Add lemon juice. Boil hard for 1 minute. Remove from heat; stir in pectin. Add thawed concentrated orange juice and mix well. Pour jelly immediately into hot containers and seal with wax. Yield: 4 or 5 (8-ounce) glasses.
Patti Lovejoy

ROSEMARY SHERRY JELLY

1 fifth cream sherry
⅓ cup freshly squeezed lemon juice, strained
1 teaspoon grated lemon rind
7 cups sugar
1 (6-ounce) bottle liquid fruit pectin
6 sprigs fresh rosemary

Combine sherry, lemon juice, rind, sugar in large kettle or heavy saucepan. Bring to a boil, stirring to dissolve sugar. Boil about 3 minutes. Remove skim from top. Add pectin and stir. Continue to stir and boil for 1 minute longer. Remove from heat and ladle into hot, sterilized glass jars, into which 1 spring rosemary has been added. Seal immediately with paraffin. Yield: seven 8-ounce jars.
Patti Lovejoy

BERRY JELLY

3 quarts berries (blackberry, black raspberry, elderberry, or your choice)
7½ cups sugar
1 bottle liquid pectin

Wash and crush berries. Extract juice using a jelly bag. Measure 4 cups juice into kettle; add sugar. Bring to a full boil, stirring constantly. Reduce heat and add pectin. Reheat to full boil and stir for one minute. Remove from heat, skim, and ladle into hot sterilized glasses and seal with wax. Yield: 4 or 5 pints.
Patti Lovejoy

RASPBERRY FLAVORED GREEN TOMATO JELLY

3 cups green tomatoes, pureed
2½ cups sugar
1 (3-ounce) package raspberry flavored gelatin
Melted paraffin

Combine tomatoes and sugar in large heavy saucepan and bring to a rolling boil over medium-high heat, stirring constantly. Boil for 2 mintues. Remove from heat and stir in gelatin until completely dissolved. Pour into hot, sterilized jars and seal with melted paraffin. Keep refrigerated after opening. Yield: 6 jelly jars.
Marie Gruss

STRAWBERRY PRESERVES

3 pints fresh strawberries
5 cups sugar
1½ cups lemon juice

Wash and stem berries. Add sugar and let set 4 hours. Bring to boil, stir, and add lemon juice. Pour into a shallow pan and let cool overnight. Ladle into hot, sterilized jars, seal, and process in boiling hot water bath for 5 minutes. Yield: four ½-pint jars.
Patti Lovejoy

WHIPPED ORANGE BUTTER

1 cup butter
½ teaspoon grated orange rind
2 teaspoons powdered sugar

Butter should be at room temperature. In a bowl whip butter until fluffy. Add grated orange and powdered sugar, blending well. Store in refrigerator. *Enjoy!* Yield: 1 cup spread.
Eileen Barlock

APPLE BUTTER

6 pounds apples (24 to 36 medium apples)
2 quarts water
1 quart sweet cider
3 cups sugar
Ground cinnamon to taste
Ground clove to taste

Wash apples and cut into small pieces, leaving skins and cores. Add water and boil apples until they are soft (about 30 minutes). Put through a food mill or rub through a sieve. Boil down cider to ½ its volume, add hot apple pulp, sugar and ground spices to taste. Cook until thick enough to spread without running. Stir occasionally to prevent sticking or scorching. Ladle into hot sterilized canning jars, leaving ¼-inch head room, and seal. Process in a boiling water bath for 5 minutes. Yield: 5 pints.
Patti Lovejoy

TIGER BUTTER

1 cup white chocolate, melted
½ cup peanut butter, creamy or chunky
½ cup milk chocolate, melted

Mix white chocolate and peanut butter together well. Pour mixture on wax paper; spoon melted milk chocolate over peanut butter mixture. With a spatula, marbelize. Put in freezer to set up. Cut into squares.
Dolores Hustack
Dee's Bakery Supply

STRAWBERRY BUTTER

2 cups sweet butter, softened
¾ cup fresh strawberries, finely chopped
4 tablespoons powdered sugar

Place all ingredients in container of blender or food processor; whip until smooth and light. Delicious as a spread for warm biscuits or beer bread. Yield: 2½ cups.
Ruth Abbott

PICKLED PINEAPPLE

2 (13½-ounce) cans pineapple chunks in juice
½ cup red wine vinegar
¾ cup sugar
⅛ teaspoon salt
8 whole cloves
2 cinnamon sticks
¼ teaspoon ground nutmeg

Drain pineapple very well, reserving 1 cup liquid. In medium saucepan, combine reserved pineapple liquid with vinegar, sugar, salt, cloves, cinnamon sticks and nutmeg. Bring to boiling. Reduce heat; simmer, uncovered, for 10 minutes. Add pineapple; bring just to boiling. Remove from heat and let stand 20 minutes. Pour pineapple and liquid into 1-quart jar; cover tightly. Refrigerate until ready to use. Drain well before using. Yield: 1-quart.
Sue Mahon

ZUCCHINI PICKLES

3 quarts thinly sliced zucchini
6 small onions, sliced
4 or 5 medium-hot yellow peppers, halved, seeded and sliced
2 tablespoons coarse non-iodized pickling salt
3 cups cider vinegar
3¼ cups sugar
½ cup pickling spice

In a large bowl or non-aluminum kettle, sprinkle salt over sliced zucchini, onions and peppers. Let stand for about 4 hours. Place in colander and drain, squeezing out as much liquid as possible. Combine vinegar and sugar in a large kettle. Add spices (in a cheesecloth bag if you do not want spices in the pickles.) Stir over high heat; cover and boil for 5 minutes. Add vegetables (unrinsed) and bring to boil. Boil 1 minute. (Remove spices if bagged.) Place in hot sterilized jars; run a rubber spatula between the jar and the pickles to rid the jar of bubbles; wipe rim with damp cloth and apply lids according to manufacturer's directions. Process in boiling water bath for 10 minutes, keeping 1-inch water above tops of jars, starting to time after the water returns to a boil. Remove from water to a rack or cloth away from a drafts. Cool completely. After 24 hours, check seals. Yield: about 3 pints.
Bernadette Caine

KOSHER DILLS

20 to 25 four-inch cucumbers
6 cloves garlic, peeled
12 to 16 heads fresh dill
6 to 8 grape leaves (adds crispness)
1 quart cider vinegar
3 quarts water
1 cup non-iodized salt

Wash cucumbers. Let stand overnight in cold water. Drain. Bring water to boil in a water-bath canner. Pack cucumbers into hot sterilized quart canning jars, not too tight. To each jar add 1 clove garlic, 2 heads dill and 1 grape leaf. In saucepan, combine vinegar, water and salt. Bring to boil. Fill jars with boiling brine, leaving ½-inch space. Wipe jar rims and apply lids—dome lids with metal rings or zinc lids with rubber rings. Place jars immediately into boiling water bath. If necessary, add boiling water so water is 1-inch above tops of jars. Start counting time immediately. Do not wait for water to come back to boiling. Process for 20 minutes. Lift out of water with jar lifter and place on towels away from drafts. Next day, check seals. For best flavor, wait a few weeks before opening. Makes 6 to 8 quarts.
Rosemary Bennett

REFRIGERATOR CUKES

4 cups sugar
4 cups vinegar
1½ teaspoon celery seed
1½ teaspoon mustard seed
1½ teaspoon tumeric
½ cup coarse kosher salt
7 to 10 cucumbers, sliced thin
3 large Spanish onions, sliced thin

In saucepan heat sugar, vinegar, celery seed, mustard seed, tumeric and kosher salt until hot, but do not boil. Remove from heat and cool. Thinly slice cucumbers and onions. Layer in plastic container, with tight fitting lid, until full. After liquid mixture is cool, pour over cucumbers and onions. Refrigerate for 5 days. After 5 days, take out of container and put into sterilized glass jars and seal. These jars must be kept in refrigerator and cold. Can be kept in refrigerator for 2 years. *The best pickles you ever tasted!*
Karen Collins

EASY PEPPER RELISH

2 cups sweet red peppers, coarsely chopped
2 cups green peppers, coarsely chopped
1 small clove garlic, minced
1 cup white vinegar
½ cup vegetable oil
¼ cup sugar
1½ teaspoons salt
¼ teaspoon pepper
1 teaspoon dried basil

Mix peppers in large bowl. Blend garlic, vinegar, oil, sugar, salt, pepper and basil in blender or jar. Pour over peppers and mix thoroughly with a spoon. Pack mixture into sterilized 1-quart jar. Seal and refrigerate overnight to blend flavors. Must be kept refrigerated. *Nice with cold cuts or hamburgers.*
Peg O'Shea

RHUBARB AND ONION RELISH

4 cups sliced rhubarb
4 cups chopped white onions
2 cups cider vinegar
1 tablespoon salt
4 cups firmly packed brown sugar
1 teaspoon each ground cloves, allspice and cinnamon
Cayenne pepper to taste

Slice rhubarb and chop onions. Combine onions and rhubarb in saucepan with vinegar, salt, sugar and spices. Cook slowly until thick; about 30 minutes. Pour into hot sterilized jars and seal with sterilized lids and rings. Yield: 8 (½-pint) jars.
Mary Kerr

CRANBERRY-BRAZIL NUT RELISH

1 envelope unflavored gelatin
½ cup cold water
1 cup cranberry juice
2 cups fresh cranberries
½ cup sugar
¼ teaspoon salt
½ cup chopped Brazil nuts
½ cup diced celery

Sprinkle gelatin over cold water and let stand 5 minutes to soften. Place over boiling water and stir until gelatin is dissolved. Remove from heat and stir in cranberry juice. Refrigerate until mixture is consistency of unbeaten egg whites (about 1 hour). Wash cranberries, drain and remove any stems. Put cranberries through medium blade of food chopper. Add sugar and salt; mix well. Gently fold cranberries into gelatin, along with nuts and celery. When blended thoroughly, spoon into a 1-quart serving dish. Refrigerate, covered, until frim (at least 2 hours). Serve with poultry, ham or pork. Yield: 12 to 16 servings.
Sue Mahon

CINNAMON-APPLE WEDGES

½ cup sugar
2 (1¾-ounce) bottles red cinnamon candies
6 cups thickly sliced, pared cored apples (2 pounds)

Combine sugar, candies and 1 cup water in a 2½-quart saucepan; stir, over high heat, to dissolve sugar and candies. Reduce heat. Add apple slices; simmer, covered, stirring occasionally, until apples are just tender (not mushy). With slotted spoon, remove apples to large bowl. Bring cinnamon syrup to boiling; cook, uncovered, until thick - about five minutes. Pour syrup over apples; refrigerate about 2 hours. *Serve as a relish with ham, pork chops, roast pork. Great change from plain applesauce.* Makes about three cups.
Peg O'Shea

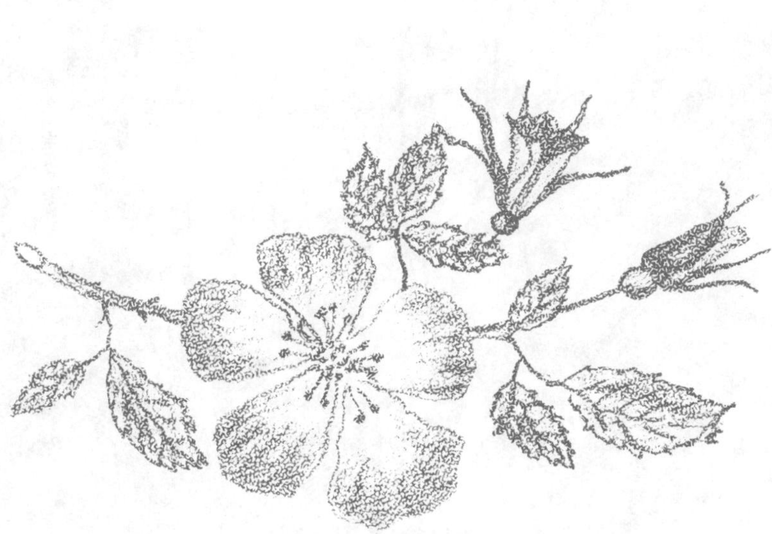

THE BUNCH FOR BRUNCH

Noontime Delectables

COFFEE KLATSCH

Café Royale

Place a sugar cube in a spoon and hold over cup of coffee. Pour brandy over sugar cube and set ablaze. When sugar has melted, stir into coffee.

Café Cappuccino

Make espresso or strong coffee. Add equal amount of hot milk. Pour into tall glasses and top with cinnamon or nutmeg.

Viennese Coffee

Make very strong coffee and top with dollop of whipped cream.

Irish Coffee

Combine 1 teaspoon sugar and 1-ounce Irish whisky in a coffee cup. Fill with very strong coffee and top with a dollop of sweetened whipped cream.

Roman Coffee

Combine 1 teaspoon sugar and 1-ounce Galliano liqueur in a coffee cup. Fill with strong coffee and top with whipped cream.

Mocha Coffee Mix

Combine 4 cups sweetened cocoa mix, ⅔ cup instant coffee crystals and 2 teaspoons ground cinnamon. Store in covered container. To serve, place 3 tablespoons coffee mix in a mug, add boiling water to fill, and stir.

APPLE-POTATO PANCAKES

½ cup grated raw apple
3 cups grated raw potatoes
1 cup chopped onion
3 eggs, slightly beaten
½ cup all-purpose flour
⅛ teaspoon ground mace
¾ teaspoon salt
½ teaspoon pepper

Combine ingredients, in order listed, in large mixing bowl. Blend well with a wooden spoon. Heat about 2 tablespoons vegetable oil in large skillet over medium-high heat. Pour in ⅓ cup batter at a time to make pancakes. Cook on both sides until lightly-browned. Lift onto paper toweling to drain. Continue, adding more oil as needed, until all batter is used. Serve immediately. Yield: 12 pancakes.
Patti Lovejoy

ZUCCHINI PANCAKES

2 cups zucchini, coarsely grated
2 large eggs, beaten
1/4 cup onion, minced
1/2 cup all-purpose flour
1/2 teaspoon baking powder

Place zucchini in strainer and press out moisture. Mix with eggs and onion. Combine dry ingredients in bowl; stir into zucchini and egg mixture. Heat oil in skillet. Add pancake batter, 1/2 cup at a time. Brown on both sides or bake for 10 to 15 minutes in a 350 degree oven.
Sharon Wachsman

FRENCH PANCAKES

4 eggs
2 tablespoons sugar
2 1/4 cups all-purpose flour
2 cups milk
1 teaspoon grated lemon rind, optional
1/2 teaspoon salt
1 tablespoon melted butter
1/2 teaspoon vanilla

Beat eggs 1 minute until thick. Add sugar and flour gradually, beating well after each addition. Add milk, lemon rind, salt, melted butter and vanilla. Beat again. Batter should be thin and light. Fry in greased, hot skillet, rotating pan to distribute batter evenly. Turn when edges brown. These should be made as thin as possible.
Eileen Barlock

CHEESE STRATA

12 slices white bread
3/4 pound sharp processed American cheese
1 (10-ounce) package chopped broccoli (optional)
2 cups diced cooked ham
6 eggs, beaten
3 1/2 cups milk
1/2 teaspoon salt
1/4 teaspoon dry mustard
2 tablespoons instant minced onion

Cut rounds out of center of bread slices. Set aside. Layer remaining crusts in the bottom of a 13x9x2-inch greased pan. Next layer cheese, broccoli and ham. Place rounds of bread over ham. Combine eggs, milk and seasonings and pour over bread rounds. Refrigerate 6 hours, or overnight, before baking. Bake in a preheated 325 degree oven for 60 minutes. Let stand 10 minutes before serving. Yield: 6 to 8 servings.
Kay Kelley
Katie Murphy

BRUNCH EGG DISH

2 cups croutons
1/4 pound (4-ounces) Cheddar cheese, grated
4 eggs
1/2 teaspoon salt
1/8 teaspoon pepper
2 cups milk

In a 1½-quart lightly-buttered casserole, combine croutons and cheese. In a medium-sized bowl, beat eggs; add milk, salt and pepper, blending gently. Pour egg mixture over croutons and cheese. Cover and refrigerate overnight. Uncover and place casserole in a shallow pan of hot water. Bake in a preheated 350 degree oven for 1 hour. Yield: 6 servings.
Kay McGorray

MAX'S NOODLE PUDDING

Noodle Layer:

1 (12-ounce) package medium wide noodles, cooked and drained
6 tablespoons butter or margarine
1¾ pounds cottage cheese
1 cup dairy sour cream
3 tablespoons sugar
1 teaspoon salt

Melt butter or margarine in 13x9x2-inch baking dish. Combine noodles, melted butter, cottage cheese, sour cream, sugar and salt in bowl; stir well. Pour into buttered baking dish. Prepare custard layer as follows.

Custard Layer:

4 eggs
1/2 cup sugar
1¾ cups milk
1/2 teaspoon vanilla extract

Beat eggs in small bowl of electric mixer; add sugar, milk and vanilla and beat until sugar is dissolved. Pour over noodles and cover with plastic wrap. Refrigerate overnight.

Topping Layer:

1½ cups cornflake crumbs
2 tablespoons brown sugar
1/4 teaspoon ground cinnamon
2 tablespoons melted butter or margarine

Next day, remove from refrigerator and bake at 350 degrees for 25 minutes. Combine topping ingredients until crumbly; sprinkle over top of pudding. Return to oven and bake for an additional 50 minutes.
Maxine Leiken

APRICOT NOODLE KUGEL

8 ounces noodles
6 tablespoons melted butter
1 (3-ounce) package cream cheese, softened
½ cup sugar
3 eggs, beaten
1 cup milk
1 cup apricot nectar

Cook noodles in saucepan and drain. In a bowl, combine melted butter, cream cheese and sugar; blend well. Add noodles to this mixture. Combine eggs, milk, apricot nectar and blend into noodle mixture. Turn into a buttered 13x9x2-inch pan.

Topping:

¼ cup butter, melted
½ to ¾ cup crushed cornflakes
¼ cup finely chopped nuts
¼ cup firmly packed brown sugar

Combine melted butter, crushed cereal, nuts and brown sugar and sprinkle over noodle mixture. Bake at 350 degrees for 1 hour. Turn off oven and leave kugel in oven an additional 20 minutes.
Sharon Wachsman

LOE'S NOODLE KUGEL

1 (10-ounce) package wide noodles
3 eggs
1 cup sugar
1 (6-ounce) jar maraschino cherries, quartered
1 cup dairy sour cream
1 teaspoon vanilla extract
1 teaspoon salt
1 (13-ounce) can crushed pineapple, drained
1 (8-ounce) package cream cheese, softened
1 cup milk
½ cup plus 2 tablespoons butter or margarine

Cook noodles according to package directions, drain and set aside. Beat eggs and sugar together in large mixing bowl until creamy. Add remaining ingredients, except 2 tablespoons margarine and noodles, and beat well. Stir in noodles. Pour into an ungreased 13x9x2-inch baking pan; dot with additional 2 tablespoons margarine or butter. Bake, uncovered, at 350 degrees for 1 hour. Remove from oven and allow to cool for about 5 minutes before cutting into squares to serve. Yield: 8 to 10 servings.
Loe Goldwasser

FRENCH TOAST BAKE

8 slices raisin bread
2 cups milk, scalded
2 tablespoons plus 1/3 cup light brown sugar, firmly packed
3 eggs, beaten
1/4 teaspoon maple flavoring
1/4 teaspoon plus 1/8 teaspoon ground cinnamon
Dash of salt
2/3 cup all-purpose flour
1/8 teaspoon ground nutmeg
1/4 cup butter, softened

Preheat oven to 375 degrees. Grease an 8-inch baking dish. Cut bread slices in 1/2 diagonally; layer slices in overlapping spirals in prepared dish. Combine milk and 2 tablespoons brown sugar. In a separate bowl, beat eggs with maple flavoring, 1/4 teaspoon cinnamon, and salt. Add milk mixture slowly, stirring until well-blended. Pour over bread. Place dish in shallow baking pan and pour in hot water to a depth of 1-inch. Bake 20 minutes.

Topping:
Combine remaining brown sugar, remaining cinnamon, and nutmeg. Stir in butter until mixture is crumbly. Sprinkle over top of French Toast Bake and bake 20 minutes longer, until set. Yield: 6 servings.
Lynne Della Donna

FAVORITE SOUR CREAM COFFEE CAKE

1/2 cup vegetable shortening
3/4 cup sugar
1 teaspoon vanilla extract
3 eggs
2 cups all-purpose flour
1 teaspoon baking powder
1 teaspoon baking soda
1 cup dairy sour cream

Topping:
4 tablespoons margarine, softened
1 cup brown sugar, firmly packed
1 cup chopped nuts
2 teaspoons ground cinnamon

Cream shortening, sugar and vanilla thoroughly. Add eggs, 1 at a time, beating well after each addition. Sift flour with baking powder and soda. Add to creamed mixture alternately with sour cream, blending after each addition. Spread 1/2 the batter in a 10-inch tube pan, greased and lined on bottom with waxed paper. Cream the topping of margarine, brown sugar, cinnamon and nuts; mix well and sprinkle 1/2 the mixture over batter. Cover with remaining batter and sprinkle remaining topping mixture over all. Bake 1 hour at 350 degrees. Cool in pan before removing. Yield: 10 to 12 servings.
Rosemary Balchak

WILLIAMSBURG BRUNCH CASSEROLE

5 cups crispy rice cereal
1 large onion, chopped
2 pounds sausage
2 cups cooked rice
8-ounces sharp Cheddar cheese, shredded
6 eggs
2 cups cream of mushroom soup
½ cup milk
Crispy rice cereal for topping

Cover bottom of buttered 13x9x2-inch baking dish with cereal. Fry onion and sausage; drain well. Spread over cereal layer in casserole. Cover with cooked rice, then cheese. Combine remaining ingredients and spread over cheese layer. Cover and refrigerate overnight. To bake, preheat oven to 350 degrees. Sprinkle additional cereal over top of casserole. Bake 40 minutes. *Wonderful for Sunday brunch.* Yield: 12 to 14 servings.
Regina Ryan

LEMON CURD

4 lemons
4 eggs
1½ cups sugar
1 cup margarine

Wash and dry lemons. Grate rind; squeeze and strain juice. Beat eggs lightly. Place sugar, margarine, grated rind and beaten eggs in a heavy saucepan. Stir with a wooden spoon over low heat until margarine is melted; stir in lemon juice. Heat slowly, stirring, until mixture comes to a boil. Reduce heat and cook slowly 3 minutes, stirring constantly. Pour into jars and chill. Keeps in refrigerator about 2 weeks. Use as spread on crackers, plain wafers, English muffins, etc.
Irene Podway
Betz Spacek

RIBBON BLINTZ SOUFFLÉ

Use cheese blintzes only if desired

1 package frozen cheese blintzes
1 package frozen fruit blintzes
¼ cup butter or margarine, melted
2 to 3 tablespoons sugar
5 eggs, beaten
2 cups dairy sour cream
½ teaspoon salt
1 tablespoon vanilla extract
3 tablespoons orange juice

Top with cherry or blueberry pie filling + sour cream.

Preheat oven to 325 degrees. Arrange blintzes in 1 layer in a greased 11x7x2-inch baking dish. Place remaining ingredients in blender container and blend 1 minute; pour over blintzes. Bake 1 hour. Freezes well. *A good luncheon dish or side dish.* Yield: 6 to 8 servings.
Gloria Rosenbush

GARDEN QUICHE

2 cloves garlic, minced
1 large onion, chopped
2 tablespoons chopped parsley
1 tablespoon chopped basil
2 cups sliced or chopped zucchini
2 to 3 hot peppers, chopped
2 cups Swiss chard, chopped
1 pound hot Italian sausage, crumbled (optional)
4 to 6 eggs
¼ cup grated Parmesan cheese

Cook sausage; drain and set aside. In sausage drippings or oil, sauté remaining ingredients until tender. Pour off all liquid and stir in cooked sausage. Pour mixture into 1¼-quart glass baking dish. Beat eggs with cheese and pour over sausage mixture. Bake at 350 degrees until eggs are well set. Yield: 4 to 6 servings.
Mary Semonetti

TEA ROOM RAREBIT

4 tablespoons butter
¼ cup all-purpose flour
½ teaspoon dry mustard
½ teaspoon salt
¼ teaspoon paprika
1 cup milk
1 cup heavy cream
1 tablespoon Worcestershire
Few drops hot pepper sauce
8-ounces sharp Cheddar cheese, shredded
Unsalted toasted, blanched whole almonds

Melt butter in heavy saucepan. In a small bowl combine flour, mustard, salt and paprika. Stir into melted butter; cook until bubbly, stirring constantly. Remove from heat. Gradually stir in milk and cream until smooth. Return to heat and cook, stirring, until thickened and smooth. Add Worcestershire sauce, hot pepper sauce, and cheese. Heat and stir until smooth. Ladle over melba toast on hot plates. Sprinkle with almonds. *Fruit salad is a nice accompaniment.* Yield: 3 cups sauce or 3 to 4 servings.
Betz Spacek

SHERRIED FRUIT MEDLEY

1 (16-ounce) package pitted prunes
1 (16-ounce) can pineapple chunks
1 (21-ounce) can cherry pie filling
1⅓ cups dried apricots
¼ cup sherry
2 cups water

Combine all ingredients in 13x9x2-inch baking dish. Bake at 350 degrees for 1½ hours. Serve warm. May be served as a side dish or over ice cream. *Great served with brunch.*
Sally Zetl
Kay Kelly

SWISS BRUNCH BAKE

2 (10¾-ounce) cans cream of chicken soup
1 cup milk
4 teaspoons minced onion
1 teaspoon prepared mustard
8-ounces process Swiss cheese, shredded
12 eggs
12 (1-inch thick) slices French bread, halved and buttered
Chopped parsley

Combine soup, milk, onion and mustard in a saucepan. Cook, stirring constantly, until smooth and heated through. Remove from heat and stir in cheese until melted. Pour ½ of mixture into each of 2 (13x9x2-inch) baking dishes. Break 6 eggs into sauce. Stand bread slices around edges of casserole with crusts up. Bake at 350 degrees 20 minutes or until eggs are set. Garnish with parsley. Brown-and-serve French bread may be used sliced, buttered and unbaked. Bread will bake while casserole bakes. Yield: 12 servings.
Lynne Della Donna
Sue Mahon

FLORENTINE EGGS

2 (10-ounce) packages frozen leaf spinach, cooked and well drained
6 eggs
Seasoning salt to taste
1 (10½-ounce) can cream of mushroom soup
2 tablespoons milk
1 cup shredded Cheddar cheese

Grease a 12x8x2-inch pan and cover bottom with spinach. Break eggs gently on top of spinach in 2 rows; 3 to a row. Sprinkle top of eggs with seasoned salt. Mix soup and milk together until smooth. Pour around eggs, completely covering spinach. Sprinkle Cheddar cheese over all. Bake in a 350 degree oven for 20 to 25 minutes or until eggs are set. Yield: 4 to 6 servings.
Lynne Della Donna

PEANUT TEA RING

1 (10-count) package plain or buttermilk refrigerated biscuits
½ cup melted margarine or butter
1 cup finely chopped peanuts
¼ cup powdered sugar
1 tablespoon water

Separate biscuits; dip both sides in melted butter, then in peanuts, coating well. Arrange in overlapping circle on greased baking sheet. Bake at 425 degrees for 10 to 15 minutes. Combine powdered sugar and water; drizzle over hot tea ring. Yield: 6 to 8 servings.
Dolores Sygula

STICKY BUNS

1 (12-count) package brown-and-serve dinner rolls
4 tablespoons butter
¼ cup brown sugar, firmly packed
24 pecan halves

Preheat oven to 375 degrees. Lightly grease a 12-cup muffin pan. Place 1 roll in each cup. With a paring knife, cut an X in the top of each roll. Melt butter and sugar over low heat. Drizzle over rolls and place 2 pecan halves on top of each. Bake 15 minutes. Yield: 12 buns.
Lynne Della Donna

PERFECT POPOVERS

6 eggs
2 cups milk
6 tablespoons butter or margarine, melted
2 cups all-purpose flour
1 teaspoon salt

Beat eggs in a large bowl until frothy using the low speed of the electric mixer. Add milk and butter. Beat until well-blended. Stir in flour and salt. Pour batter into twelve, greased 2½-inch muffin pan cups, filling each about ½ full. Bake at 375 degrees for 50 minutes or until golden brown. Quickly, make a slit in the top of each popover to release steam. Bake 5 to 10 minutes longer. Remove popovers from the muffin cups immediately. Serve hot with melted butter. *Wonderful!* Yield: 12 popovers.
Ron Barlock

APPLE MUFFINS

1¼ cups bran
⅔ cup milk
2 eggs
1 cup sugar
½ cup melted vegetable shortening or vegetable oil
1 cup all-purpose flour
2½ teaspoons baking powder
½ teaspoon salt
1 teaspoon ground cinnamon
¼ teaspoon ground cloves
1 cup chopped raw apple
1 cup raisins

Preheat oven to 400 degrees. Combine bran, milk, eggs, sugar, and shortening or oil in a bowl. Sift flour, baking powder, salt, cinnamon and cloves together, then stir into batter. Stir in apples and raisins. Spoon into greased muffin tins. Bake 25 minutes. May be served as a dessert, topped with whipped cream. Yield: 20 (2-inch) muffins.
Dolores Sygula

ROSEMARY'S DANISH PUFF PASTRY

1 cup all-purpose flour, sifted or lightly spooned into cup
½ cup margarine, softened
2 tablespoons water
Chopped nuts

Cut margarine into flour until mixture resembles coarse corn meal. Sprinkle on water and mix with a fork as for pie crust. Shape into a ball, divide in ½ and pat into 2 long strips 12x3-inches long. Arrange on a 15x10x1-inch baking sheet at least 2 inches apart. Divide filling between the 2 strips and bake at 350 degrees for 1 hour. Cool 1 hour and spread on frosting. Sprinkle with nuts if desired. Yield: 8 to 12 servings.

Filling:

½ cup butter or margarine
1 cup water
1 teaspoon vanilla extract
1 cup all-purpose flour
3 eggs, slightly beaten

Combine margarine and water in saucepan. Bring to a boil over medium-high heat. Add vanilla, remove from heat and immediately add flour. Beat well. Add eggs 1 at a time, beating constantly until smooth. Divide mixture between 2 dough strips on baking sheet.

Frosting:

2 cups powdered sugar
4 tablespoons margarine, softened
2 tablespoons milk

Combine ingredients in order listed. Beat until well-blended and spreading consistency is reached. Add a small amount of additional milk if needed.
Rosemary Balchak

WAFFLES FOR A WEEK

1 cup cold milk
¼ cup vegetable oil
1 tablespoon sugar
2 teaspoons salt
1½ cups warm water
1 package active dry yeast
2 eggs, slightly beaten
3 cups all-purpose flour

Dissolve yeast in warm water. Mix all ingredients in order given in blender or with electric mixer. Store in closed container in refrigerator. Keeps 1 week. Use as needed. Follow directions for your waffle iron.
Sally Vlasik

THE GANG'S ALL HERE

Crowd Pleasing Fare

BAKLAVA

4 cups finely chopped walnuts
½ cup sugar
1 teaspoon ground cinnamon
1 pound strudel leaves
1 cup butter or margarine, melted
1 (12-ounce) jar honey

Combine first 3 ingredients in a large bowl. Mix until well-blended. Set aside. Place 1 sheet of strudel leaves in a greased, 13x9x2-inch baking dish letting it extend up the sides of the dish. Brush with butter. Repeat, making 5 more layers of strudel leaves. Sprinkle with 1 cup of walnut mixture. Cut remaining strudel leaves into 13x9x2-inch rectangles. Place 1 sheet strudel leaves in baking dish over walnut mixture. Brush with melted butter. Repeat to make at least 6 layers of strudel leaves. Sprinkle with 1 cup walnut mixture. Repeat layering 2 more times, ending with a layer of strudel leaves. With a sharp knife, cut halfway through all layers in a diamond pattern making 28 servings. Bake at 300 degrees for 1 hour 25 minutes or until top is golden brown. Heat honey over a low heat until it is hot but not boiling. Spoon evenly over the Baklava. Cool in the pan for at least 1 hour. Cover and leave at room temperature until serving time. To serve, finish cutting through the layers with a sharp knife. Yield: 28 servings.
Ann Karpac

BLACKEYED SUSANS

Cake:

1½ cups all-purpose flour
1 cup sugar
1 teaspoon baking soda
½ teaspoon salt
¼ cup cocoa
1 cup water
1 teaspoon vanilla extract
⅓ cup vegetable oil
1 teaspoon white vinegar
30-36 tart papers, tart pans or foil tart papers

Combine ingredients in order listed in a large mixing bowl. Mix until well-blended. Fill paper lined tart tins or foil tart papers ½ full of mixture. Spoon ½ teaspoon of filling mix into the center of the cake mix. Bake at 350 degrees for 15 minutes. *This is great for showers and kids love them.* Yield: 30 to 36 tarts.

Filling:

1 egg
1 (8-ounce) package cream cheese, room temperature
Dash of salt
1 (6-ounce) package mini chocolate morsels

Cream eggs, cream cheese and salt until smooth and well blended. Stir in chips.
Ellen Curran

ELEGANT TRUFFLE

2 (6-ounce) packages vanilla pudding mix, cooked according to package directions
2 frozen pound cakes, cut into ½-inch slices
¼ cup sherry (not cooking type)
1 (12-ounce) jar strawberry or raspberry preserves
2 cups heavy whipping cream, whipped
Grated lemon or orange rind for garnish

In a large bowl layer a small portion of cooled vanilla pudding mix, top with several slices of pound cake. Sprinkle about 1 tablespoon sherry over pound cake, then spread with a layer of preserves. Continue layering pudding, pound cake, sherry and preserves until all ingredients are used. Cover with plastic wrap. Refrigerate 4 to 5 hours or overnight to develop flavors. When ready to serve, whip cream and spread over top of truffle. Garnish with grated lemon or orange rind. *Wonderfully delicious! An elegant dessert for company or for the holidays, especially if served in a crystal bowl.*
Betty Carlisle

TEXAS SHEET CAKE

1 cup margarine (not butter)
1 cup water
4 tablespoons cocoa
2 cups all-purpose flour
2 cups sugar
½ teaspoon salt
2 eggs
1 teaspoon baking soda
¾ cup dairy sour cream

In a large pan, heat margarine, water and cocoa until it boils. Remove pan from heat and add flour, sugar and salt. Mix well. Beat in eggs, baking soda and sour cream. Pour mixture into 10x15-inch cookie sheet pan and bake at 375 degrees for 20 to 25 minutes.

Frosting:

½ cup margarine
4 tablespoons cocoa
6 tablespoons milk
1 pound powdered sugar
1 teaspoon vanilla extract
chopped nuts (optional)

Heat together margarine, cocoa and milk until it boils. Remove from heat, add sugar and vanilla. Spread on cake as soon as it is removed from the oven. Sprinkle with chopped nuts, if desired. Yield: 15-18.
Sue Mahon

SAUERBRATEN

4 cups water
1 cup dry red wine
1 cup red wine vinegar
1 large onion, sliced
2 tablespoons packed brown sugar
1 teaspoon whole allspice
1 teaspoon crushed bay leaves
1 teaspoon pepper
6 pounds beef chuck roast
All-purpose flour
½ cup butter
1 large onion cut in wedges
2 carrots, cut in 2-inch pieces
2 tablespoons tomato paste
½ cup ground gingersnaps

In a saucepan, heat water, wine, vinegar, sliced onion, brown sugar, allspice, bay leaves and pepper. Bring to a boil; pour over meat in a large bowl. Cool. Cover and place in refrigerator for 1 to 3 days. (The flavor improves the longer meat is marinated. Turn meat several times daily). Drain meat, reserving 1½ cups of marinade. Coat meat with flour. In Dutch oven, brown meat with butter; add reserved marinade, onion, carrots and tomato paste. Cover and simmer 2½ hours until meat is tender. Remove meat and cover to keep warm. Place cooking liquid and vegetables in food processor and blend until smooth. Heat mixture to boiling in Dutch oven, add gingersnaps and boil until sauce is desired consistency. Serve over meat. Yield: 10 to 12 servings.
Patti Lovejoy

CHICKEN BREASTS SUPREME

1 pint dairy sour cream
¼ cup lemon juice
1 clove garlic, crushed
½ teaspoon celery salt
2 teaspoons paprika
½ teaspoon pepper
6 whole chicken breasts, skinned, boned and halved
1¼ cups dry breadcrumbs
½ cup butter
½ cup vegetable shortening

Combine sour cream, lemon juice, garlic and seasonings. Add chicken and stir to cover breasts with sour cream mixture. Marinate in refrigerator overnight. Shortly before baking, roll each sour cream covered chicken breast in breadcrumbs. Place rolled breasts in a greased 13x9x2-inch casserole. Melt butter and shortening over low heat. Pour ½ mixture over chicken breasts. Bake at 350 degrees for 45 minutes. Baste with remaining butter mixture. Bake an additional 15 minutes. Yield: 12 servings.
Shirley Ziegler

HOMEMADE PIZZA

Crust:

1 (5/8-ounce) cake yeast
2 cups warm water
4 cups all-purpose flour

Sauce:

3 cups tomato sauce
2 tablespoons olive or salad oil
1 1/2 teaspoons oregano
1 teaspoon garlic powder, or 1 large clove garlic, minced
2 to 3 tablespoons Parmesan cheese
1 pound Italian sausage, optional
1 (8-ounce) package sliced pepperoni, optional
8 ounces fresh mushrooms, sliced and sautéed
2 (16-ounce) packages pizza cheese

Crumble yeast in warm water; stir and add flour. Stir well to moisten all flour. Turn onto floured surface and knead until smooth, about 5 minutes, adding more flour if necessary. Place in greased bowl, cover with a damp cloth and allow to rise in a warm place until doubled in bulk, 45 minutes to 1 hour. Combine sauce ingredients and set aside. Grease 2 jelly roll pans and spread 1/2 the dough in each. With greased fingertips, spread dough evenly to edges of pan. Divide sauce between pans, cover with pizza cheese and choice of toppings (to use sausage, remove casings and crumble). Bake at 425 degrees 20 to 25 minutes. If baking both pans in one oven, switch positions of pans halfway through baking time so both crusts will brown on bottom and cheese will bubble on top. Cut into slices to serve. Yield: 24 to 30 pieces.
Jean Croyle

LEG-OF-LAMB BARBECUE

1/2 cup olive oil
1 cup dry white wine
3 cloves garlic, minced
1/2 teaspoon dry mustard
1/4 cup parsley, minced or 2 tablespoons dried parsley flakes
1/2 teaspoon cayenne pepper or hot pepper sauce
1 whole leg of lamb, boned and well trimmed

Combine first 6 ingredients in a shallow pan. Marinate roast in this mixture for 2 hours, turning every 30 minutes. *Do not* refrigerate. Broil outdoors over very hot charcoal for 20 minutes. Turn and broil for an additional 20 minutes. Yield: 10 to 12 servings.
Don Badjun

CHIPPED BEEF CHICKEN

2 (2.5-ounce) packages chipped beef
8 chicken breasts, skinned, halved and boned
8 thin slices bacon
2 (10¾-ounce) cans cream of chicken soup, undiluted
1 pint dairy sour cream
¼ cup dry sherry

Shred beef; pour boiling water over beef and drain well. Pat into the bottom of a buttered 13x9x2-inch casserole dish. Place chicken breasts that have been folded over to resemble a roll, on top of the beef. Top each chicken breast with ½ strip of bacon. Combine soup, sour cream and sherry. Pour over chicken. Bake, covered, at 275 degrees for 2½ hours. Uncover and cook for an additional 30 minutes or until browned. Yield: 10-12 servings.
Lynne Della Donna

HOT SALAMI APPETIZERS

1 whole salami
¾ cup barbecue sauce
1 tablespoon orange marmalade
3 tablespoons catsup
2 tablespoons prepared mustard
1 tablespoon Worcestershire sauce
1 tablespoon brown sugar

Cut salami into ½-inch slices, but not completely through to bottom. Place whole salami in greased baking dish. Combine remaining ingredients in small bowl; pour over salami. Bake at 275 degrees for about 2 hours. Baste often. Serve on rye rounds or crackers. Serves a crowd.
Nancy Kumin

HEARTY BEEF-BARLEY SOUP

1½ pounds short ribs with bone
1 to 1½ pounds boneless short ribs, cubed, or lean stew meat
1 (2½-to 3-pound) can tomatoes in purée sauce, chopped
1 (15-ounce) can beef broth
2 to 3 tomato cans water
1 teaspoon garlic salt (or to taste)
1 to 1½ cups chopped celery
1 cup chopped onion
1½ to 2 cups dry barley, washed

Put meat, chopped tomatoes with purée, broth, water and garlic salt in a large soup pot. Bring to a boil, turn heat down, and simmer, covered, 1½ hours, until meat falls from bones. Remove bones and fat. Add celery and onions; cook, covered, 30 minutes longer. Add barley and cook 1½ to 2 hours more. (Amount of barley used may vary according to preferred thickness of soup. Barley will increase in volume about 4 times.) Yield: 10-12 servings.
Jo Lawrence

SLOPPY JOES FOR A CROWD

3 pounds ground beef
1 cup chopped onions
1½ cups chopped celery
¾ cup chopped green pepper
¾ cup chopped mushrooms
1 teaspoon cayenne pepper
1 teaspoon black pepper
1 tablespoon dry mustard
2 tablespoons salt
1 quart tomato purée
½ cup brown sugar, firmly packed
¼ cup vinegar
2 cups water, if needed
25 sandwich buns

Start browning beef in skillet and add onion, celery, pepper and mushrooms; cook until almost tender. Transfer to large saucepan and add remaining ingredients, stirring well. Cook until thickened, about 1 hour. Add water if mixture becomes too thick, but it should not be soupy. Spoon onto sandwich buns. Yield: 25 sandwiches.
Rosemary Balchak

FLUFFY CORN FRITTERS

2 eggs, slightly beaten
¼ cup milk
1 cup pancake mix
1 (12-ounce) can whole kernel corn, drained

Blend eggs and milk well with wire whisk. Gently stir in pancake mix and drained corn with a wooden spoon. Do not beat, but mix lightly to obtain a light, fluffy fritter. Drop by teaspoonsful into hot oil (approximately 1-inch deep) and cook slowly until golden brown (about 4 minutes). Serve plain or with syrup. Leftovers can be refrigerated and used the following day for snacks without reheating. Yield: about 34 fritters.
Ruth Abbott

LIMA BEAN CASSEROLE

2 (16-ounce) packages dry large lima beans
4 large onions, quartered
2 to 2½ cups diced ham
1 tablespoon prepared mustard
Salt and pepper to taste (about 5 teaspoons salt)
1½ cups brown sugar

Combine all ingredients, except lima beans, in crockpot or large oven-proof casserole dish. Rinse and pick beans; add to casserole dish and add enough water to cover. Bake at 350 degrees (or cook in crockpot) for 4 hours. Check hourly to see if more water needs to be added. Do not add water during last hour of cooking time. Yield: 16 servings.
Sister Eleanor

MUFFINS FOR A MOB

1 (15-ounce) box bran cereal with raisins
1 quart buttermilk
1 cup vegetable oil
2⅓ cups sugar
4 eggs, slightly beaten
5 cups all-purpose flour
5 teaspoons baking soda
1 teaspoon salt

Combine cereal, buttermilk, oil, sugar and eggs in large mixing bowl. Sift dry ingredients together and add to mixture, stirring just until all flour is moistened. Cover and refrigerate at least 6 hours before using, preferably overnight. (Batter will keep for 6 weeks in refrigerator. *Do not freeze.*) Bake at 375 degrees for 15 to 20 minutes in greased muffin tins, returning remaining dough to refrigerator each time. Yield: about 6 dozen muffins.
Sally Vlasik

SIX HOT BEAN DISH

1 (16-ounce) can kidney beans
1 (16-ounce) can pork and beans
1 (16-ounce) can green beans, drained
1 (16-ounce) can yellow beans, drained
1 (16-ounce) can lima beans, drained
1 (16-ounce) can chili beans
1 pound Italian sausage, mild, without casing
2 onions, chopped
1 cup chopped celery
2 tablespoons mustard
1 cup light brown sugar, packed
1 (10¾-ounce) can tomato soup
1 (12-ounce) can tomato paste
5 slices bacon, cut into small pieces

Place beans in a large roaster or casserole. Fry sausage over medium heat until well-browned on all sides. Sauté onions and celery in grease until transparent. Drain off excess grease. Add sausage, mustard, brown sugar and tomato soup. Mix until well-blended. Spread tomato paste over the top of the beans. Top with bacon pieces. Bake, uncovered, at 350 degrees for 1 hour and 15 minutes. Mix in bacon pieces. Yield: 16 to 20 servings.
Sister Joan

LUMBERJACK BEAN BAKE

8 slices thick bacon, diced
1 cup minced onion
1/3 cup brown sugar, firmly packed
1/2 cup wine vinegar
1/2 teaspoon dry mustard
1/2 teaspoon garlic salt
1 (16-ounce) can butterbeans, drained
1 (16-ounce) can kidney beans, drained
1 (16-ounce) can lima beans, drained
1 (16-ounce) can pork and beans

Fry bacon and onion until onion is tender, about 5 minutes. Stir in sugar, vinegar, mustard and garlic salt; simmer, covered, 15 minutes. In a 4-quart casserole, combine the 4 kinds of beans and toss lightly to mix. Spoon bacon mixture over beans. Bake, uncovered, at 350 degrees for 50 to 60 minutes, or until bubbly. Yield: 10 to 12 servings.
Teddie Wise

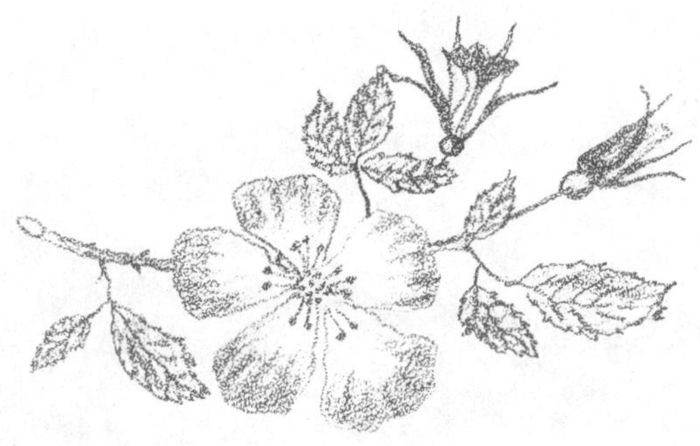

CATHOLIC POTATOES

12 medium potatoes, cooked
1 (8-ounce) package cream cheese
1/4 cup margarine
1/2 cup dairy sour cream
1/2 cup milk
2 eggs, beaten
1/4 cup minced onion
1 teaspoon salt
Pepper

In a large mixing bowl, mash hot potatoes. Add small pieces of cream cheese and butter, beating until both are melted and completely blended into potatoes. Blend in sour cream. Combine eggs, milk, onion and seasonings and fold into potatoes. Beat until light and fluffy. Turn into greased 9-inch round oven proof casserole and refrigerate for several hours or overnight. Bake at 350 degrees for 45 minutes until top is lightly browned. Yield: 10 to 12 servings.
Charles Eanes

INDEX

Index

Index

THE GANG'S ALL HERE,
Crowd Pleasing Fare

Notes

Mail to: **BEYOND THE VILLAGE GATE**
Parmadale
6753 State Road
Parma, Ohio 44134

Please send me _____ copies of
BEYOND THE VILLAGE GATE at $10.00 each $________
Postage and Handling at $2.00 per book $________
Ohio residents please add 6.5% sales tax $________
TOTAL $________

Enclosed is my check for $________; additional donation ________.
Please charge to My Master Charge Card #________
Bank No. ________ Expiration Date ________ Signature ________
Name ________
Address ________
City ________ State ________ Zip ________

*Make all checks payable to *PARMADALE COOKBOOK.*
COOKBOOKS MAKE GREAT GIFTS!

Mail to: **BEYOND THE VILLAGE GATE**
Parmadale
6753 State Road
Parma, Ohio 44134

Please send me _____ copies of
BEYOND THE VILLAGE GATE at $10.00 each $________
Postage and Handling at $2.00 per book $________
Ohio residents please add 6.5% sales tax $________
TOTAL $________

Enclosed is my check for $________; additional donation ________.
Please charge to My Master Charge Card #________
Bank No. ________ Expiration Date ________ Signature ________
Name ________
Address ________
City ________ State ________ Zip ________

*Make all checks payable to *PARMADALE COOKBOOK.*
COOKBOOKS MAKE GREAT GIFTS!

Reorder Additional Copies